7-Day Menu Planner
FOR DUMMIES®

by Susan Nicholson, RD/LD

Wiley Publishing, Inc.

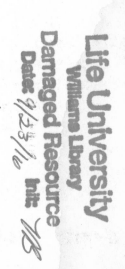

7-Day Menu Planner For Dummies®

Published by
Wiley Publishing, Inc.
111 River St.
Hoboken, NJ 07030-5774
www.wiley.com

For general information on our other products and services, please contact our Customer Care Department within the U.S. at 877-762-2974, outside the U.S. at 317-572-3993, or fax 317-572-4002.

For technical support, please visit www.wiley.com/techsupport.

Wiley also publishes its books in a variety of electronic formats. Some content that appears in print may not be available in electronic books.

Library of Congress Control Number: 2010934752

ISBN: 978-0-470-87857-6

Manufactured in the United States of America

10 9 8 7 6 5 4 3 2 1

WILEY

About the Author

Susan Nicholson is a columnist, speaker, cookbook author, and consultant in the area of food and nutrition. Her weekly syndicated column from Universal Uclick, "The 7-Day Menu Planner," is a practical, quick, healthy eating guide for budget-minded families. Nicholson's columns appear in newspapers with total circulations of more than 6 million.

Known for her humorous, down-to-earth style and creative, healthy recipes, Nicholson has appeared more than 125 times on Atlanta network television and on CNN and The Discovery Channel. She also has participated in many radio and newspaper interviews.

"The 7-Day Menu Planner" began in *The Atlanta Journal-Constitution* in 1995. Before Nicholson began writing the column, she owned and operated a microwave specialty store and cooking school. She attended La Varenne Ecole de Cuisine in Paris. Her book, *Save Your Heart with Susan — Six Easy Steps to Cooking Delicious Healthy Meals in a Microwave,* was published in January 1991 (William Morrow & Co.).

Prior to her full-time culinary endeavors, Nicholson held regional sales positions with Mead Johnson's Nutritional Division and the former Marriott Corp.'s Contract Food Services Division.

Nicholson is a registered and licensed dietitian and a member of the American Dietetic Association and the International Association of Culinary Professionals. She is a member of the Association of Food Journalists. Nicholson also is a founding member and past president of the Atlanta chapter of Les Dames d'Escoffier.

Nicholson is a native of the Shenandoah Valley of Virginia and now lives in Atlanta.

For musings, misadventures, and more from Susan, visit the Making the Menu blog at www.makingthemenu.com, and find more menus at www.7daymenuplanner.com. Follow Susan on Twitter at http://twitter.com/7DayMenu.

Dedication

To my family here on earth, Nick, also known as Cupcake and the Virgo, and our four-legged "children," Smoke and Flash, feline brothers who are destined to rule the universe.

And to my mother, Mary Rupp Orebaugh, the woman who taught me more than anyone, in and out of the kitchen. I wish she were here on earth to read this book. It would make her laugh. And, to our first four-legged "children," Magnolia Blossom and Casey Bubba, neither of whom ever missed a meal.

Author's Acknowledgments

To friends who were always ready for "test" meals, no matter what was on the menu, even Christmas brunch on Labor Day. To Vicki Adang and Brooke Goetz, my Wiley and Universal Uclick editors who dragged so much information out of my brain for this book that I will have to take a nap every afternoon for the rest of my life. Of course, Christy Pingleton, my copy editor, and Emily Bailey, RD, who were right there, making all the copy perfect and the details accurate. Then there are those two editors for my newspaper column, the "7-Day Menu Planner": Alan McDermott, my editor for 10 years, who never saw a piece of butter he didn't like nor a peanut that he did, and Gillian Titus, my current editor, who loves kitties almost as much as I do, which makes her a good person all around. And, she would certainly catch my mistakes (should I ever make any). Of course, hats off to Lee Salem, who discovered me in the first place. I owe you all so much.

Publisher's Acknowledgments

We're proud of this book; please send us your comments at http://dummies.custhelp.com.
For other comments, please contact our Customer Care Department within the U.S. at 877-762-2974,
outside the U.S. at 317-572-3993, or fax 317-572-4002.

Some of the people who helped bring this book to market include the following:

Acquisitions, Editorial, and Media Development

Project Editor: Victoria M. Adang

Acquisitions Editors: Mike Baker, Erin Calligan Mooney

Copy Editor: Christine Pingleton

Assistant Editor: David Lutton

Technical Editors: Emily Bailey, RD, LD, NASM; Emily Nolan; Patti Santelli

Editorial Manager: Michelle Hacker

Editorial Assistants: Jennette ElNaggar, Rachelle S. Amick

Art Coordinator: Alicia B. South

Cover Photos: National Chicken Council/U.S. Poultry & Egg Association, National Onion Association/Souders Studios, U.S. Highbush Blueberry Council

Cartoons: Rich Tennant (www.the5thwave.com)

Composition Services

Project Coordinators: Katherine Crocker, Kristie Rees

Layout and Graphics: Carrie A. Cesavice, Shawn Frazier, Rashell Smith, Erin Zeltner

Proofreader: Jacqui Brownstein

Indexer: Johnna VanHoose Dinse

Illustrator: Liz Kurtzman

Publishing and Editorial for Consumer Dummies

Diane Graves Steele, Vice President and Publisher, Consumer Dummies

Kristin Ferguson-Wagstaffe, Product Development Director, Consumer Dummies

Ensley Eikenburg, Associate Publisher, Travel

Kelly Regan, Editorial Director, Travel

Publishing for Technology Dummies

Andy Cummings, Vice President and Publisher, Dummies Technology/General User

Composition Services

Debbie Stailey, Director of Composition Services

Contents at a Glance

Recipes at a Glance

Family

Heat and Eat

Meatless

Easy Entertaining

Bonus Recipes

Table of Contents

Introduction

Welcome to *7-Day Menu Planner For Dummies!* What you'll find in between the shiny yellow-and-black covers of this book will change your life forever. Instead of standing with the refrigerator or freezer door wide open (didn't your mother ever tell you not to do that? Mine did) and wondering what in the world you're going to serve for dinner in less than an hour, or just giving up and dialing the number of the nearest pizza joint, this book gives you a healthy, budget-friendly menu for every night of the week.

Menu planning is not brain surgery; it's not even rocket science, even though some would have you believe that only a genius can do it successfully. When I show you how simple it is, you'll be amazed. All you need to become a menu planner is a desire to eat healthier, save money, reduce stress, and enjoy delicious meals.

But, I want you to be able to do more than re-create my menus. I want you to be able to follow my guidelines and create your own menus. You'll be the master planner in your house. How's that for something to be proud of? I couldn't agree more. It gives you a lot of power, too, in case you needed more.

I show you step by step how to create your own plans. And while you're at it, I encourage you to teach someone else in the family so that the skill can be passed on to the next generation. Remember, you want to be invited to your daughter's or son's house for dinner sometime in the future.

The whole truth is, we *don't* hate to cook; we just haven't figured out how to plan *what* to cook. That's about to change, starting right now!

About This Book

You've bought this fabulous book (well, I think it's fabulous and so would my mother if she were here on earth), and now you want to know exactly why you're going to love it so much that you'll take it with you to bed for your nighttime reading material. Who cares about steamy novels or scary mysteries when you have the *7-Day Menu Planner For Dummies* to keep you awake with excitement? No falling asleep with the *7-Day Menu Planner* by your side.

One of the biggest advantages of this book is that it provides you with 52 weekly menu plans — that's right, 365 nights of meals. (Yes, I've even included holiday meals. You're welcome.) Some of the meals are straightforward. Other meals might take a little bit of work, and for those I provide "formal" recipes. These recipes don't take a lot of time (who wants to spend all afternoon in the kitchen?), and they taste delicious. Another benefit is that the meals are good for you (there are a lot of ways to season food that don't involve bacon and butter). Plus, they use common ingredients to save you time and money at the supermarket.

These days, money is a top concern for many families. The amount of money you'll save with your new menu plans will knock your socks off. The faithful readers of my "7-Day Menu Planner" column tell me this all the time. How will you save money? You'll spend wisely and not overbuy. You'll use leftovers in interesting and creative ways instead of wasting food, you won't stop for fast food on the way home, and you'll shop by season, to mention a few ways.

In addition to the menu plans and recipes, I include some information that I hope you'll find helpful. I explain what goes into a healthy meal, how I plan my menus, and how you can plan your own menus. I also offer tricks to minimize your time in the kitchen, tips for saving money at the grocery store, and a list of meals you can count on when you're short on time.

Conventions Used in This Book

By their very nature, cookbooks are about rules. How else would you get your meals to turn out the way I've planned them for you? Here's what you need to know about the recipes:

- Milk is fat-free or 1-percent.
- Eggs are large.
- Butter is salted.
- Flour is all-purpose unless otherwise specified.
- Sugar is granulated unless otherwise noted.
- Brown sugar is packed.
- All herbs are fresh unless dried herbs are specified.
- All temperatures are Fahrenheit. (If you need to convert temperatures to Celsius, check out the metric conversions in the Appendix.)
- All fresh ingredients come directly from the refrigerator unless otherwise noted.

- Liquids are measured in glass measuring cups; dry ingredients and semi-solids are measured in metal measuring cups. Spices and herbs are measured in metal measuring spoons.

- Chicken should not be "enhanced" with salt, sodium, broth, or brine. (Check the label.)

When you're reading the chapters, know that

- All Web addresses appear in `monofont`.

- New terms appear in *italic* and are closely followed by an easy-to-understand definition.

- **Bold** is used to highlight key words in bulleted lists.

- "The Virgo" is my husband. I often refer to him that way because he is logical, orderly, and methodical — traits of some of those born under the Virgo sun sign as he was.

What You're Not to Read

It will break my heart if you don't read every word I've written (sniff!), but I'll get over it. You do, however, have my permission to skip the sidebars (the text in the gray boxes). The information in the sidebars isn't essential to menu planning, but it may improve your cooking skills or make meal preparation a little smoother. You can come back to the sidebars when you have the time or the interest.

Foolish Assumptions

In the grand design of the *7-Day Menu Planner For Dummies,* I had to answer some profound questions to create top-notch meals for you. Here are the questions I asked and the answers I came up with — sort of a one-way communication to help you get into my brain:

- Who are my readers? You!

- Where do they live? All over the United States.

- Who is "the family"? I'm not sure, but I'm thinking of Mom, Dad, and a couple of elementary school children. However, the family may be one person or a couple. I hear from all walks of life.

- How much money do they have? They're neither rich nor poor.

✔ Do the adults work, or is there a stay-at-home adult in the house? Some work; some stay at home.

✔ Do they like to cook? Sometimes, but not always.

✔ Do they know the value of healthful meals? Do they care? Yes, to both questions.

✔ How much time do they have to prepare and enjoy meals? During the week, not so much; they have more time for food, family, and fun on the weekends.

✔ Do meals depend on their schedules? Of course.

✔ Does the reader do/cook everything I say? Well, hope springs eternal, but I doubt it.

✔ Is it likely that readers pick and choose which meals to follow? Under duress, I have to admit this is true.

✔ Does this make me throw a tantrum? Occasionally.

How This Book Is Organized

I've divided *7-Day Menu Planner For Dummies* into three parts. Here's what you'll find where.

Part 1: The Path to Quick, Healthy, Budget-Friendly Meals

You may be skeptical that planning your menus in advance is worth the time and effort it takes. In this part, I outline the benefits of doing so, show you how I plan menus, and then arm you with what you need to know to plan your own meals. It's not as painful as it sounds — trust me!

Part 11: A Year's Worth of Weekly Menu Plans

All the menus, from Week 1 to Week 52, are contained in this one part, and I've organized them by season. (This may not seem important now, but it will when you want to take advantage of seasonal foods for their cost and quality.) Week 1 corresponds with the first week of January; Week 52 is the last week of December. Week 26 marks midyear around the Fourth of July. I encourage you to figure out what week of the calendar you're in, and turn to that week's menu when you're ready to get started. Then follow along from there. When a holiday is on the horizon, know that I've planned a special menu for that night, but you may have to look ahead or back a few days or a few weeks because of the fluid nature of the calendar and the concreteness of this book.

The other thing to know about this part is that each week's menu contains seven themes, marked by a fun little picture in the margin. Here are the themes (flip to Chapter 1 if you want more details about each theme):

 On Family night, you'll prepare a recipe the whole family will enjoy, commonly known as family favorites or sometimes comfort food.

 Kids night does not mean simple food. Although these recipes are lightly seasoned, they do not lack in flavor.

 Express meals take the form of leftovers, a very quick and easy recipe, or a convenience food.

 You'll save some money with the meals I've planned for Budget night. Look for braised or canned meats in stews or salads. Here's where you'd use ground instead of whole meat.

 When you Heat and Eat, you'll often be cooking in the microwave and using leftovers in new ways to get dinner on the table. Sometimes, these meals won't even require heating.

 Meatless nights often feature beans, pasta, or rice.

 A personal favorite is Easy Entertaining night. Invite friends over, splurge a little, and try something new!

Part III: The Part of Tens

In this part of the book, you find chapters on saving time in the kitchen, saving money at the grocery store, my favorite foods to eat for better health, and recipes for meals you can fix in a hurry. I've also included an appendix in this part that can help you convert the measurements in the recipes to metric measurements.

Icons Used in This Book

I want you to pay special attention to some of the main points I make in the chapters in Parts I and III. To call your attention to these must-read ideas, I mark them with icons.

The text next to this icon contains an idea that you simply must know. It may have to do with your health, or it may be something important to remember in the kitchen.

This icon draws your attention to shortcuts, ideas to save you time and money, and other helpful information. You won't want to skip these paragraphs.

You have to be careful when planning meals and cooking. I want you to stay safe in the kitchen and live a long and healthy life, so when I write about something that could cause you harm, I mark it with a Warning icon.

Where to Go from Here

The logical place to go from this point is to Chapter 1! That's where I tell you all the wonderful benefits of menu planning. But if you want to skip the appetizer and head straight for the main course, figure out what week of the calendar it is, and turn to that week in Part II. Then start enjoying the ease of knowing what's for dinner for the next seven nights, seven weeks, or seven months. Expect your plan to go slowly at first, but know that it will grow as a snowball grows into a snowman in no time. The main mandate is that you don't give up too soon. Take the attitude of *I can do it.* Remember: It's never too late to get organized. This book leads you down a path that ends with the family sitting at the table enjoying stress-free, healthful, delicious meals.

Part I
The Path to Quick, Healthy, Budget-Friendly Meals

The 5th Wave   By Rich Tennant

"I'm not actually buying this stuff, I'm just using it to hide the fruit, legumes, and greens until we get checked out."

In this part . . .

Because this isn't your average cookbook, I explain the benefits of mapping out a menu plan in advance, and then I introduce you to the strategies behind planning a week's worth of meals and show you how it's done. I'm so confident that you'll fall in love with the convenience of menu planning that I explain how you can create your own plans. Just follow my lead.

Chapter 1

The 7-Day Menu Planner: A Friend in the Kitchen

. . . .

In This Chapter

▶ Understanding what the 7-day menu approach can do for you

▶ Realizing why planning ahead is a good thing

▶ Staying organized with themes

. . . .

There are almost as many recipe books published as there are grains of sand on the beach. Many cookbooks are wonderful; some are not so good. The reason you can have other cookbooks *and* the *7-Day Menu Planner For Dummies* is that *this book is unique.* You have 365 meals planned for you, along with recipes and ideas, shopping lists online, and nutritional analysis for many recipes, all between two covers at a reasonable price. No other book like it exists.

In this chapter, I introduce you to the benefits of planning meals seven days at a time and give you an overview of how the menus are organized.

The Benefits of Planning

Coming home from a hard day at work or elsewhere and having dinner either cooking (in your slow cooker) or crying out for you in the refrigerator (a left-over) is a way to increase your life span and decrease your heart rate! That sounds a little extreme, but it's true.

I remember my days as an early married, working in a hospital until 6:30 p.m. and arriving home around 7 with no dinner ideas looming in my head. What did the uncertainty produce? A headache on the way home and a not-too-cheerful new bride to my (always) hungry husband. I wasn't a menu planner for us at the time. At the hospital, yes, but not at home.

Saving time is the goal of many people. Planning gets them to the goal line faster in the long run. Granted, it means spending time at the beginning, but the turtle versus the hare analogy is true here. You remember the result.

In the following sections, I reveal how planning meals ahead of time can save you time, make you and your family healthier, and save you moolah.

Taking control of mealtime and your evenings

When you plan your meals a week at a time, you have so much more time to do what you'd really like to be doing, and you have the enthusiasm to present your family with the absolute best meals in town.

How can this happen, you ask? For starters, consider the time savings: Because your meals have been planned (pat yourself on the back), you've already bought what was on your list at the grocery store (thus cutting out spontaneous purchases and forgetting items), and you have everything ready when it's time to cook. All this planning has given you a big, fat block of time. No more rooting around in the pantry, under the bed, and in the garage for ingredients. You're ready to roll!

Now that you're less stressed and have more energy, it's time for your family to go to a movie, play a board game, or take a walk around the neighborhood. These are all plusses of gaining quality time.

As far as having enthusiasm to present your family with delicious meals, when you incorporate themes into your nightly menus, you'll experience a catchphrase you've probably heard many times before and never believed, "the joy of cooking." *7-Day Menu Planner For Dummies* gives you first, *time,* and second, *joy,* through theme nights and a little dessert with every menu to show you that dining at home can be just as much fun as dining out.

I explain how to use the menus I've created for you in Chapter 3, and then I give you 52 weeks of menus in Part II of this book. In Chapter 4, I explain how you can create your own menus. Why should you know how to plan your own menus? Here's the easy answer: You'll probably want to take control of your food and your life because you may not like everything I've planned for you. You may want to substitute your family's preferences for a day or two of my theme menus when you're first getting started. Eventually, you'll find that menu planning takes less and less time. That's the point.

Improving your family's health

Menu planning will improve overall health and establish good eating habits for younger children as well as tweak eating habits for the rest of the family. Lowering sodium and saturated fat while increasing fiber in your diet does wonders for your overall health and wellness. By planning, you can choose foods and recipes that take your family's nutrition needs more into account. Lowering sodium and saturated fat helps overall heart health, and fiber contributes to colon health. These choices certainly contribute more to good health than a bag of chips and a soft drink for dinner.

Experts agree that losing as little as 10 percent of your body weight can greatly influence your blood pressure, cholesterol, and blood sugar. Additional benefits of dropping those extra pounds include reducing the risk of heart disease, stroke, diabetes, arthritis, certain types of cancer, and breathing problems.

If you took a survey, you, like everyone else, would probably say that you want better health, more energy, and to look good in a bathing suit. Of course you know that eating out of paper bags is not the way to up your health quotient any more than eating cookies while sitting on your behind is the way to improve your muscle mass. Imagine the survey-taker asking what you plan to do about your — okay, I'm just going to say it — your slovenly ways. There, I got it out. Believe me, I've been into slovenly ways (which I don't care to reveal at this time) more than once.

Suffice it to say that slovenliness isn't the way to go. You want to follow your menu plan, get some exercise (consider getting a dog), and take better care of yourself. You know you want to live to be old enough to allow your children — who drive you nuts from time to time — to take care of you when you're old, and one of the ways to do this is to eat healthier food. (I cover the basics of healthy eating in Chapter 2.)

Saving money

Planning saves money. Who doesn't want to give the food budget some relief, especially when times are tight? Follow these tips to make your dollars stretch (and for even more ideas, check out Chapter 7):

- **Take advantage of sales and coupons.** When you plan your meals a few days before you plan to serve them, you can check out what foods are on sale at the grocery store and work those into your menu. And if you can pair a sale and a coupon, so much the better! Oh, how I love to save money at the grocery store. I just wish I was as good at using coupons as some of the "specialists." Alas, I'm not, but I'm pretty darn good at it if I do say so myself (I just patted my own back).

✔ **Make a list.** I recommend making a grocery list; don't mosey into the store empty-handed, just to wander around and buy whatever sounds good at the moment. If you do, you'll blow your grocery budget for sure. (See Chapter 3 for more tips on grocery shopping.)

✔ **Don't overbuy.** Buy what's on the list; don't overbuy. Overbuying and tossing food in the landfill is not a money-saving routine. Cooking only what you'll eat for a meal (unless you've planned for leftovers) prevents full garbage cans and gives you a fatter wallet. If you buy 2 pounds of something because the price is less and throw away half of it, you're not saving money. Buy one; get one free is another favorite of mine — *but only when I know I can store the freebie and will use it before too long.*

Most grocery stores will offer the sale price when you only buy one of the item. Be sure to ask your local grocer.

✔ **Make wise use of leftovers.** Leftovers save money. Use leftovers by repurposing them into a totally different dish. Only you will know the magic you performed for Thursday's meal that was originally served on Tuesday. For five years I produced a column called *Double-Duty Dinners* that did just that. Cook once/eat twice was the focus.

For example, imagine you have Happy Trails Pot Roast for your first meal. In it, besides beef, are onion, diced tomatoes, green chilies, and spices. The next meal is a natural for Tex-Mex Tortillas. Shred the left-over meat and heat it with the vegetables, soften corn tortillas, spoon meat onto the tortillas, roll 'em up, and top them with salsa and sour cream. Or, say you roast a chicken for one night. You can turn it into Open-Face Italian Chicken Melts a couple days later. Spread pesto on toasted sandwich rolls, and layer them with leftover sliced chicken, roasted red peppers, tomato sauce, and mozzarella cheese. Broil until the cheese melts. See how easy it is to turn two meals into four? And you haven't even been to magician school.

✔ **Buy in-season produce.** Take advantage of seasonal products. Buying and eating what's in season and closest to your home is a wonderful idea. However, sometimes you want fresh blueberries or cherries or nectarines in February and are willing to pay for them. Many people (myself included) are hooked on fresh tomatoes year-round. I accept that they aren't as good as the ones grown in mid-summer in a neighbor's garden, but I don't have the luxury of a generous neighbor with a garden any time of year, so I just have to realize the limitations and buy what's in the market.

Check your local farmers markets for seasonal deals.

✔ **Consider canned and frozen options.** Some times of year, canned tomatoes are a better choice in recipes than fresh ones, just as sometimes frozen vegetables beat their fresh counterparts. I love green peas from the garden, but not many of us have access to them. And who has the time to shell them?

Try to purchase the low-sodium or no-salt-added versions of canned vegetables to keep your eating healthy.

The 7-Day Menu Planner Approach

One reason to love the *7-Day Menu Planner For Dummies* is that it requires no thinking on your part. I've done it for you. The truth is, I've been thinking nonstop about you and your meals for years and years (no kidding). Through my 15-year career to date as a menu-planner, I've planned about 5,500 dinners with you in mind already.

What were you doing during this time? Getting your nails done, having your teeth straightened, or taking a world cruise? You may even have been eating out of bags, but I don't want to go there. No, I'm not bitter, I'm just happy for us both because I now have the opportunity to tell you how to increase your happiness, wealth, and health through this book. You're worth it!

These menus are not written for modified diets. The menus are for folks who have no dietary restrictions and want to eat healthier, with easy recipes, on a budget. I've always emphasized that the 7-Day Menu Planner is not a "diet" program, although it is healthful for you. This book doesn't replace your physician's or registered dietitian's advice. If you're on a modified diet, please consult your doctor.

To locate a registered dietitian in your area, go to www.eatright.org, the Web site of the American Dietetic Association.

Even though the 7-Day Menu Planner is not intended to address special dietary needs, please understand that I do try hard to pay attention to salt, fat, and calories in the recipes. You'll see "low-fat," "reduced-sodium," and other such descriptors for ingredients often in recipes and menus. I'm thinking of your health and wellness all the time.

The following sections tell you how the menu planner in Part II is organized. It also explains the themes that are represented throughout the menus (with a few suggestions for creating your own themes as well!).

Providing a week's worth of dinners

The mission of the 7-Day Menu Planner is to provide a week of healthful, easy recipes and menus with a moderate food budget in mind. I like to plan menus by season. My philosophy is that it's more fun to eat hearty stews and soups in the winter and cheaper to eat fresh vegetables in the summer. Grilling has no season; neither does my slow cooker. The Menu Planner likes holidays (especially the ones where I get gifts) and special occasions, too, so you'll find menus honoring New Year's Day, Valentine's Day, St. Patrick's Day, Mother's Day, Memorial Day, Father's Day, and other special days throughout the year.

Special occasion, holiday, and seasonal meals are an important part of life and a component in planning the week's meals. Good recipes and menus can last a lifetime, especially when you add your family's favorites and your special touches.

The menus follow the seasonal winter-spring-summer-fall routine in a given year, as well as seasonal holidays. Think of Week 1 as January 1-7. If you are reading this book for the first time in June, please thumb to Week 26, for example, and get started!

What this book shows you about menu planning will last you a lifetime; no one can take it away from you. While menus and recipes can come and go with trends, fads, and new nutrition information, the skills you gain stay with you. Like riding a bike, you'll never forget how to do it, even many years after you first discover how.

Labeling the days of the week

If you want to stir up the family dining enthusiasm, tell them that tonight is "All the Dessert You Can Eat" night. That's what's known as a theme night. The 7-Day Menu Planner has a theme every night with a specific group or type of cuisine in mind. Your group will be your own family.

Before you post your menus in your kitchen, give each night's menu a theme. It could be: "Susie Cooks Night," "Find the Leftovers Night," "Guess Where This Recipe Came from Night," "No Meat Tonight Night," or "Bring It from the Deli Night." You get the idea. You can have the same themes each week (although I'd limit the "All the Dessert You Can Eat" night to once or twice a year).

When there's a birthday in the family, it's "Susie's Birthday Dinner" (note how Susie becomes a theme unto herself). If my name were Louise, the theme would be "Louise's Birthday Dinner." You get the point.

When you begin to plan your own menus later (see Chapter 4), you can decide on themes. You can ask the family what themes they think are fun, interesting, and easy. Try not to be dictatorial with your themes or sarcastic about your family's ideas.

As you go through the weeks (see Part II), you'll see that not every Monday is the Kids theme, and not every Wednesday is the Budget theme. That would be boring; I'm trying to avoid boring. To me, however, Family is almost always a Sunday theme, and Saturday is almost always for Easy Entertaining. This may change according to your family and work schedule, and that's okay! The 7-Day Menu Planner is a very flexible kitchen guide.

The following sections describe the themes I use in each week's menu.

Family

 Sundays are usually "Family" days. It's one of the days of the week when everyone should gather and enjoy a meal together. Often the Sunday meal involves preparing a whole meat, making enough for leftovers that can follow any day of the week. On Sundays, you might find a roast chicken or pot roast menu like the sort of old-fashioned, gather-'round-the-table entrees your grandmother may have prepared. Some people call these "comfort foods." Eating with your family should be a pleasurable experience, and the food should reinforce that idea.

Kids

 How could we have theme nights without including kid-centric meals? These are the meals designed for Mom, Dad, and elementary-school-age children in particular. I plan for these meals to be lightly seasoned in opposition to what I usually prefer. I mince the onions, tuck in vegetables where you wouldn't expect them (such as in meatloaf), and cut down the spiciness.

I find it's one of my most challenging nights because kids' palates are not as well developed as adults'. I've been known to follow children and mothers around the grocery stores to quiz the kids on what they like to eat besides pizza, hot dogs, hamburgers, spaghetti, and tacos (which, as any mother knows, rank high on the kid-preferred list!). You wouldn't believe how much kids have to say on the subject. Out of their little angelic mouths roll salmon, broccoli, green beans, and other such surprises. Sometimes Mom is surprised, too, because she's never seen her child eat such foods. The secret: Kids eat these foods at their friends' houses.

That being said, I will now contradict myself. Kids need to learn to develop a taste for a variety of foods. How do they do that? Parents, it's your job to help them by introducing new foods at the table and encouraging the kids to taste them. If mom and dad are eating it, it can't be such a bad idea! Monkey-see, monkey-do.

 Keep in mind that you might have to serve a food seven or eight times before your kids are willing to eat it. I see nothing wrong with having a "taste" requirement for any new foods.

Kids have unique likes and dislikes. I was one darn picky eater as a kid, and so was my brother. The worst part is that we got away with it for the most part. I honestly didn't like fatty meat or chicken skin (and still don't), even though both my parents ate fried chicken with gusto. I ate the meat; I just removed the skin. That was one of my better eating habits as a kid.

There were times when I had to stay at the table until those carrots disappeared. They disappeared all right — and my cat never spoke to me again. (I do eat carrots now.) Now, my husband Virgo's mother took no prisoners. You ate it or you stayed at the table until you grew old. Virgo (see my disclosure) now eats most foods. (By the way, his mother always denied her dictatorial ways until the day she left this earth. She was also a Virgo.)

(*Full disclosure:* Virgo's birthday is September 18. He's very particular, orderly, logical, and methodical. I won't go further into Virgo traits because you might find one or two Virgos who are slobs and don't fit the mold. Most of you know which mold you fit. You'll read about more of Virgo's personality type throughout the book!)

Express

"Express" night is the night to enjoy a new convenience food. It also might be a night for leftovers or a very quick recipe. The sky's the limit on quick recipes.

I could just as well call this night "No Stress Night." I try not to make this meal one that requires lots of ingredients, lots of time to prepare, or much cleanup time. The time required to get it on the table varies from 10 minutes to maybe 30. When you factor in eating and cleanup times, you should be able to be in and out of the kitchen in an hour or so. The rules aren't rigid, but that's the goal.

You might also check your freezer for something to thaw for dinner. I don't count the time it takes to thaw something in your refrigerator as part of the prep time!

If you don't already, take advantage of your microwave for reheating leftovers and cooking rice and vegetables. It takes less time, and the cleanup is minimal.

When you're at the grocery store shopping for convenience foods, read those labels (check out Chapter 2 for more on reading nutrition labels). I have a much harder time suggesting convenience foods these days because of the amount of sodium many manufacturers insist on putting in their processed foods. I've heard that some food manufacturers say that consumers demand it, but I've always wondered how a consumer can demand something from a manufacturer. Do consumers stand outside the corporate headquarters, carrying signs and shouting "Up with sodium!" or some other such nonsense?

Budget

"Budget" night is right up my alley! What you'll cook and eat this night could be ground beef, chicken, or turkey rather than their whole counterparts. You won't have lamb chops on this night, but you might have lamb stew because of the difference in cost per pound. *Braised* meats (these are usually tougher cuts cooked in or with liquid) versus roasted meats are another good option. The slow cooker gets a gold star for braised meats and might be your appliance of choice for this night. Another idea for cooking on a budget is to serve tuna salad paninis this night instead of grilled tuna steaks.

It's hard to put an exact dollar amount on a budget meal, but somewhere between $2 and $3 per adult and less for children is a ballpark number. The meal could be higher or lower and could vary from week to week. A good idea would be for you to do the math on each meal (or dish) to see exactly what you're spending. You might be thrilled, or you might be horrified. Whatever you learn, apply the knowledge to your menu planning.

Heat and Eat

 The "Heat and Eat" night uses a leftover from another night. Sometimes you just heat the other half of the recipe; other times you turn it into something new (flip to Chapter 3 for more on this). Either way, it's an easy meal. Personally, I feel rich when I open the refrigerator and find leftovers. Some folks shun the word "leftovers," but I embrace it. You can be assured that my freezer and refrigerator are almost always full of leftovers because I cook all the time — except when I'm at the computer or grocery store!

When I think Heat and Eat, I think of one of my favorite appliances — the microwave! No, it's not just for popping popcorn. Reheat your leftovers and serve them just as you would any other meal. Heat and Eat doesn't mean "microwave meals;" it just means "repurposing leftovers." Your family won't know the difference.

Meatless

 The menu plans skip meat one night a week for a "Meatless" meal, another theme night. The star of this show could be beans, pasta, rice, or another food that doesn't breathe. We eat nothing that moves on this night — not even fish or seafood! This may be your most economical night because using plant-based food often saves money. Protein foods (meat, fish, poultry), while not usually budget-breaking, are more expensive sources of protein than the starches or beans mentioned. This night does not include tofu. I leave cooking tofu to the experts who know better how to prepare it than I do.

 You might try one of the natural food stores for tofu cooking inspiration and lessons, or dine in an Asian restaurant where tofu is on the menu, and ask if they teach classes. Many do.

Easy Entertaining

 My favorite meal of the week is the one designated "Easy Entertaining," a time when you can splurge a little more and experiment with new foods or recipes. Your guests will thank you for it.

Some experts say that when you're planning to entertain, you should always prepare the dish you plan to serve at least once before. Those entertaining experts are right, but I don't always do it. I invite friends for "test meals." "Easy Entertaining" can be one of those meals. It's most often on Saturday night, when most of us have more time to prepare meals. This is the night for lamb chops, shrimp, or steak, served on your best china with cloth napkins alongside. Over the years, I've found that adding dinner music adds a nice touch to the ambiance too.

Chapter 2

Choosing Healthy Foods

- -

- -

We've all been told over and over and over to eat healthy, exercise often, and help little ol' ladies across the street. This is all good advice, but how do we manage to accomplish these goals and still live the way we want to? I'm skipping the exercise and little ol' lady parts, and concentrating on the food you put in your mouth — what it is and how much of it is in your best interest. The 7-Day Menu Planner menus and recipes use lean meats, fresh fruits, vegetables, whole grains, and simple low-fat preparation and products, all of which lead the way to better health.

Defining Healthy Meals

How much and what you eat can help define your overall health status. Making the right choices makes life more enjoyable and helps you to be more active. When you're at the right weight for your height and age, you feel and look so much better. Feeling better leads to a more positive outlook on life. Isn't that what most people really want? I say yes.

Getting the right amount of nutrients

To get technical (which I'm not), a nutrient is a chemical that an organism (that's you) needs to live and grow. Nutrients are substances that provide food or nourishment, such as proteins, fats, and carbohydrates along with vitamins and minerals. The body uses them all for the ever-changing and ongoing functioning of its metabolic processes. Without these essential elements, you'd be up a creek without a paddle, to put it figuratively.

Life is all about balance, and that applies to the nutrients — that is, food — that you eat. Eat a variety of foods in moderation for optimal health.

What you need a lot of

You can't have too much of a good thing, and that holds true for certain categories of nutrients. Try to eat foods high in the following nutrients:

- ✔ **Fiber:** Fiber can help reduce the risk of diseases and should be eaten in generous amounts. Generous amounts of fiber, however, can also decrease your number of friends. What you want is increased understanding from your friends to offset your increased fiber intake. You can eat as much as 50 grams of fiber a day, but more has not been shown to be beneficial. Most of us eat much less fiber than that so there's little need for worry about going over 50 grams.

  As you increase your fiber, increase your water intake to keep more friends. Easy ways to add fiber are to include beans in your salads, soups, and casseroles. You can even pop some beans into your tacos. Eat oatmeal for breakfast, and add some raisins for a good dose of extra fiber. Forget fruit juices in favor of whole fruits and vegetables. Make the fruits and vegetables part of every meal.

- ✔ **Vitamins and minerals:** These, like fiber, promote good health and should be included in your diet. The majority of Americans don't get enough vitamins and minerals, so try to include good sources of these daily.

  A balanced diet contributes greatly to your overall intake of vitamins and minerals. Sometimes, a supplement is needed to get all the vitamins and minerals that you need, but eat right first; take supplements last. Megadoses of vitamins and minerals are not in your best interest unless your physician or dietitian recommends them to you. Try not to consume more than 100 percent of the RDA (recommended daily allowance).

  All ages need plenty of calcium, and, as we age, we need even more. Vitamin D needs are in the news now because most people have a deficiency of this vitamin.

What you don't need a lot of

Doesn't it just figure that the tastes that people like the best are the ones they should eat the least of? Hey, just because I'm a registered dietitian doesn't mean that all I want to eat is carrots and bran cereal (pass the ice cream, please). Here are the nutrients that you should try to limit in your diet, because too many can increase your risk of diseases such as heart disease and cancer.

- ✔ **Fats:** This category is broken into three parts: saturated fat, unsaturated fat, and trans fat. Saturated fats raise cholesterol levels in the blood (more on cholesterol in a minute). Unsaturated fats are the "heart healthy" fats and are found as monounsaturated and polyunsaturated. Monounsaturated fats help to raise blood levels of good cholesterol, HDL, and lower blood levels of bad cholesterol, LDL. Polyunsaturated fats lower LDL but leave HDL alone. Trans fats are partially hydrogenated oil (the main source of trans fats). They're dangerous because they raise blood levels of LDL, while lowering HDL cholesterol. These trans fats are created when vegetable oil is put through a process called hydrogenation to make it thicker in consistency.

Look on the label for "partially hydrogenated," and if you see it, run for the exit!

One of the jobs of fat is to carry flavor. That's why bacon is so popular — it's so full of flavor. Think about butter: Is there really any substitute for the flavor? Not in my book. You might like to eat a lot more of the stuff, but remember the reasons for holding back — it's high in calories and saturated fat.

Ideally, people should keep their percentage of fat intake to 20 to 30 percent of total calories, with a mere 7 percent of that coming from saturated fat. If you eat 2,000 calories, limiting fat intake to 44 to 66 grams is a worthy goal, with 4 to 5 grams of saturated fat.

- **Cholesterol:** You want to eat foods low in cholesterol. Cholesterol is found only in *animal* fats, so fats derived from plant sources are a better choice (think olive oil). High cholesterol levels in your body increase your risk of heart disease and stroke.

- **Sodium:** Sodium is the scientific name for salt, and Americans love their salt. (Just take a look at the amount of sodium in any processed food. I bet you'll be shocked at the number.) According to experts, eating too much salt can lead to high blood pressure, which can cause kidney failure and strokes. Americans eat more than twice the amount recommended. We can all aim to do better.

A reality check on sodium consumption

The new recommendation (2010) for sodium consumption has decreased from 2,300 milligrams to 1,500 milligrams per day. Usually, I'm ranting and raving about reducing sodium in our diets (see the section "What you don't need a lot of"). However, while I have no proof, I'm pretty certain that no one who is recommending this reduction has ever been on a 1,500-milligram diet for longer than 10 minutes. I'll probably be burned at the stake for saying this, but I'm a practical person, and 1,500 milligrams a day is not practical in my book. If most Americans could just adapt to a 2,300-milligram sodium diet, they'd be a lot better off. Many folks get up to 5,000 or 6,000 milligrams of sodium a day now, and that's awful. To show you what I mean, here are the amounts of sodium contained by some everyday foods found today in my kitchen:

- Skim milk, 1 cup: 130 milligrams
- Whole-grain bread, 1 slice: 170–200 milligrams
- Butter, 1 tablespoon: 90 milligrams
- Bacon, broiled: 101 milligrams (and who eats *broiled* bacon?)
- Banana: 1 milligram
- Egg: 62 milligrams
- Ketchup, 1 tablespoon: 178 milligrams
- Ready-to-eat cereal, ¾ cup: Kashi Go Lean (in my pantry), 85 milligrams; Cornflakes and Rice Krispies (not in my pantry), 203 and 319 milligrams, respectively
- Vegetable juice, 1 cup: 883 milligrams (not in my pantry)

Studies show that 77 percent of our sodium intake comes from processed foods. Five percent comes from cooking, and 6 percent comes from adding salt at the table. The other 12 percent comes from natural sources (food in general, and sometimes water).

I've been on a too-much-sodium-in-processed-foods kick for years, so I look hard at milligrams of sodium per serving.

Companies are beginning to lower sodium in their products but are a long way from doing what they should. They do have to meet U.S. government standards, but believe me, they don't make their products 1 milligram lower than they have to. The recommendation for a healthy adult is to consume no more than 2,300 (soon to be 1,500) milligrams per day. People with high blood pressure and other health conditions need even less. Most people, including me, could do with a lot less.

Just remember: Taste before you shake!

✔ **Carbohydrates:** Ah, carbohydrates — don't you just love them to death? Where would we be without potatoes, rice, beans, sugar, fruits, desserts, and so on? Most people have a real fondness for foods with lots of carbohydrates (just the thought of carbohydrates makes me swoon and my mouth water). If you're a diabetic or pre-diabetic, you have to count the darn things to protect your health. That's so important for those with this disease.

Even if you're not diabetic, you better pay attention or you're likely to overdo it and gain weight, especially with simple carbohydrates such as sugar, desserts, and fruit juices. Watch your intake and take in more complex carbs, such as whole grains, beans, and legumes. They take longer to digest, and most contain fiber, which keeps you from feeling hungry as fast. That's a good thing for most people. It is for me, anyway.

Carbohydrate is also the most easily digestible nutrient and the most instant source of energy, leaving you feeling hungry shortly after consumption. In a 2,000-calorie diet, 50 to 60 percent of your daily calories should be carbs. Whole grains, fruits, and vegetables should add up to 250 to 300 grams a day.

✔ **Protein:** You need it, but you don't need as much as you think you do. Because most proteins are a combination of protein and fat, they give us *satiety,* another word for satisfaction. (Can you imagine Mick Jagger naming his famous song, "I Can't Get No Satiety?") Proteins are the building blocks of our bodies. The most important functions of proteins are to build up, keep up, and replace body tissue as needed. Call it maintenance — just like you have to keep up your house and car and make repairs, you must keep up your body. It needs constant attention, and the way to pay attention to its needs is by eating a healthful diet. Sorry if this sounds like preaching from your mama. It is. About 15 to 20 percent of your total calories should come from protein.

In addition to meats, main sources of protein are dairy, eggs, and cheese. Other sources are beans, legumes, soy products, nuts, and nut butters.

Proteins are the most expensive foods we eat. With that in mind, why not skip meat once or twice a week? It's good for your health, good for your budget, and good for the environment.

Keeping the food groups in balance

Expect a little controversy over portion sizes, because the amount we *like* to eat and the amount we *need* to eat are often at odds. So how much do we *really* need?

The U.S. Department of Agriculture (USDA) has revamped the food pyramid to help Americans improve their diets. The pyramid is divided into slices of varying sizes (see Figure 2-1); the different widths suggest how much of your daily diet should come from each food category. The person climbing the steps of the pyramid is meant to remind you to get some physical activity each day. Exercise is your friend!

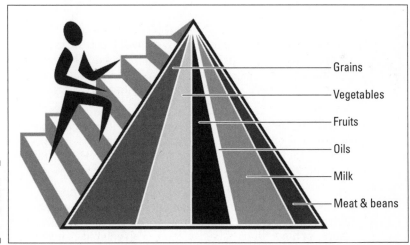

Figure 2-1:
The Food
Guide
Pyramid.

— Grains
— Vegetables
— Fruits
— Oils
— Milk
— Meat & beans

Source: U.S. Department of Agriculture

The bad news about the pyramid is that it makes it a little harder to generalize how much of each category I can recommend to all of you readers as a group. The good news is that you can go to www.mypyramid.gov and get a personalized recommendation of how much of each category you should eat (click MyPyramid Plan on the left side of the home page). You can enter your age (don't lie!), gender, height, weight (be honest!), and activity level, and the Web site will generate a plan specifically for you. Isn't our government wonderful?

How a registered dietitian can help you stay healthy

Has the family doctor gently suggested (or threatened) that if someone doesn't change their eating habits, the consequences will be severe? It's better to head off diseases before they happen, and watching what you eat plays an important role. Seek the counseling of a registered dietitian (RD) if you have special dietary needs. Ask your doctor for a referral or find an RD at www.eatright.org, the Web site of the American Dietetic Association, which can help you locate an RD in your area if your doctor can't refer you to one.

The Virgo sees a dietitian (not me) for his hypertension and pre-diabetic condition. Through counseling with his RD, he has managed to decrease and control his blood pressure, and he hopes to head off diabetes before it develops further. He's done this solely with his diet, meaning that he takes no medication for either condition. So far, so good. To look at him, you'd never suspect either condition because he's within normal weight limits, exercises regularly, and has followed a healthy diet for years. He doesn't fit the pattern, but looks can be deceiving.

If you need to lose weight, an RD can help with that too.

Following is an overview of how each slice of the pyramid fits into an average daily diet

- ✔ **Grains:** Starches (potatoes, rice, corn, pasta, beans) have great appeal for many people — too much appeal for some. The USDA recommends eating at least 3 ounces per day. Hold the line at ½ to 1 cup cooked starch per serving, depending on your ideal height and weight.

  Aim for whole grains (whole wheat, whole oat, quinoa, and barley), and check the ingredients listed on the packaging. If grains are described as "enriched" or "refined," they're not whole grains, even if the front of the package says "wheat," "multi-grain," or "made with whole grain."

- ✔ **Vegetables:** Aim for nine servings of vegetables and fruits (see the next item in this list) per day. For cooked vegetables, enjoy a minimum of ½ cup per serving. I'm talking about broccoli, bell peppers, cabbage, cauliflower, squash, tomatoes — you get the picture. Eat more if you like (and try hard to "like" them). For raw vegetables, such as green salads, 1 cup is a serving. Eat all you want, but go easy on the salad dressing.

- ✔ **Fruits:** Eat about ½ cup of fresh fruits per serving rather than fruit juice to up your daily fruit and vegetable consumption to nine servings.

- ✔ **Oils/fats:** Most of your fats should come from polyunsaturated and monounsaturated fatty acids, such as fish, nuts, and vegetable oils. When preparing and selecting meats, poultry, milk, and milk products, choose lean, low-fat, or fat-free.

- ✔ **Milk/calcium:** Milk and dairy products contribute protein, carbohydrates, and fat. Choose the fat-free version for your heath and waistline. Look for reduced-fat cheeses, yogurt, and other dairy products. Dairy foods make a huge contribution to calcium intake.

✔ **Meats and beans/proteins:** Half a cow is too much protein; instead, plan on 50 to 175 grams a day in a 2,000-calorie diet. Generally speaking, 1 ounce of meat has about 7 grams of protein.

The exact amount needed is age- and gender-specific, but generally speaking, a healthy adult needs 0.8 grams per day per kilo (or 2.2 pounds) of body weight. Here's the formula: Divide your weight by 2.2. Multiply that number by 0.8, and that's the number of grams you need.

For example, if I weighed 125 pounds (dream on, girlfriend), that would be about 57 kilos (125 ÷ 2.2 = 57). Multiply that by 0.8 for about 45 grams of protein a day for me. Guys get more because they weigh more (usually).The Virgo, who weighs about 165 (75 kilos), needs 60 grams. That's why he gets the bigger piece of chicken.

Reading the Nutrition Facts Label

The familiar Nutrition Facts panel has been a part of food packages since 1991, when the U.S. Food and Drug Administration (FDA) began requiring that the standardized box of information be included on most food products. Since that time, some changes have been made to the panel, such as what nutrients are required to be listed, but the layout of the label has remained consistent.

The Nutrition Facts label (see Figure 2-2) gives information for one serving of the food product, and then compares that nutrient information to a 2,000-calorie daily diet.

You have to hand it to our government for giving us these important facts in label form on our food. I remember when the bill first passed the legislature; I truly jumped up and down. I'm not kidding. These fact panels are one of the best things our government has done in terms of looking after the public's nutritional health. I wasn't the only person jumping up and down, either. Dietitians, physicians, healthcare workers, and consumers interested in nutrition were jumping with me. It's a wonder the earth didn't tilt with all that jumping.

Some foods aren't covered by the FDA's labeling requirements. The USDA oversees the labeling of meat and poultry. Food sold in unpackaged form, such as raw fruits and vegetables and raw seafood, are exempt from food labeling. Most alcohol doesn't require nutrition information on the label. (I find the fact that alcohol doesn't need a label scintillating information.)

Grocery stores are supposed to list the point of origin or the area where the food item is harvested — for example, salmon from Alaska or blueberries from Chile. Some stores make available a chart that shows the nutritive value of each fruit and vegetable. If you don't see it in your store, ask where it is.

Nutrition Facts

Serving Size 1 cup (228g)
Servings Per Container 2

Amount Per Serving

Calories 250   Calories from Fat 110

% Daily Value*

Total Fat 12g	18%
Saturated Fat 3g	15%
Trans Fat 1.5g	
Cholesterol 30mg	10%
Sodium 470mg	20%
Total Carbohydrate 31g	10%
Dietary Fiber 0g	0%
Sugars 5g	
Protein 5g	

Vitamin A	4%
Vitamin C	2%
Calcium	20%
Iron	4%

*Percent Daily Values are based on a 2,000 calorie diet. Your daily values may be higher or lower depending on your calorie needs:

		Calories:	2,000	2,500
Total Fat	Less than		65g	80g
Saturated Fat	Less than		20g	25g
Cholesterol	Less than		300mg	300mg
Sodium	Less than		2,400mg	2,400mg
Total Carbohydrate			300g	375g
Dietary Fiber			25g	30g

Figure 2-2:
A Nutrition
Facts panel.

Breaking down the label

The label is a guide — it's a good one, but still a guide. Canned tomatoes or a jar of marinara sauce may have tomatoes from different locations. These tomatoes might have a slightly different nutritive analysis because a tomato grown in one location in a particular climate with different watering techniques and different soil cannot be exactly like one grown 3,000 miles away. Just know that the analysis of tomatoes and other foods is the best it can be. This label is the standard we have for now and is a lot better than it was before the government required labels.

Not being from the government, I can't write and explain the label like I was one of "them." It takes special training to be that kind of technical writer, and I'm not a techie kind of person. As proof, I'm writing a *For Dummies* book, which means I'm doing my best to enliven this text so you don't fall asleep. I know this isn't scintillating reading, but bear with me. Here's a breakdown of the specific parts of the label:

✔ **Servings and serving size:** This section gives the portion of food considered to be one serving, according to the USDA guidelines. All nutrition information listed is based on one serving. Got it? One serving. This amount may vary from the amount you actually eat. Serving size is listed in a standard measurement, such as cups or tablespoons, as well as in gram weight. A bucket is not considered a standard serving.

Companies have been known to base the information on a tiny serving size to make the nutritional analysis look better. For example, 8 ounces of a regular cola beverage is not a typical serving size for most people. If you drink more than that, you have to multiply "up" to get the correct amount of sodium, calories, and so on. Companies are doing a better job of correcting this so that consumers don't have to do the math in the grocery aisle. Some soft drink labels now show the number of calories per bottle, rather than per 8 ounces.

The number of servings per container is listed on the next line of the label.

✔ **Calories:** In this line, total calories for one serving are listed on the left and the number of calories that come from fat is listed on the right. Comparing these two numbers helps to promote a balanced diet by giving you an idea of how many of your total calories come from fat. Calories are such fun to talk about. Fat, not so much. Not everyone agrees with me on this.

✔ **Nutrients:** Here are the nutrients you'll find listed on a Nutrition Panel:

- Fat (saturated and trans fats). Some labels include mono and poly-unsaturated fats, too.

- Cholesterol.

- Sodium.

- Carbohydrates (fiber and sugar).

- Protein.

- Vitamins and minerals.

The amount of each nutrient is listed in grams or milligrams, so you can use those numbers to figure whether you're meeting your requirements.

The first nutrients listed — total fat, saturated fat, trans fat, cholesterol, and sodium — should be eaten in limited amounts, because excessive amounts can increase your risk of diseases such as heart disease and cancer.

Looking at the numbers

The Nutrition Panel wouldn't do you much good if it only listed which nutrients a food contained. The panel also includes numbers that help you know how that food's nutritional content fits into your dietary needs for the day.

Percent daily values

Most of the nutrients on the label list a number known as the *percent daily value (%DV)* to the right of the nutrient amount. It tells you what percentage of your daily requirement for that nutrient is provided by one serving of the food (based on a 2,000-calorie diet). The percentage allows you to quickly recognize whether the food is high or low in a particular nutrient. As a general rule, 5 percent or less is low; 20 percent or more is high. That makes sense.

Use this percentage to help balance your diet. If you eat a food with a high fat percentage, balance that by including other foods in your diet with low fat percentages. If you need to limit your intake of a nutrient, such as fat, try not to let your daily total intake of that nutrient exceed 100 percent of the daily value. This is all about math. As one nutrient goes up, something else has to go down, percentage-wise.

The %DV notation isn't required for trans fat, sugars, and protein. However, if a label makes a particular claim, such as "Good source of protein," a %DV for protein will be listed. You won't see "good source of protein" on chocolate chip cookies or beer.

The main point to remember is that when it comes to percent per nutrient (carbohydrates, fat, and protein), the total must add up to 100 percent. If one goes up, something else has to go down. The nutrients have to add up to 100. That's just the way it goes!

Daily values footnote

This section is included at the bottom of larger labels and gives daily values of particular nutrients for a 2,000- or 2,500-calorie diet. The footnote does not change from product to product. Consistency is good.

The values for total fat, saturated fat, cholesterol, and sodium are *maximum* amounts. You should make a major effort to consume less than these amounts each day. Try to eat no more than 30 percent of your calories from fat; less is best. All mothers agree on this, which is amazing because all mothers don't agree on much of anything else, other than that their kid is the smartest, best-looking, and most likely kid to succeed in the entire universe.

The values listed for total carbohydrate and dietary fiber are *minimum* amounts recommended for each calorie level. For these, try to eat at least the amount listed on a daily basis. Earlier in this chapter, you see carbohydrates listed in the "What you don't need a lot of" section. Don't get me wrong — you need to eat some carbohydrates because they're a ready source of energy. Just don't go overboard with them. "All things in moderation" is a motto to etch in stone.

Eyeing ingredient lists

In addition to the Nutrition Facts panel, an ingredient list is included on each food package. The ingredients are listed in descending order according to weight. So if you pick up a product, cereal for example, and sugar is at the top of the ingredients list (first or second), that cereal is high in sugar.

The ingredient list not only lets you know exactly what's in the food, but can also be used for comparing similar products. For instance, compare two juice drinks. The first drink has fruit juice listed as its first ingredient, and the second drink has water listed first and fruit juice listed near the end of the ingredient list. By weight, the majority of the first drink is juice, whereas the second drink contains more water than anything else. The first few ingredients are what you want to pay attention to.

As a general rule, the healthier the product, the fewer ingredients listed. Also, as a general guideline, you want to try to only eat ingredients you can pronounce and are familiar with. Why would you want to put some chemical in your body when you don't know what it does?

Preparing Healthy Meals

How much and what we eat can help define our overall health status. Making the right choices makes life more enjoyable and active. When you and I are at the right weight for our height, age, and activity, we feel and look so much better. Feeling better leads to a more positive outlook in life. Isn't that what most of us really want? I say yes.

The ideal place to start making healthy food choices is with your menu planning, followed by how you prepare the items on your menu. For example, baked chicken without skin is a better choice than fried chicken, and a baked potato or steamed brown rice is a better choice than French fries.

Finding ways to cut the sodium

I'm not going to beat around the bush about sodium. (*Me*, beat around the bush?) You need to reduce the amount of sodium you're consuming. Me, too. I've already told you that. I'm working on it, and so should you.

Here are some ways to help you. Whenever you can, use fresh ingredients. Okay, I know sometimes it's the middle of winter, there's no fresh food in the refrigerator, the temp is below zero, and the snow is piled up in your driveway so you can't get to the store. What to do then? It's time to punt. You can use frozen vegetables, rinse the canned beans in your pantry to reduce their sodium content by 40 percent, limit your intake of proteins (they're higher in sodium), and fill up your plate with complex carbohydrates. When the weather changes, you can go back to the "fresh is best" philosophy.

Replace sodium with seasonings like herbs and spices to perk up the flavor. Use lots of ground black pepper, lemon juice, or assertive spices such as cayenne pepper, chili powder, or curry. Almost anything that comes in a can has high sodium (unless the cans are labeled "no salt added"), except fruits.

Some reduced-sodium and no-salt-added canned items are now available, and I applaud the companies that make them. Bush's beans and Hunt's and Del Monte's tomatoes come to mind. Swanson and Campbell's offer lower-sodium soups. Expect manufacturers to offer lower-sodium versions of their products (and request them from those that don't). Consumers can make a difference.

While you're at it, skip the highest sodium products, and if you do use them, use them sparingly. Start your serious look at labels with processed meats, and read every label of everything you buy starting now.

A good place to start with label reading is in your own pantry and refrigerator. This will save you time at the grocery store because we tend to purchase some of the same staple items. Now when you're at the store you can just read new items you pick up.

Using low-fat items when you can

Call me crazy, but I do like to use reduced-fat and even fat-free ingredients sometimes. Some people would rather use half as much of an ingredient than the full amount of a reduced-fat version. I have no problem with that, if that's what they really do. If I find a reduced-fat (or reduced-sodium) product that I like, I use it.

Be aware, however, that if the label boasts "fat free," the manufacturer may have increased the sugar content.

On my bread, baked potatoes, and sometimes vegetables, I usually use *light* I Can't Believe It's Not Butter. I also use their "butter" spray on vegetables and corn on the cob. It's lower in calories and much healthier than lots of butter; I use it for that reason, plus I don't mind the taste.

As for cheese, which I love and use often, I like Cabot's 50-percent-reduced-fat cheese and use it almost exclusively when I need cheddar, jalapeño, or pepper jack. I buy it in blocks and shred it myself. Some reduced-fat cheeses don't melt well. I skip them. I recently used fat-free cream cheese for an unbaked tart, and it was just fine. Usually I use reduced-fat cream cheese or Neufchatel cheese. If I want a little creamier texture in a sauce, I use 1-percent-fat milk; otherwise, I use (and drink) fat-free milk, usually Smart Balance for the extra calcium. Sometimes, I use fat-free half-and-half, depending on the amount needed in a recipe.

Obvious ways to cut the fat are to trim as much fat from the protein as possible before cooking, chill and skim after cooking, and avoid eating the skin from poultry. For example, if I'm going to make a pulled pork recipe in the slow cooker, I trim a lot of the obvious fat (and there's a lot of obvious fat) before I put it in the cooker. Recently I bought a 4.1-pound pork shoulder (pork butt), and I trimmed ¾ pound of fat before adding it to the cooker. At $2.39 per pound, I threw away $1.79. It's better in the trash than in your body. You wouldn't pour grease down your drain because it would clog the pipes; why would you pour it into your body to clog your pipes (arteries)? After the pork is done, I use a fat-separator to remove more fat, and after chilling, I take out the collected fat. It's a fatty piece of meat with a lot of flavor; I use it for the flavor and cost savings. Because you're going to cut out so much fat, you may want to buy a larger pork shoulder to start with.

Oh, and of course, skip fried foods. Because my favorite foods are French fries and burgers, I have to break that rule, and I do at least twice a month (and sometimes more). I order both, cut the burger in half, take it home or give it away at the table, and eat ten French fries. The leftover French fries aren't a problem, because anyone I have this meal with will refrain from ordering the fries, but surreptitiously remove them from my plate. It's a game I play often, and the thieves are usually women. Men order their own fries in the first place.

Freezing and thawing instructions

How you handle foods before you prepare them is part of serving healthy meals. I'm a huge fan of buying foods on sale and storing them in the freezer (if appropriate) until I'm ready to use them or I need a meal in a hurry. Here are some tips when it comes to freezing foods:

✔ **Know how long you can keep foods in your freezer:** According to the USDA, frozen foods remain safe to eat indefinitely. But the quality of the taste declines the longer you keep the food in the freezer. The following chart shows the USDA's recommendations for the maximum amount of time to freeze certain foods.

Item	Months
Bacon and sausage	1 to 2
Casseroles	2 to 3
Egg whites or egg substitutes	12
Frozen dinners and entrees	3 to 4
Ham, hot dogs, and lunchmeats	1 to 2
Meat, cooked	2 to 3
Meat, uncooked ground	3 to 4
Meat, uncooked roasts	4 to 12
Meat, uncooked steaks or chops	4 to 12
Poultry, cooked	4
Poultry, uncooked parts	9
Poultry, uncooked whole	12
Soups and stews	2 to 3

✔ **Know what *not* to put in the freezer** (besides your secret money and your good jewelry): Some foods just don't freeze well. Better to prepare these and eat them right away:

  • **Cooked eggs.** By the way, don't ever try to cook a raw egg in the shell in the microwave. The result (which I've witnessed) is neither a pretty sight nor inexpensive to repair.

- **Cooked chunks of potatoes.** Mashed potatoes and twice-baked ones, on the other hand, can be frozen. Mashed potatoes get watery, but when you reheat them, they're just fine. I am the voice of experience who loves mashed potatoes (and all potatoes).

- **Potato salad.** I never have any leftover, so it's not an issue.

- **Raw watery vegetables.** This includes lettuce, cucumbers, radishes, tomatoes, celery, and cabbage. If these are in a cooked dish, like vegetable soup, they freeze better. Why would you freeze lettuce anyway? Ditto any other watery vegetables.

- **Yogurt, sour cream, and mayonnaise.** These can separate. However, I freeze milk all the time to keep it from spoiling. Leave plenty of room in the bottle or container for expansion or it will crack. Remember learning about the expansion of liquids in physics?

- **Fried foods with coating.** These get gummy. Ick. Ditto for crumb toppings. Double ick.

✔ **Know what's in your freezer.** Label everything that goes into the freezer with the date, number of servings, and whether it's raw or cooked. Then keep a running list of inventory so that when you need a quick meal, you can locate it in a hurry. All I have to say about this advice is *good luck.*

✔ **Periodically check the contents of your freezer.** Make an effort to go through the freezer a couple of times a year, and toss anything that you can't identify, that looks like an art project from your 6-year-old, or is older than one year. Then, you'll have more room to add more food to toss next year. It's comforting to open your freezer and see lots of neat little packages — sort of like Christmas with lots of surprises in store for you. Except, these packages don't surprise those who do as I've instructed. That would be 17 people.

If you've ever wondered why the quality of the foods you freeze doesn't seem as good as that of manufactured frozen products, you can take heart in the fact that you're not to blame. The makers of commercially frozen products have special equipment that costs zillions of dollars and freezes food lickety-split, giving it a better quality.

Of course, if you freeze foods, you usually have to thaw them before you can prepare or eat them. Thaw them right! This does not mean on top of the radiator or in the hot sun.

Thawing slowly in the refrigerator is the absolute best and safest way. The last thing you want to do to is give your family and friends a food-borne disease. Allow one day per 5 pounds of weight as a general rule. Thaw on lower shelves of the refrigerator, and place food on a plate to catch drips and to protect other foods in the refrigerator.

If you must thaw food in the microwave, use 20- or 30-percent power and then cook it immediately. The microwave heats the food that bacteria love, so be careful.

Chapter 3

The 7-Day Menu Planner Users' Guide

*W*hen you think of a menu, it's much more than "what's for dinner." It's a complex plan of taking multiple elements and putting the parts together to make a perfect picture, flavor profile, and nutritional power-house. (I can't believe I wrote that. It's beautiful. But I digress.) And while the process may sound complicated, it isn't.

In this chapter, I show you the true "secrets" of the 7-Day Menu Planner and how I design, plan, and make menus for the week. We call this the exposé part. Who knew you'd find such thrills in a menu-planning book? Then I tell you how to put these menus to work for your family.

What's on the Menu?

When I start to build a menu, I begin with the main course. From there, I fill in with different kinds of side dishes (starches, vegetables, and salads), and finally, I wrap up with a dessert (you didn't think I would skip that, did you?). Designing a menu may sound pretty basic, but because I can choose from so many dishes, I outline my strategy in the following sections so you can see how it's done.

One of the keys to successful menu planning is to choose dishes based on the time of year. When summer is here, I can't wait to get to the grocery store and buy all those fresh fruits and vegetables that aren't around in January (unless you live below the equator). Cooler salads and no-cook meals are so appeal-ing when the temperature climbs. As fall approaches, not only do I drag out my orange- and rust-colored clothes, but I begin to think of recipes with root vegetables and pumpkin and other "heartier" ingredients. As the north winds howl, those heavier stews and soups warm our chilled bodies. Spring blows in with warmer temperatures and the beginning of fresh vegetables again. And so the cycle continues. Whatever the season, enjoy the foods that bring it alive.

Laying down the foundation: Entrees

Entrees come in two forms: combination dishes that combine a protein with a starch or vegetable — think casseroles — and plain old protein by itself — think a chicken breast, a slice of roast beef, a pork chop, or a piece of fish (I cover combination dishes and stand-alone entrees in more detail in Chapter 4). Which type of entree does your family prefer? When I'm thinking of you and how I'm going to design a menu for you and your family, I figure that you like some of both types of entrees, for different reasons.

In choosing an entree, I take into account how much protein it has and whether it's a whole meat or a combo dish. If the protein isn't as much as I think it needs to be, I have to add other sources of protein to the meal. I plan for 3 ounces of cooked weight for a whole meat serving or about that amount for a total meal. The raw portion may be 4 to 5 ounces, depending on fat and moisture content.

Can you afford whole meats, such as steak, chops, or roasts, every night? Most of my readers can't, nor can I. Here's the secret to getting the most bang for your grocery buck when buying meat for an entree: The leaner the meat or fish, the less raw weight you need to buy to get the recommended amount of protein. For example, if I buy one pound of fatty ground beef at $3 a pound and lose 40 percent in the cooking process due to moisture and fat, as opposed to buying 93- to 95-percent-lean ground beef at $4 per pound and losing 10 percent of it, have I saved money? Initially, yes, you paid $3 versus $4 at the store, but how much cooked weight is left in one versus the other after cooking? It isn't until after you cook the meat and lose fat and moisture that you see you didn't save by buying the least-expensive meat. Paying less doesn't mean you should expect the same result. You get what you pay for. Raw cost versus cooked-weight cost is what I have to figure when I'm planning menus for you.

Of course, during this planning phase, I consider where a particular entree fits into the themes I design for each night during the week. You may or may not have your own themes. (Check out Chapter 1 for more on themes.)

Choosing sides: Starches, vegetables, and salads

Once the entree is chosen for each night, I think about what foods go well with what I've selected. I think of the sides as perfect partners to compliment the entree. Remember, I'm looking at the overall design of all the dinners during the week, not just one meal. Take a bag of baby carrots, for example.

For Family Night the carrots may be steamed, but for Express Night they may be a used as a colorful, crunchy side. I also consider the ratio of casseroles to whole meats, whether a particular food is repeated too many times, and whether the colors of the dishes make the meals attractive. The goal is for all meals to be equally successful, healthful, attractive, and budget-friendly.

In terms of cost, sides generally aren't an issue because you can choose canned, frozen, or fresh according to season and budget. Starches are almost always inexpensive (that's why some populations eat too many of them). The protein is usually the most expensive item in the meal or on the menu.

If I'm having a stand-alone entree (such as baked chicken, pork chops, or meat patties), I add a starch. The starch could be brown rice, baked sweet potatoes, corn on the cob, starchy beans (black, pinto, or navy, for example), pasta, and so on. Now, I add vegetables and salad. The vegetables I'm thinking of are broccoli, cabbage, carrots, cauliflower, eggplant, greens (such as kale, spinach, or collard greens), mushrooms, squash, or tomatoes. (Potatoes, starchy beans, and corn are *not* considered vegetables, as much as I wish they were.) A green salad is next. It can be as simple as chopped lettuce.

Combination dishes receive the same treatment as stand-alone entrees. Even though a casserole can be a combination of meats, starches, and vegetables, add a green salad or a side of green beans, broccoli, kale, spinach, cabbage, or something along those lines to that meal, as well as some whole-grain bread to complete the combination dish!

Okay, I need to say a little more about vegetables — no one is allowed to be excused, and no hall passes will be issued during the vegetable discussion! I know some of you would be happy if you never ate a vegetable again, and I know where you live, so watch it! Forgoing vegetables is not acceptable behavior for a couple of reasons. I'm not going to beat a dead horse and expound on the benefits of eating vegetables for their nutritional benefits because, as I point out in Chapter 2, you're supposed to be eating nine servings of fruits and vegetables a day (shocking as that number is).

What I *am* going to wow you with are the many other benefits of veggies as side dishes. Let me count the ways:

- ✔ The different colors look fabulous on your plate, and increase nutrient value.

- ✔ Vegetables are much less expensive than whole proteins.

- ✔ Veggies add all sorts of crunch, texture, and interest (like the perfect wine) to the meal.

- ✔ They're easy to prepare.

- ✔ Perhaps most important, vegetables fill you up so that you don't overeat. Broccoli and other fresh vegetables can be your secret weapon against overeating. It's mine.

For the best nutrient punch, darker greens for salads are better than iceberg lettuce. Also, the bagged salad mixtures have a vast combination of greens and are certainly convenient, but they're more expensive than a head of lettuce or cabbage and a bunch of kale. Some people clean and spin their own salad greens: My honey does; I don't. However, I do eat what he cleans, and it tastes better than the bagged kind.

I really want you to up your vegetable intake, and that's why you see veggies in my recipes and menus for every meal. I aim for nine vegetables and/or fruits a day. Two of these can be at breakfast and lunch, with three for dinner. Between meals, select three more, and you've exceeded the recommendation. Keep in mind that people who are overweight probably didn't get that way by eating too many fruits and vegetables.

As a side note, a serving isn't as much as you may think: ½ cup of raw or cooked veggies, 1 cup of raw lettuce, or ½ cup or one medium piece of fruit. Now take out your ½-cup measuring cup and take notice: It's not that much! The task isn't as daunting as you may have first thought.

As you advance in age, your taste buds continue to mature, which means you have the opportunity to increase your list of favorite vegetables (and other foods). You'll influence your children to try new foods, too. When mom and dad try a new food, they send a positive message to the kids.

The finishing touch: Desserts

Finally, dessert (yes, I know this is your favorite part of the meal). You can have dessert during the week, but keep it simple — a piece of fruit is ideal. The weekend is a good time to have a special sweet.

I'm not an ogre when it comes to desserts, but some folks eat too darn many. I've been known to knock off a half-dozen cookies myself, but I do try to talk my way out of that rut. I'm not even going to tell you about the time I arrived at Krispy Kreme Doughnuts and ate a half dozen of the warm, sweet, dreamy wonders in one sitting. Yes, have a bite or a piece, but don't eat the whole package. I do include desserts on the 7-Day Menu Planner because I know lots of you want a sweet at the end of your meal. Make it fruit more often than not. It's coolness and sweetness can declare that the meal is over, not to mention it counts as one of your nine daily servings!

If you're challenged to have "a little" sweet before you go to bed even though you're not really hungry, you may need a little behavior modification. When I'm in that state of mind, I march myself to my toothbrush and dental floss, salute, and go at it. For me, it's a good way to knock off that "feed me a sweet" call.

Consider storing your dessert for a little later in the evening. Then if you have a tendency to nonchalantly (yeah, right!) wander into the kitchen 30 minutes after you've had a nice dinner and open the refrigerator (didn't know I had spies everywhere, did you?) looking for a little snack, your dinner dessert will be waiting for you. You're so smart!

Maybe if you're entertaining, you'll want to leave the dining table and serve coffee or tea in another place. That's a good time to have dessert, too.

Peeking at My Strategy

You may be wondering why I choose the recipes for you that I do. Well, suffice it to say I don't actually choose them for *you*. It's all about me (again). The choices I make relate to what I want to eat. It's that simple. (I'm not even thinking about you at this point. Sorry. Eventually, you'll pop into mind.) I look at the recipe, and decide whether it sounds and looks good (if there's a photo) and whether the Virgo and I would want to have it for a meal. These are the questions I routinely ask myself during the workday.

Next, I think of *you*. Would you like to eat it, too? If I want to, then you will, too, is what's going through my mind. How many ingredients does the recipe have? Where do I buy the ingredients? Are they in my grocery store? How much does it cost? How much chopping is there? How many pans/dishes will I dirty? Will this work on the weekend or during the workweek? How long does it take to cook? Do I marinate it? These questions may seem like a lot of work to you, but I'm used to it. The best part is, I answer them all for you in the 365 menus in this book!

Let me answer these questions, one by one, for you so you get a better idea of how I put the menus together. You may want to use the same checklist when you start planning your own menus (see Chapter 4).

- ✔ **Would I like to eat it?** I have a fairly broad base of food likes with few real dislikes. My husband has essentially no food dislikes. If the recipe makes the first cut of flavor and it's a yes, I move on.

- ✔ **How many ingredients?** Usually if I have to count them, there are too many. When it comes to spices, I allow more ingredients because spices add so much flavor without fat and calories, and they are easy to come by. Notice I said "easy to come by," meaning that they are in my grocery store and I don't have to make a trip to a specialty market.

- ✔ **Where do I buy the ingredients and are they in my store?** I might go to a specialty store once a year for an ingredient, but no more. It's too much trouble for me (and I think for you, too). The ingredients have to be convenient or I won't choose that recipe for us.

✔ **How much will the ingredients cost?** I worry about this all the time. I try to be respectful of my food dollars and also of yours. I've had to eliminate certain kinds of fish and seafood from some of the menus because I don't like to pay the price. I hate doing this, but I believe it's necessary in these tougher times. Readers who live in seafood areas may see this differently, and I would, too, if I lived there.

✔ **How much prep work does the recipe take?** Chopping, dicing, and cutting meat and veggies into pieces doesn't appeal to everyone. In Chapter 5, you read about having good knives, and I do (but half the time they aren't as sharp as they should be). If you want to spend the money for convenience, then you can buy chopped and ready-to-use vegetables and fruits, fresh or frozen.

✔ **Will I spend all night cleaning up?** Two pans, maximum three, are the limit. I try to limit bowls, too. It's hard to truly enjoy a meal if the kitchen looks like a tornado dropped by. In all fairness, a clean-as-you-go cook should have major help with clean-up. I do, and I certainly appreciate it. Ask for help if you don't have it already. You should not take on the role of Kitchen Queen or King.

✔ **How long will the recipe take to prepare and cook?** Cooking and prep time are important elements. Who has hours and hours to make dinner? I try to keep the preparation time under 15 to 20 minutes during the week and the cooking time no more than 45 minutes (and often less than 30). Sometimes, when I find a really wonderful recipe, I might fudge that time a little. If it's a slow-cooker meal, it might take 20 minutes of prep, but dinner is ready when you come home. Man, do I love those evenings.

When company is coming, I allow for a little leeway when I'm choosing recipes. The meal will probably be a little more expensive and may take longer and use more dishes and pans. It's usually on Saturday night.

Working with the Recipes

The recipes I include in Part II don't have a huge number of ingredients or steps (which often leads to more dishes and pans to wash). I also like recipes with ingredients that are easy to find in my supermarket, thus eliminating the need to run all over town looking for a particular ingredient and running out of gas in the process. (True story! It happened to me.)

I'm a simple person and I like simple recipes. I hate to say it out loud, but maybe I like the easier recipes because not only am I simple, I'm lazy, and I don't want to complicate my life any more than I want to complicate yours.

No matter how easy a recipe is, you still need to know some essential points before preparing it, such as how long it takes to make and how many hungry mouths it feeds. I cover those points in the following sections and also explain my philosophy about leftovers.

It's all in the timing

Beyond planning, I believe that timing for meal preparation is one of the hardest things to master. Timing requires strategy and — you guessed it — planning. I'm such a nag.

For your planning purposes, each recipe in this book lists two times:

- ✔ **Prep time:** This time represents the actual labor required to get the recipe together. It includes opening packages or cans, washing, slicing, chopping, and so on. Call it the verb part: Action!

- ✔ **Cook time:** This time represents the application of heat: browning, boiling, baking, braising (I love alliteration), grilling, and microwaving. Microwaving doesn't actually apply heat, but its mechanism or "energy" (agitation of molecules) causes food to cook.

When you combine the two times, you have the amount of time to get the dish on the table from A to Z or start to finish. It's the checkered flag time; you cross the finish line and ring the "dinner is served" bell!

Here's a sample plan for getting an entire meal to the table. Say you're preparing chili, which takes a while to simmer. While the chili cooks, heat the oven. Stir up a cornbread mix to go with the chili. It can be baking while the chili is simmering. After the cornbread is in the oven, that's the time to make a green salad or create a raw vegetable tray of carrot and celery sticks, cherry tomatoes, and salad greens. It's also a good time to set the table or teach the kids how to do it. While they practice their table-setting skills, you can stir the chili and check on the cornbread in the oven. Before the timer dings, get the fresh fruit ready to portion for dessert and refrigerate it. Ding! Dinner is ready.

One of the best ways to perfect your timing is by planning ahead. Read the recipe a few days before you plan to prepare a dish. Make sure you have all the ingredients you need for a meal. Defrost the entree in the refrigerator the day before you plan to use it.

Looking at a few timing factors

Several factors go into determining how long it takes to prepare a given food. For example, how long does it take water to boil for pasta? That depends on the following:

- ✔ **The stove:** Does your stove heat fast, or do you feel as if you're on the prairie starting a fire at the back of a covered wagon? (Please don't write to me and tell me never to have a stove/fire on the back of a covered wagon. This is just a ridiculous example.) I'm somewhere in between the two. My stove isn't very good nor does it heat very fast or evenly. If I sell a lot of books, I'll buy a new one.

✔ **The amount of water:** For example, if I'm boiling water for pasta, it takes longer than boiling water for couscous. Why? There's more water to bring to boiling.

Boiling small amounts of water in the microwave might be quicker, but for larger volumes, use the stove. The time it takes a microwave to cook something is determined by volume and density: The more you have, the longer it takes.

✔ **The type of pan:** A long, shallow, 3-quart baking dish (a 9-x-13-inch dish, for example) cooks food faster than a smaller, taller dish with the same volume of food. In the latter case, it takes longer for the heat to reach the center and cook the ingredients. All methods of cooking (including microwave cooking) rely on transferring heat from the outside to the center. This is why, when you test for doneness via temperature, you test the center of what you're cooking. Temperature is the most accurate measure of doneness.

When I want to "dry" (not cook) frozen chopped spinach to add to a recipe (such as vegetable lasagna), I spread the spinach in a skillet and place it on a burner that's the same size as the skillet for maximum heat contact. I turn the burner on low heat and press the spinach to the bottom of the skillet (where it's hottest) so the water evaporates. I use heat in this instance because it's more effective than squeezing the spinach dry with my fist or pressing it into a colander. If I put the same spinach in a straight-sided pan, it would take longer to dry.

On the other hand, if I had a lot of water to boil, I'd use a saucepan or large pot on a large burner and cover it, because a saucepan is more convenient. I wouldn't use a skillet to boil water. The point is to match the size of the cooking utensil to the size of the burner, when possible.

Having everything ready at the same time

When you're cooking a meal, you have to worry about the timing of several dishes. Following several different recipes for one meal is difficult until you get your timing honed. One of the hardest skills for many cooks is figuring out how to have all menu items done and hot/cold at the same time. That, too, takes planning and experience.

I start with the recipe that takes the longest and write down how long it will take from start to finish. In determining the amount of time to allot, I figure in boiling water, heating the oven, chopping, trimming, cooking time, standing time, and any other variables. Most likely, all of these variables aren't in one recipe — if they were, I'd toss the recipe. So, lucky for you, I haven't included any recipes in this book that require that much time and effort.

Next, I decide when I want all the food to go on the table, so I have both start and finish times. Between the two is the prep, cooking, and standing time. Write it down. I always do this when I have guests for dinner and may be preparing four or five different dishes. I create an informal chart that tells me when to start each dish. For example, say you have guests arriving at 7 p.m., and you plan to serve dinner at 8. You prepared a dish earlier that you need to bake for 20 minutes just prior to serving. Allowing five minutes or so to get guests to the table and place the food, you should plan to put the dish in the oven at 7:35. I also drag out the serving containers and label them with regard to which recipe goes into which serving dish. Gosh, might I have some Virgo in me, too?

I use kitchen timers (often, more than one) for everything because I simply cannot remember when I put something in the oven or in the skillet. Just remember to set the timer!

Serving up the right portion sizes

Most recipes make four, six, or eight servings. The recipes in the 7-Day Menu Planner follow that lead. If you're a family of four and you make a recipe that yields 8 servings, lucky you. You have another meal waiting for you!

When you're dishing out portions, you can either measure the precise amounts (see Chapter 2 for more information on correct serving sizes), or you can eyeball them according to these guidelines:

- ✔ **½ cup cooked rice, pasta, or vegetables, or a piece of whole fruit:** A rounded handful or a woman's fist
- ✔ **1 cup leafy greens:** A baseball or a softball (the more leafy greens you eat, the better)
- ✔ **¼ cup dried fruit:** A golf ball
- ✔ **3 ounces cooked meat:** A deck of cards or the palm of your hand without fingers (I'm not talking about the hands of a professional basketball player, either)
- ✔ **8 ounces cooked meat:** A small paperback book (no, *War and Peace* does not qualify)
- ✔ **1 medium baked potato:** A computer mouse — *not* the mouse pad
- ✔ **1 teaspoon butter, margarine, or peanut butter:** A thumb tip

Get used to measuring amounts of food until your eyeball measurements are accurate. I still measure amounts, especially starches, because I have a "starch tooth."

Why it's wise to keep an eye on portion sizes

Be careful about portion distortion, especially if your weight is an issue. Guilty as charged. In former days, if I made a recipe for four, a minimal amount would be left over. That's the behavior that sent me to Weight Watchers. It wasn't that I didn't know what to do; I just didn't choose to use my knowledge to maintain a healthful weight. I needed the discipline of getting on a scale every week. I did weigh myself every week, and now I pay a lot more attention to portion sizes. I continue to weigh in monthly and plan to continue to do so.

Making use of leftovers

In Part II's 7-Day Menu Planner, you'll find "plan ahead" instructions on some days. This is where I help you use leftovers in creative ways. Sometimes, you can even reuse the leftover leftovers. I feel triumphant when I can do that. Here are a few examples.

On Sunday, I tell you to roast a large chicken (6 to 7 pounds total). Monday, I have you make it into Chicken Enchiladas (which use cooked chicken). On Wednesday, I have you reheat the leftover enchiladas. (Your family may not want chicken three days in a row, so I skip serving it on Tuesday night.) You can follow suit by turning roast beef into a roast beef stir-fry, open-face roast beef sandwiches, or barbeque roast beef (by adding barbecue sauce). An extra baked (or grilled) salmon fillet can morph into an ingredient in a pasta sauce — all you have to do is add the pieces of cooked salmon on top of the pasta and sauce, or stir the cooked salmon into heated Alfredo sauce and cooked pasta.

However, don't go too far with redoing leftovers. A case in point: When I was still a bride, thinking my new husband would love everything I cooked, I re-created a cream cheese-based dessert to turn it into something new and exciting. My attempts caused great consternation for him. As I recall it, I added pink gelatin to the cream cheese mixture, which made it even stiffer. He did eat it like a good, loving husband, but years later he told me he thought I was trying to collect on his insurance when I fed him "pink plaster." I had gone too far. A better idea would have been to make cupcakes and give him one every night in a row, but decorate them with a variety of candy pieces. Lesson learned!

Tweaking the Menus for Your Family's Tastes

Because I don't live with you — even though I am up for adoption — I can't know all your family's likes and dislikes. The menus in the 7-Day Menu

Planner are designed so you can change what you don't like into what you and your family do like.

However, there are limits to what you can swap. You can make exchanges only within groups of foods. What am I talking about? You can't change roast pork to chocolate chip cookies or substitute an extra serving of mashed potatoes for broccoli. That would drive me bonkers! You *can* substitute roast beef for roast pork (no cookies) or broccoli for spinach. Get it? You must color inside the lines for this one. If you don't like peaches, how about pears? That's what I'm talking about. I'm very strict about this rule.

If your family likes bread, serve whole-grain and whole-wheat varieties for added nutritional value. If you're going to enjoy bread, why not enjoy a kind that has fiber and a better nutritional profile? In my opinion, most white bread is like eating air with a crust.

If a loaf of bread lasts into its moldy days at your house, freeze the number of slices you need for each meal. By freezing it, you create your own Mold-Be-Gone system instead of wasting the bread. Save money any way you can.

Hitting the Grocery Store

When you're using the menus I provide in Part II, you'll have some of the ingredients in your pantry and refrigerator (more on those in Chapter 5). But you'll probably need to buy other ingredients, like the protein, vegetables, and fruits.

If you're lucky, you can buy all your staples for the week in one trip; for perishables it's more difficult, unless you have a cow and a garden full of vegetables. For most of us, it takes two or three visits. The more planning you do and the more organized you are, the fewer trips you'll need to make. With good planning, you can reduce it to two trips. I've heard some folks suggest eating all your produce at the first of the week so it doesn't spoil. The theory is that you can use frozen vegetables and fruits when the fresh ones run out. I can't do that. I'd much rather make another trip and have a variety of fresh produce daily.

In the following sections, I explain how you can streamline your shopping by using a grocery list, and then I offer tips on how to make the most of your trip through the grocery store aisles.

Drafting a weekly shopping list

I suggest making a list and hitting the grocery store once a week for what's on the list plus half of the nonperishables you've planned for in your menus. Depending on the size of your family, you may need to shop for fresh produce, milk, and fresh meat in a second trip. Using a list allows you to make one trip to the store to buy almost everything at once, and it discourages you from buying what you don't need because it's not on the list.

Perhaps you buy some of the same items routinely. Create your own personal shopping list that contains these items. Organize the list by the route you typically take through the store. When you're sitting at home with your coupons and grocery ads planning your trip, you can check off those staples on your master list that need replenishing.

Figure 3-1 shows you what my basic shopping list looks like. It doesn't include foods that will be prepared for the evening meals. I add those as needed. The one on the left is more of a fall/winter list and the other one is a spring/summer list to accommodate seasonal fruits and vegetables. Some items are for my husband's pre-diabetic diet as recommended by *his* dietitian (not me). The brands, when listed, are strictly our personal preferences. Some items we buy by price alone. We use store-brand or generic products when they fit our needs — we've found that the quality of these products has improved greatly in the last several years.

Try to buy most of your items from one store unless shopping at multiple stores is convenient and you save enough money to justify the extra time and driving. One or two shopping trips a week should cover most families unless there are a lot of mouths to feed.

Using sanity-saving strategies at the grocery store

To make your fabulous meals move along smoothly, you must visit the grocery store (unless you have a delivery service, of course). It's best to prepare yourself for what's to come. You've already armed yourself with the perfect shopping list (see the preceding section), now it's time to march off to the store and shop wisely. Following are a few tips:

- ✔ **Eat before you go.** If you're starving when you're in the store, I can assure you that nothing good is going to happen. You'll be loving Twinkies at first sight along with any food that involves free samples. Who knows what other trouble you'll find yourself in? In a word: Don't!

- ✔ **Shop the perimeter *and* up and down the aisles.** Shop anyway you darn please — good food choices are all over the store, just like there are bad choices everywhere. Forget that always-shop-the-perimeter routine; move up and down the aisles as well!

Some experts recommend shopping the perimeter of the store. I look at it this way: If you spend all your time in the suburbs (perimeter of the store), how will you know what other opportunities exist in the inner city? If you only shop the perimeter, you'll miss spices, pasta, rice, canned tuna and chicken, oatmeal, canned vegetables and fruits, and a host of other important products that are in the grocery store's "inner city."

✔ **Know your store and the store manager.** The manager is your friend and can order special items for you when you need them. He's the best person to complain or give compliments to. Start at the top!

Fall/Winter List	Spring/Summer List
Apples Avocado Bananas Pears	Apples Avocado Bananas Blueberries Cherries Cantaloupe Nectarines
Broccoli Red bell pepper Winter squash Lettuce – bagged or head Spinach Tomatoes Mushrooms	Broccoli Red bell pepper Summer squash Lettuce – bagged or head Spinach Tomatoes Mushrooms
Fish – Tilapia ( ); Salmon ( )	Fish – Tilapia ( ); Salmon ( )
Chicken breasts	Chicken breasts
Lowest-carb bread	Lowest-carb bread
Oatmeal	Kashi Go Lean
Paper towels Toilet paper Tissues	Paper towels Toilet paper Tissues
Laughing Cow Light Swiss Spread Cheese, Cabot, Jalapeño Cheese, Cabot, Sharp Cheddar, 50% Smart Balance I Can't Believe It's Not Butter Light Sour cream (low-fat) Yogurt, fat-free plain, Greek Eggs ___Gallon Milk, Skim	Laughing Cow Light Swiss Spread Cheese, Cabot, Jalapeño Cheese, Cabot, Sharp Cheddar, 50% Smart Balance I Can't Believe It's Not Butter Light Sour cream (low-fat) Yogurt, fat-free plain, Greek Eggs ___Gallon Milk, Skim

Figure 3-1: Examples of seasonal grocery lists.

✔ **Shop alone.** Like most tasks that are new and different, shopping with your new plan may take a little longer the first few times. After that, you won't have any problem. If you're the lone meal preparer, if at all possible, shop alone. If that's not possible, try to make the trip as fast as you can for your good humor and for the sake of whoever is with you, especially children.

✔ **Share the experience . . . sometimes.** If you can shop with someone who knows your "ropes," do so. If not, leave others at home or at the babysitter's house. You'll save time and money (kids are notorious for pleading for items that aren't on your list). If you do take someone with you, enforce a no-whining policy.

You may laugh at this, but my husband and I power shop together. *Power shopping* is giving each person a cart and his or her own list. We do it this way: He gets all the routine things to meet our household needs, such as produce, products that he eats regularly but I don't (like Greek yogurt for his diet), buttery spreads, paper supplies, and detergents. I, on the other hand, buy for recipe testing, which may involve ingredients that we don't keep on hand (and which he therefore doesn't know where to find in the store). We find this saves time.

✔ **Get supermarket savvy online:** To give yourself an extra heads-up on supermarket shopping for the new menu planner in you, go to www. supermarketsavvy.com. You'll find tools to help you make the best nutritious food choices that fit your family's specific health needs. You can even browse the aisles of the virtual supermarket that includes 1,000 healthful foods to keep you up-to-date on the latest. Or, you can subscribe to the "Supermarket Savvy" newsletter. It's another timely helper offering info on new, healthful foods, food label claims, nutritious ingredients, and menu ideas. A registered dietitian, Linda McDonald, runs the service. I subscribe and think Linda does a great job.

Besides the supermarket, you can also buy food at Marshall's, TJ Maxx, Tuesday Morning, pharmacies/drug stores, and IKEA, to name a few places. You can often find gourmet items such as jellies, jams, salsa, pasta sauce, vinegars, olive oils, and other items at these stores. Other food stores include Trader Joes, farmers' markets, dollar stores, and co-op stores (in Atlanta, Sevananda is our favorite). I rarely buy at gourmet-type stores, except for an occasional gift.

Chapter 4

Creating Your Own Two-Week Menu Plans

In This Chapter

▶ Getting together everything you'll need

▶ Deciding what to serve

▶ Making your meals enticing

▶ Appraising your plan

Chances are, sooner or later you'll want to learn to plan your own menus. You might not like my choices all the time, hard as that is to believe. And what about five years from now, when the family says something like, "Hey, don't we have the same meal every third week in August?" Please explain how you're going to answer that question! Don't worry, you won't have to, because you'll have created your own plans. Stay tuned!

In this chapter, I give you a recipe for cooking up your own two-week menu plans. I tell you what you need, how to put it all together, and how to refine the process when you're ready to make another plan.

You're only going to plan two weeks at a time for now. You have to crawl before you walk. When you get more proficient in your planning, you can look more than two weeks ahead. When I'm planning for you, I plan four weeks at a time. That way, I don't repeat the same recipes too often and bore you. When you're really movin' and groovin', you might want to plan even farther ahead. Start with baby steps, and soon you'll be off and running!

Gathering the Ingredients You'll Need

Every good recipe starts with an ingredient list. Drawing up a menu plan is no different. You need paper, pencils, and a few other items (these are your utensils), a bit of time, and most important, your ideas and energy (the main ingredients). Oh! And don't forget your family (think of them as your sous chefs, diners, and critics rolled into one). The following sections give you more details about each of these.

Who you'll need

Menu planning is a family affair. Try to get a commitment from everyone, and form a committee. Those who participate in planning, shopping, and cooking are much more likely to buy into the entire process. You want that support. This is the time to be hard-nosed with the family and tell it like it *will be*. Explain that those who don't participate in the planning don't get to have an opinion regarding what's on the menu, no matter what role they play in the family (dad, teenager, grandma, and so on).

After several sessions of planning, it's a good idea to assign family members specific tasks for which they'll be responsible at each meal. Rotate the duties as age and skills demand. Be prepared to explain these roles — shopping, preparation, cooking, and cleaning duties may be brand new concepts to one or more family members! You may also want to give an estimate of how long each task will take. For example, setting the table takes about 5 minutes.

After about a month of planning, you'll find that the family will really appreciate their meals (and you) much more, along with their time together. The children will be learning some life lessons about cooperation, trust, and what it takes to make the mealtime an "event" as well as lessons in good nutrition, math, and manners.

Expect to encounter resistance. Whoever volunteered for braces on their teeth or to get a shot at the doctor's office? But ask how happy those who get them were when the shiny metal came off or they missed the flu, and they'll sing a different tune! Relate this menu-planning session to braces and emphasize how happy the family will be when the planning is complete. If that doesn't work, *think bribes*. This may be a good time to offer a prize. For example, promise that after the planning session, you'll go out to a favorite simple restaurant, to a movie, or to do something everyone shares an interest in.

Children ages 6 and up can help with *something*. I'm not recommending they take on the heavy lifting of using an 8-inch chef's knife, but they can set the table, tear up bread, pick out fruit, and do other simple tasks. Kids ages 10 and up can handle more complex tasks. Just remember, the more they do, the better the experience will be (for everyone).

This exercise of planning, shopping, cooking, and sitting down at the table as a family is a terrific learning experience for the children's futures. They'll be able to follow in your footsteps when they begin to practice what they learned at home. Your reward: beaming with pride at how well you taught them.

What you'll need

Your meeting will go better if you have a couple of handy items at the ready. Think of these as your ingredients and utensils:

✔ **Recipes:** These can include

• **Favorite family recipes**

Make sure to ask your extended family and friends for copies of the recipes they're known for. I like to share (recipes, yes; cookies, no), and most other people do, too. Your mother-in-law has some good recipes (at least mine did). We don't need to mention your own mother — that's a given, unless she's a lousy cook. Try to find something nice to say about her meals if necessary.

• **Recipes and ideas from this book**

• **Recipes from other cookbooks, magazines, and the Internet**

✔ **Your family calendar:** This keeps you apprised of special events, meetings, appointments, and so on that you need to take into consideration.

✔ **Sharpened pencils and three-ring notebooks:** Have one of each for each family participant. (See the later section "First things first: Setting a dinner time" for tips on how to use them.) The notebooks are also a reliable way for each person to write down his or her responsibilities for the week.

✔ **Newspaper or advertising fliers:** If you subscribe to the paper or get fliers in the mail, haul them out to see what's on sale and which fruits and vegetables are in season that week.

✔ **Anything else that helps you plan menus:** An open mind will be one of the most important "ingredients" to bring to the planning table. If you're like some folks who say "I'd rather do it myself," that's fine. But then you don't have the privilege to whine, complain about how no one helps you, or have a sour face when the family is tired of your meals.

As head of this project, you're the one who has to get the momentum going, so don't forget to bring your enthusiasm along with everything else. And tell the family to bring their thinking caps, too.

Setting aside time to get started

Give everyone over the age of 6 a few days' notice about when your menu-planning meeting is going to happen. Tell them it will only take about 30 minutes.

When the meeting time comes, turn off the TV, cellphones, music, video games, and any other distractions. It may be helpful to have a snack on the table. Be sure to give a two-minute warning before the sit-down time, and tell everyone to go to the bathroom (because you won't allow anyone to leave the table once the clock starts except for an extreme emergency — and fire is about the only thing extreme enough to be considered an emergency).

Whipping Up the Plan

When everyone is settled in around the table, pass out the notebooks and pencils. Explain the goal — to plan menus as a family for the next two weeks, taking schedules, food likes and dislikes, and skill levels into account — and lay down some ground rules:

- ✔ No whining.
- ✔ Listen when someone else is talking.
- ✔ Wait your turn to speak.
- ✔ Take notes.
- ✔ Be prepared to discuss your food likes and dislikes.
- ✔ After a period of time, the group will reconvene to discuss the successes and opportunities.

As you and your family talk about what you want to have for dinner, keep in mind how much money you have to spend on food, how much time you have to shop for and prepare it, and which foods are your family's favorites. These will be the guiding principles for your personal menu planning.

In the following sections, I help you figure out how to set a dinner time and then decide what you're going to serve for the next 14 nights.

First things first: Setting a dinnertime

First, establish a dinnertime. Maybe it's 6, 7, or 8 p.m. (8 is a little late for kids), but set a time most everyone can live with. The Virgo and I eat between 7:30 and 8, but we don't have small children to feed. Our time is also a compromise because I'd like to eat closer to 7, and he'd rather eat at 8.

Of course, your mealtime can be a moving target that changes according to jobs, seasons, activities, and other factors.

To determine a dinnertime that works best for everyone, give each person a blank two-week grid in a 3-ring notebook. I always start with Sunday, but the day you begin with doesn't matter. First, fill in your family's social, school, church, and other activities (and their times and duration) on the grid. (See Figure 4-1 for an example of what this might look like.) Ask the question: How will the activity affect dinner plans?

TIP

If you find that five or more activities wreak havoc with the dinner hour, maybe it's time to look at the reasons for having so many activities that prevent your family from gathering for a meal. You may need to make adjustments in that area.

Eww, I don't like that! Leaving foods off the menu

Allow each person to state two or three dislikes, with the stipulation that the dislikes can't be *all* vegetables, *all* fruits, or *all* of anything. Instead, make your kids (or spouse) pick the worst of the offending category. You can't rule out all vegetables, but you can rule out Brussels sprouts or a vegetable that no one likes.

	SUNDAY Family	MONDAY	TUESDAY	WEDNESDAY	THURSDAY	FRIDAY	SATURDAY Entertaining
Week 1	Dinner: 6:00 p.m.	Kids' practice: 4–6 p.m. Dinner: 7 p.m.	Dinner: 6:30 p.m.	Choir: 7–8:30 p.m. Dinner: 6 p.m.	Dinner: 6:30 p.m.	Ballgame: 7–10 p.m. Dinner: 6 p.m.	Entertaining for adults Dinner: 7 p.m.
Week 2	Dinner: 6:30 p.m.	Dinner: 6:30 p.m.	Kids' practice: 4–6 p.m. Dinner: 6:30 p.m.	Choir: 7–8:30 p.m. Dinner: 6:30 p.m.	Dinner: 6:30 p.m.	Grandparents visit (Friday p.m. through Sunday a.m.) Dinner: 7 p.m.	Dinner out (Grandparents pay) Dinner: 7 p.m.

Figure 4-1: A sample two-week grid with activities and dinner-times filled in.

After everyone has written down their dislikes, call for a vote. Majority rules. For example, if one person has a strong dislike for liver and the majority of the family agrees, you never have to have it. Or maybe one person has a "thing" about coconut, and the majority of the family is willing to do without it. These foods aren't hard to work around. Fresh fruits and vegetables are! If there's a tie, you can agree to serve the food in question half as often as you ordinarily would, and the person who dislikes it can agree to try it. Choose your battles.

Sounds delicious! Choosing delectable dishes

After filling in all your family's activities, decide what protein or entree (beef, pork, chicken, lamb, no-meat, and so on) you'll have for each of the 14 days. I recommend avoiding the "Sunday is chicken, Monday is meatloaf, Tuesday is pasta" routine unless your family is rock solid on that system. It's time to branch out.

You can go in one of two directions when choosing an entree: You can opt for a stand-alone protein (like a pork chop or hamburger), or you can select a combination meal where you throw everything in one pot or dish and leave it to cook itself. I explain the pros and cons of each of these approaches in the following sections.

Don't feel like you have to stick to one type of entree. On hectic Mondays, plan to have a combination meal; maybe Thursday nights are open, so you have more time to cook individual dishes. You enjoy meals more and eat better when you mix up your menus like this. See Figure 4-2 for a sample two-week menu.

When you're talking about what you want to eat for dinner in the next two weeks, check out grocery ads to see what's on sale and to spur your imagination. You can also flip through your cookbooks or the collection of recipes you've torn out of magazines to come up with some new dishes to try.

The more meat, fish, and poultry you have on the menu, the more expensive your food costs will be. Generally speaking, more convenience items run up the cost, too. You have to decide which is more important: time or money. Sometimes it's one; other times it's the other.

When you're planning a meal, start with the entree and then choose side dishes that complement it. See Chapter 3 for more on creating an appealing meal.

	SUNDAY Family	MONDAY	TUESDAY	WEDNESDAY	THURSDAY	FRIDAY	SATURDAY Entertaining
Week 1		Kids' practice: 4–6 p.m.		Choir: 7–8:30 p.m.		Ballgame: 7–10 p.m.	Entertaining for adults
	Dinner: 6:00 p.m.	Dinner: 7 p.m.	Dinner: 6:30 p.m.	Dinner: 6 p.m.	Dinner: 6:30 p.m.	Dinner: 6 p.m.	Dinner: 7 p.m.
	Grilled chicken *Make or use a bottled marinade *Grill extra	Chicken wraps *Tortilla with shredded lettuce, diced chicken, with salsa and sour cream garnish *Use corn or flour	Meatloaf *Make 2; freeze 1 *Recipe from Week 51	Deli tuna salad and tomato soup *Put tuna on whole-grain bread or lettuce	Pasta with spinach, gorgonzola, and tomatoes *Use any pasta *Recipe from Week 49	Pizza *Ready-to-heat crust *Toppings: shredded low-fat cheese, pasta sauce, assorted vegetables	Island Shrimp *Recipe from Week 26
Week 2			Kids' practice: 4–6 p.m.	Choir: 7–8:30 p.m.		Grandparents visit (Friday p.m. through Sunday a.m.)	Dinner out (Grandparents pay)
	Dinner: 6:30 p.m.	Dinner: 6:30 p.m.	Dinner: 6:30 p.m.	Dinner: 6:30 p.m.	Dinner: 6:30 p.m.	Dinner: 7 p.m.	Dinner: 7 p.m.
	Pork loin *Use a rub or recipe from Week 25 *3 or 4 pounds	Bow-Tie Pasta with Spinach and Mushrooms *Recipe from Week 33	Leftover pork stir-fry *Use bottled sauce *Assorted veggies *Leftover pork cut into strips *Thaw meatloaf from last Tuesday	Leftover meatloaf sandwiches *Use whole-grain bread with lettuce and sliced avocado	Chicken Chili *Make extra and freeze *Recipe from Week 49	Santa Fe Grilled Steak *Company tonight *Recipe from Week 24	Dinner out with grandparents (they pay!)

Figure 4-2:
A sample
two-week
menu.

Combination meals, or putting all your eggs in one basket

In combination meals (also known as "casseroles," "bakes," and "skillets"),
all the ingredients end up in one vessel, often a casserole dish or skillet, and
are baked or cooked on top of the stove. The dish often combines a protein
and vegetables or a protein and starch. Depending on your combination, you
might serve a side to round out the meal. So for a protein-veggie combo, you
could add a starch (macaroni, spaghetti, beans, corn) as a side, whereas for a
protein-starch dish, you might add a salad or vegetable.

For example, say tonight you decide to have Chili-Mac. You brown the meat
and seasonings while you cook the macaroni separately. When both are
done, you combine them, spoon the mixture into a casserole dish, top with
breadcrumbs or another topping, and bake until bubbly.

Or, you might brown meat in a skillet, and then add diced canned tomatoes and
seasoning, water, and uncooked pasta. You cover, lower the heat, and simmer
for 15 minutes or as directed. You're cooking everything together in one vessel
without having to cook the pasta separately. The recipe might be called Beef
and Rotini Skillet. Sometimes, a green or other vegetable might be added such
as shredded carrots, broccoli florets, or green peas. All you need now is a salad.

The upside of combination meals is that they're often quick and inexpensive. These mixed dishes or casseroles are food-budget friendly. It's fine to eat whole meats every night if you have an unlimited budget for groceries, but combination dishes are more economical. Plus, a casserole can contain two or three nutrient groups. It's an all-in-one that can save time, money, and a "what-to-fix" headache. And sometimes there's nothing more delicious than an ooey-gooey casserole. That kind of dish can provide great comfort.

On the downside, sometimes casseroles are laden with high-fat ingredients such as huge amounts of cheese, breadcrumbs, or even cream. These ingredients are another definition of "ooey-gooey."

Meat and four, or putting a different egg in each basket

If you live in certain areas, you're familiar with "meat and three" or "meat and two" restaurant promotions. Usually this consists of a fried meat and two or three highly seasoned vegetables with bacon fat or ham.

You can plan your own "meat and two (or three)" meals, but skip the restaurant method of preparation. Your approach consists of the following:

- ✔ A piece of chicken, a pork chop, or a slice of beef
- ✔ A steamed vegetable
- ✔ A green salad
- ✔ A complex carbohydrate (beans, rice, whole grains)
- ✔ Fruit for dessert

I call it a "meat and four"! An example of this type of meal would be pork chops, steamed fresh broccoli, a mixed-greens salad, whole-grain rolls, and pineapple spears. This type of meal is more expensive because the protein is in one piece, and you need a serving of protein for each person you're serving. Each addition to the meat is a stand-alone item. Some family members (I call them children) might enjoy seeing each individual part of the meal rather than all of the ingredients mixed together. And, the appearance of the meal with separate foods might be more appetizing to some.

Selecting the recipes

After the grid has been filled in with entrees, you'll need recipes for each dish that requires preparation. You'll also need foods to go with the main course. Those foods may require recipes, or they may be as simple as a salad you have to assemble or a vegetable that requires microwaving. Check out the "What you'll need" section, earlier in this chapter, for suggested recipe sources.

Planning ahead to eat out

Just as all work and no play makes us dull as dirt, eating every meal at home could be dull. Plan on an evening out for dinner every so often. Besides a change of scenery, you can experience some new foods, a different atmosphere, and the joy of not having to plan, cook, and clean up every night of the week. I try to "close" our kitchen Friday and Saturday nights, but

I don't have small children to feed — just the Virgo. Remember, invite friends to your house for dinner sometimes, and if they have any manners at all, they'll reciprocate with an evening out at their place. If they don't invite you to their house, don't ask them to yours again. Fair is fair.

Sampling three or four new recipes a week is an ideal goal, but at least try one or two new ones. Choose them according to the expertise of the cook, and the time and money available. I like recipes that use ingredients you can find in the supermarket better than those that require trips to gourmet or specialty food stores. I don't want to make several stops for ingredients, and I'm guessing that you don't either.

Many favorite family recipes are in someone's head! It's a good idea to get them on paper in case someone else wants to prepare them or the person with the recipe suddenly leaves home.

Your two-week chart can incorporate using leftovers. Think of ways to put them to good use. Can the stew be served in a bread bowl? Can the roast beef be shredded, heated, tossed in barbecue sauce, and served over cornbread? Can the turkey breast be turned into a salad with almonds, grapes, celery, and mayo, or maybe into enchiladas?

After you've chosen the recipes you want to use, make sure you have all the ingredients that you'll need on hand (more on this in Chapter 5). Then the only thing left to do is to follow the plan and enjoy two weeks of healthy, stress-free meals!

Putting Together an Appealing Meal

You can choose from hundreds of entrees and thousands of sides when you're planning a meal. How do you know what foods go well together and which foods don't? You can decide based on your senses. What will look nice together? How will the foods feel in your mouth? Will the tastes clash or complement each other? I give you answers to each of these questions in the following sections.

In the weekly menus in Part II, I've done the work of creating appealing meals for you. When you start putting together your own weekly menus, you can try your hand at serving different dishes together.

Focusing on flavor

Flavor is at the top of the list. The accompaniment must enhance the flavor of the entree rather than fight it, the way some colors fight each other. If you don't have favorite flavor pairings already, keep in mind these ideas. If you have an assertive or spicy food such as chili or barbecue, compliment it with a milder side like coleslaw or potato salad. Or, put a dollop of sour cream on the chili to tone it down. If the side dish packs a flavor punch, make the entree a mild flavor such as baked chicken. In other words, don't make every entree or side hot, spicy, or bland — mix them up.

When you're choosing side dishes, keep your entree in mind. Some foods just naturally partner well. For example, ham, sweet potatoes, and apples are a good combination of flavors and colors. Grilled beef, oven roasted potatoes with rosemary, and a fresh green vegetable, such as green beans, are a good combination, too. Roast chicken along with mashed potatoes, gravy, and fresh broccoli have a pleasant taste profile as well. These examples are very basic, but they're a start. You'll also note that the colors work well together, as do the textures.

Personally, I don't like spaghetti with a grilled steak (and I'm the one in charge of the 7-Day Menu Planner!). For me, it doesn't work. I like both, just not together. Nor does oven-fried chicken go with couscous. It's a personal preference. Your family might love these combinations, which is fine. I'd rather have corn on the cob, roasted potatoes, or pasta salad with steak, and oven-fried chicken demands mashed potatoes or rice to me.

Concentrating on color

Don't get me started on color. If the colors don't compliment the plate, it's like wearing the wrong lipstick with an outfit (sorry guys, I know you don't get this). It hurts your eyes or the eyes looking at you. Remember the old saying, "You eat with your eyes." Corny as it is, it's so true. Don't be lulled into "brown night" where everything is the same color. Keep in mind that an attractive, colorful plate doesn't necessarily have to cost more.

A boring combination of colors is roast chicken breast, mashed potatoes, and cauliflower. It's all white and looks unappetizing. What could you do to improve it? Add color! Garnish the chicken with chopped fresh parsley, spoon an au gratin sauce over the cauliflower and sprinkle it with paprika, and change the potatoes from mashed to baked. Garnishes are your friends. Problem solved!

Touching on texture

Texture is another criterion I consider when planning a menu. For example, soft foods (mashed potatoes, pudding), creamy foods (ice cream, milkshakes), and crunchy and crispy foods (chips, nuts) all add different textures to different entrees.

Combining foods that have similar textures, such as mashed potatoes and baked fish, is dull, dull, dull. You might as well be eating pureed food for all the excitement this combination brings to your taste buds. If taste buds could talk back, they might say, "Hey, how about oven-roasted potatoes and some crunchy broccoli with that baked fish?" I also advise you to avoid serving multiple casseroles at the same meal. A baked casserole cries out for a crunchy mixed green salad or a crisp, colorful vegetable alongside it. In the case of textures, opposites attract!

Evaluating Your Plan

At the end of each meal, ask your family what they thought and make notes in your menu planner. If the meal was a success, put that day's menu in the permanent file, and make sure to note why everyone all but licked their plates clean. Failures should be noted, along with the reason why. The *why* is important. Was it because of flavor or expense? Maybe it was too complicated or too time-consuming. Read on for more tips on meal assessment.

Taking an inventory of the meal

When you're careful to make notes (put down your cellphone for this), the next time this meal comes around you can give it a thumbs-up or thumbs-down according to your notes. Why re-create an unsuccessful endeavor? You'll want to consider ease of preparation, cost, appearance, and, of course, flavor.

Answer these questions after every meal:

- **Was the receipe too difficult?** What needs to be changed? Perhaps the method of preparation?

- **Was the time needed to prepare the meal/recipe acceptable?** Were you eating at midnight instead of 7 p.m.?

- **Were there too many dishes or pans to clean up?** Were you still washing dishes when you should have been drinking your morning coffee?

- **Was the recipe too spicy, bland, sweet, or sour?** Was your mouth on fire, asleep, high on sugar, or pickled?

✔ **Did the food "feel" good in your mouth?** Crispy, creamy, tart, smooth, or crunchy?

✔ **Was the meal appropriate for all family members?** Did mom, dad, and the kids lap it up?

✔ **Was the meal too expensive?** Did you spend half the food budget on one item?

✔ **Was the meal all one color?** Say, turmeric chicken, sweet potatoes, carrots, and apricots? If you eat too many meals like this, you'll turn as yellow as your food.

Write down any important notes on your menu planner. Then refer to the notes the next time your family meets to draw up another two-week plan.

You'll know the meal was a hit when everyone at the table has eaten the expected amount of each dish, and at least one person has asked for seconds. Other signs? There was no whining, moving the food around the plate in a playful way, feeding it to the dog, or hiding it in a napkin or a nearby plant. I call this success.

If your efforts weren't so successful, you have two options. You can try the recipe again, referring to your notes about what didn't work to try to revise the dish, or you can toss the recipe and forget about the dish. There's absolutely nothing wrong with the latter, and you still get points for trying something new!

Giving the plan a thumbs-up or thumbs-down

After you've eaten a week's worth of menus and made notes about the meals, it's time to gather the family again to see what the definite likes and dislikes are. Highlight or circle the meals that your family agrees they would eat again. Put an "X" through any meals that the dog wouldn't even touch (I hope you don't have too many of these). Put a question mark or asterisk by the meals that you're willing to try again, but with some modifications.

Make adjustments to the second week of menus, if appropriate. You may have found that a recipe that looked easy and tasty was a complete flop. Toss the recipe. Another night, the food might have had potential, but needed some extra spices. Make a note and add the spices next time. Because you've already prepared it once, round two will be easier. If the family loves everything about a meal — looks, taste, cost, and ease of preparation and cleanup — give that meal a gold star and plan to have it again in a couple of weeks. File Week 1 in your notebook. Proceed with Week 2 as with Week 1. Once you've created two weeks of menus, it's time to move on to Weeks 3 and 4. The procedure is the same; before you know it, you'll be planning meals like the pros!

Chapter 5

Preparing Your Kitchen for the Weeks Ahead

In This Chapter

▶ Stocking your pantry

▶ Taking advantage of your refrigerator and freezer

▶ Having the right cookware and appliances

▶ Taking a strategic approach to grocery shopping

The way many men stock their workshops with saws, wrenches, screwdrivers, hammers, nails, and so on is no secret. Everything in the workshop has a place. The walls, cabinets, and drawers are used to store all their paraphernalia. They may never repair anything, but the tools are there, just in case.

The kitchen also holds a variety of paraphernalia, but the difference is that it does get used — all the time! Like the workshop, it needs to be attractive, efficient, and organized. I take you down this path in this chapter.

Hopefully, you don't have to store your pots and pans under the bed like my mother-in-law used to because her kitchen was so tiny and she was such a great cook and hostess. When she started hanging her utensils in the shower, I told her she had gone too far. She did the best she could with what she had to work with. You have to do the same.

The Well-Stocked Pantry

Think about those nights when you get home from work around 6 p.m. or later with no take-out in hand, and you have to feed your family fast. The children are grumpy, the dogs are barking, and your significant other is late coming home, but will be there soon.

With a well-stocked pantry (plus refrigerator and freezer, which I cover later in this chapter) you'll have no trouble producing a healthy, quick, and budget-friendly meal in short order. If you plan your menus and shop accordingly, you can pat yourself on the back and have great meals with minimal stress.

The ideal pantry is one that always contains the ingredients you use often. In the following sections, I tell you what foods I keep in my pantry. Your tastes and preferences may differ. If you hate an item, forget it. On the other hand, if you see a recipe in this book you think you'd love, try something new! I don't expect you to buy something you don't like or will never use, but I do ask that you keep an open mind while reading the next few pages. Personalize the lists according to your family's preferences, and add to them as you discover new recipes.

If you like something I missed, add it. You're in charge of your pantry.

Ingredients and condiments

You can't ride a horse without a horse. I bet you think I'm reaching here with that statement, but the truth is you can't cook without ingredients and condiments. See? I'm being profound again.

Here are the condiments and ingredients I keep in my pantry at all times:

- ✔ **Broths:** Reduced-sodium chicken and beef broths, and vegetable broth are good to have on hand. I generally use Swanson's reduced-sodium (Natural Goodness) chicken broth and their lower-sodium beef broth. You'll need vegetable broth, too, but you may have to search a little harder for a low-sodium version. Use whatever suits your taste and pocketbook.

  Using various flavors of broth can perk up the flavor of a variety of dishes, including soups, stews, rice, couscous, and sometimes pasta. Beware that broth may increase the sodium content of a dish. If that's the case, use water instead.

- ✔ **Vinegars:** Balsamic, cider, sherry, red wine, tarragon, unseasoned rice wine, and other vinegars add flavor without adding salt. All of these are in my pantry. Choose the ones you like the most.

  Vinegars add flavor without calories or salt. I use different flavors of vinegar all the time for just that reason. They're generally inexpensive except for balsamic, which is aged and higher-priced. Use the ones that appeal to you.

- ✔ **Ketchup:** One of our past presidents tried to make it a vegetable, but it's really a condiment. I use it in barbecue sauce, meatloaf, and other "mixture" dishes.

✔ **Mustards:** Yellow, Dijon, grainy, dry, and Dijonnaise (a combination of mustard and mayonnaise that's low in calories) add flavor, but are higher in sodium. Use ground mustard if you're watching your sodium intake.

A huge variety of mustards is available. They're practically calorie-free and really add some zing to otherwise boring dishes.

✔ **Mayonnaise:** Choose low-fat or light mayonnaise.

Some folks live and die with their brand of mayonnaise. If you're from the South, you may prefer Duke's. Other areas may opt for Hellman's or Best. I opt for lower-fat versions to reduce calories and fats. You can also find mayos made with olive oil or canola oil.

Dried herbs and spices

Back in your grandmother's time, most spice cabinets contained salt and pepper. (If you lived in Texas, you might have chili powder, too.) These days, people use a variety of spices — I have at least 25 in my pantry. Why use spices? Foods are all about flavor, and herbs and spices play a big role in perking up the flavor of all kinds of dishes. Another benefit is that herbs and spices have *no calories or sodium.*

If your spices/herbs are still in little metal boxes, toss them, except for black pepper. I use the smell test for herbs. If an herb has a pleasant aroma, it's okay. Use it. If it doesn't have an aroma, toss it. It's just taking up space. If you have spices that you bought when your first child was born and he's now in middle school, toss those, too.

For easy accessibility, put your favorites in alphabetical order on a Lazy Susan. This is a timesaver for those nights when you're really in a hurry and don't feel like digging through 25 jars to find the one you want.

In the list that follows, I include the herbs and spices I think need to be in a basic collection (hat tip to McCormick for their assistance in compiling this list). Choose others according to your family's preferences. Many dried spices are excellent. Others are a waste of money. For example, I don't spend money on dried parsley when I can buy it fresh. Parsley is everywhere, and it's not expensive. If I lived on a deserted island, I might use the dried kind. I feel the same way about dried cilantro and chives. I use fresh! Some spice "blends" contain loads of salt, so be sure to read the label.

✔ Allspice

✔ Basil leaves

✔ Bay leaves

✔ Black pepper, ground

✔ Black peppercorns, whole

✔ Celery seed

✔ Chili powder

✔ Cinnamon

✔ Cinnamon sugar

✔ Cumin

- ✔ Curry powder
- ✔ Dill weed
- ✔ Garlic powder
- ✔ Ginger
- ✔ Italian seasoning
- ✔ Marjoram leaves
- ✔ Mustard, ground
- ✔ Nutmeg
- ✔ Onion powder

- ✔ Oregano leaves
- ✔ Paprika
- ✔ Poppy seed
- ✔ Red pepper
- ✔ Rosemary
- ✔ Sage
- ✔ Tarragon leaves
- ✔ Thyme
- ✔ Turmeric

Fats and oils

The two oils I use most often are canola and olive. I don't refrigerate these oils because I use them quickly. Other oils that add a distinctive flavor to a recipe are light and dark sesame oils, and walnut and almond oils. I keep the latter ones in the refrigerator because I use them less often than canola and olive oils, and they tend to become rancid due to their high saturated-fat content. They also cost more. Enough said for refrigerating them.

I rarely use solid shortenings such as Crisco, and when I do, I buy the least amount available. If I baked more bread, cakes, pies, and other desserts from scratch, I'd use more. Because I don't deep-fry any foods, I don't use solid shortening for that either. Solid shortenings contain saturated fat, and its appearance is like the gunk that builds up in human arteries. (Sorry to be a nag about saturated fat, but I'm encouraging you to choose healthy fats and oils!) Lard does not cross my threshold.

Cooking spray is a staple. I use it instead of more oil to coat the pan. I also spray it on foil when I'm roasting foods like chicken breasts, pork tenderloins, potato wedges, and vegetables at higher temperatures to prevent them from sticking to the foil.

Beans

Beans are your friends because they're nutritious, low-cost, and easy to prepare and store. (See Chapter 8 for more on the health benefits of beans.)

I keep a variety of canned and dry beans in my pantry all the time. The Virgo has hypertension and cooks dry beans from scratch because of their low sodium content. Here are the beans I keep in my pantry:

- ✔ Black
- ✔ Pinto
- ✔ White Great Northern
- ✔ Navy
- ✔ Cannellini
- ✔ Chickpeas or garbanzo (they're the same bean)

Rinsing canned beans removes about 30 to 40 percent of the sodium, whether they're the regular or low-sodium varieties. Dry beans have essentially no sodium and are low in fat. And, beans are inexpensive (especially the dry ones).

Grains

When you think "grains," think "whole" grains. Whole grains are the most nutritious form. Foods made from whole grains contain all the essential parts and naturally-occurring nutrients of the entire grain seed. If it has been cracked, crushed, rolled, extruded, and or cooked (processed), the grain should give us exactly or nearly the same nutrients as the original seed. That's very comforting, because most people prefer that their whole grains have one of these verbs (cracked, crushed, rolled, and so on) applied to their whole condition. We'd still be chewing some of them if they hadn't gone through the processing part. I can sleep better knowing this.

Following are a few good grains to keep on hand:

- ✔ **Barley:** Usually, I use the quick-cooking kind when I'm looking for a "different" starch.
- ✔ **Oatmeal:** I eat it most mornings in the winter. It's cheap and good for you.
- ✔ **Rice:** I recommend brown, long-grain white, jasmine, and basmati rice. Quick-cooking varieties are convenient, but they add to your grocery bill.

Cook rice from scratch, and then freeze, label, and date it so that you don't get stuck having to delay dinner when the menu calls for rice. Rice thaws quickly in the microwave. Another way out of this dilemma is to keep quick-cooking rice in your pantry.

I prefer to cook rice in the microwave. It takes just as long, but the cooking container is a lot easier to clean. I never have learned to cook good rice on top of the stove. The Virgo always cooked it before the microwave (he's from Texas where they eat a lot of rice), because I always turned it into "glob." We didn't call it rice. He'd say, "I see we're having *glob* with our chicken tonight?" The microwave cooking method changed my rice-cooking expertise forever. This includes brown rice.

Achieving the impossible: Perfect rice

Knowing that rice is such a hard food to cook perfectly for some of us (me), I provide you with the following tips for cooking light and fluffy rice, courtesy of the USA Rice Federation (www.usarice.com):

✔ Accurately measure the rice and liquid.

✔ Set a timer to prevent under- or overcooking.

✔ Know your own stove.

✔ Keep the lid on the pot during cooking to prevent steam from escaping.

✔ Rice triples in volume. Use cookware appropriate for the amount of rice you're preparing or it will boil all over the place.

✔ Don't stir. Stirring releases the starch, resulting in rice that's sticky or gummy (also known as *glob*).

✔ At the end of the cooking time, remove the lid and test for doneness. If the rice isn't tender or the liquid isn't absorbed, cook two to four minutes longer.

✔ When rice is cooked, fluff with fork or slotted spoon to allow steam to escape and keep the grains separate.

If you follow the preceding tips to the letter and your rice still isn't to your satisfaction, try these suggestions the next time you cook rice (assuming you do try again):

✔ If the rice is crunchy, add additional liquid, cover tightly, and cook until grains are tender.

✔ If you desire more separate grains, sauté the rice in a small amount of butter or margarine before adding liquid.

✔ If you burn the heck out of it, including the pan (in the microwave), open all the windows, turn on the fans, say bad words, and leave home to allow the stench to leave the premises. Boy, do burned plastic and burned rice turn you into a person who pays more attention to what's cooking! It's a memorable experience. Just ask the Virgo.

Pasta

Before we dive into pasta, note that you'd have to rent an arena to store all the various kinds. Stock the ones you like, and buy the others as you need them. I always have spaghetti and some tube-shaped pasta handy. The rest I buy as I need it.

Pasta is low in sodium and fat. It's what you add to it that can be a source of high calories. Look for the newer high-fiber and whole grain pastas for better nutritional choices.

I include the most common pasta shapes in Table 5-1, courtesy of the National Pasta Association (www.ilovepasta.org). Choose the ones that your family likes the most to keep in your pantry.

Table 5-1	Popular Pasta Varieties	
Pasta Name (and Nickname)	**Shape**	**Uses**
Alphabet pasta	Letters of the alphabet	A favorite of kids, usually used in soups for a fun meal.
Angel hair, capellini ("fine hairs")	Thin, delicate, cylindrical strands	Best with thinner, delicate sauces; may also be used in salads or stir-fry, or broken in half and used in soup.
Bow ties, farfalle ("butterflies")	Rectangular, pinched in the middle; resemble miniature bow ties	Thick enough for a variety of sauces; also a perfect addition to many salads and soups.
Egg noodles	Flat; available in varying widths	Medium or wide egg noodles can be baked, tossed in soups or salads, or topped with cream, tomato, cheese, or meat sauces.
Elbow macaroni	Narrow, curved tubes about 1 inch long	Traditionally used to make macaroni and cheese; can be topped with any sauce, baked, or put in soups, salads, and stir-fry.
Jumbo shells	Large-sized; resemble ridged seashells	Best when stuffed with your favorite mixtures of cheese, meat, and vegetables.
Lasagna	Flat; about 3 inches wide; usually with curly edges	Create original lasagna casseroles by using chopped vegetables, cheeses, and any kind of sauce; freezes well in prepared casseroles.
Linguine ("little tongues")	Thin, slightly flattened strands; about ⅛ inch wide	Compliments a variety of sauces; also a good choice for salads and stir-fry.
Manicotti ("small muffs")	Thick tubes with ridges; sometimes cut on an angle	Good when stuffed with a mixture of meat, cheese, and/or vegetables, topped with a favorite sauce, and baked.
Medium shells, conchiglie ("shells")	Smaller than jumbo shells; resemble ridged seashells	A great addition to soups or as the base of a salad; can also be used as a substitute for elbow macaroni in recipes for macaroni and cheese.

(continued)

Table 5-1 *(continued)*

Pasta Name (and Nickname)	Shape	Uses
Orzo ("barley")	Resembles grains of rice	Can be topped with any sauce, added to soups, or baked as a casserole; perfect as a side dish as well as a main course.
Penne ("quills" or "feathers")	Tubular shape; may be smooth or ridged	Compliment virtually every sauce, exceptional paired with a chunky sauce; pairs nicely with chunky meat, chunky vegetable, cream, or oil-based sauces; also great in baked dishes.
Ravioli	Resemble square, hollow pillows with rounded corners	Contain a filling of cheese, meats, and/or vegetables, plus seasonings; can be served with a red sauce or with butter, oil, or cream.
Rigatoni	Thick, ridged tubes about 1½ inches long	Perfect with any sauce, from cream or cheese to the chunkiest meat sauces.
Rotini	Twists and spirals, as in wrapping a knitting needle with thin strands of pasta	Twisted shape holds bits of meat, vegetables and cheese; works well with any sauce; good for creating fun salads, baked casseroles, or stir-fry.
Spaghetti ("a length of cord")	America's favorite; thin, round, solid strands	The perfect choice for nearly any sauce (go beyond tomato to find your favorite); can be used to make casseroles or stir-fry.
Tortellini	Ring-shaped	Typically stuffed with meat, cheese, or vegetables; commonly served in a broth or cream sauce.
Vermicelli ("little worms")	Slightly thinner than spaghetti	Good topped with any sauce, or as a salad or stir-fry ingredient.
Ziti ("bridegrooms")	Medium-sized tubes	Perfect for chunky sauces and meat dishes; also makes wonderful salads, baked dishes, and stir-fry meals.

Vegetables

Man (or woman) cannot live by meat and potatoes alone! This is an old proverb (about 10 minutes old). Vegetables add a different dimension to your meal and its flavors. Can you imagine a world without vegetables? It would be a dull place.

Always eat fresh vegetables in season and whenever you can, which means buying what you need at the store on a semiweekly or weekly basis. But some veggies, such as onions, keep just fine for a few weeks when stored in a cool, dry place like your pantry. In the following sections, I give you some pointers about which vegetables to keep in your pantry (either fresh, or in cans or jars).

Garlic and onions

My middle initial is "O," and sometimes I think it should stand for "onions" because I use them in so many recipes. Why? Flavor, of course. Not to mention that onions are inexpensive and essentially calorie-free. They store well in a cool place and quietly stand by to serve you. I even keep some diced ones in the freezer for emergencies. I use yellow onions for most dishes.

Assuming you choose onions that are in excellent condition at the store, you can expect them to last in a cool, dark space at your house two to three weeks or even longer. When they're soft, shrunken, spongy, sprouting, or moldy, take them to the nearest trash can.

In the past, I used mostly fresh garlic. Now, I often use fresh, diced garlic in jars. (Look for it in the produce section.) You know the reason — convenience — and I find the flavor acceptable too. I noticed that I was throwing out most of the bulbs I bought after using just one clove. You know I'm much too frugal for that. Professional cooks and chefs would be horrified, but I'm not thinking about them; I'm thinking about you (and me).

Potatoes

Boy, do I love potatoes — about as much as I love tomatoes. Growing up, my family rarely had a meal without them (even if Mother tried to sneak in some rice from time to time). When rice appeared, my father always asked in a disappointed way, "Aren't there any potatoes tonight?"

At the store, choose clean, smooth, firm-textured potatoes without cuts, bruises, or ugly colors. Store them in a well-ventilated place. If you have a cooler basement, that's ideal, but don't refrigerate them. Keep them dry.

The ones I use often are russets. They're high in starch and light and fluffy when cooked. You can bake, mash, fry, or roast them. Red-skinned potatoes are well suited for salads and roasting along with boiling and steaming. I use yellow potatoes often when I serve mashed potatoes because you can pretend the yellow color is butter. Sometimes it works, because they do have a creamy texture.

Tomatoes

Holy cow, do I love tomatoes — anyway they come, in any color. I use them in everything except apple pie. Why? They have great flavor and color; they're low in calories, high in nutrition, and inexpensive; and they make wonderful sandwiches in the summer with bread and mayonnaise. Who could ask more of a vegetable?

I love them so much that my father used to send me a box via UPS from Virginia to Atlanta every summer with the beauties enclosed. I didn't share them, and I don't feel a bit bad about it.

I use all varieties of tomatoes in recipes: fresh, canned, diced with various additions (onions, garlic, herbs). Use them any chance you get. Here are the tomato staples I keep in the pantry:

- **Tomato paste:** The frugal cook (that would be me) portions the leftovers into 1-tablespoon amounts, wraps them in plastic wrap, and freezes them. You can also buy tomato paste in a tube. That makes a lot of sense.

- **Tomato sauce:** Look for "no-salt-added" on the label.

A few other essentials

Listed here are a few more of the essentials in my pantry. You may or may not need them in yours:

- **Lentils:** Green and brown are the most readily available in the supermarket. They're especially handy because they take less time than beans to cook.

- **Flour:** Keep all-purpose and self-rising flour on hand. If you like to bake cakes, you'll want cake flour, too.

- **Cornmeal:** This is good for coating foods before pan-frying or baking.

- **Cornstarch:** Cornstarch is a thickening agent, often used to thicken gravy or sauces.

- **Panko:** These Japanese breadcrumbs are coarser than the traditional breadcrumbs most people are used to and create a crunchier crust. I rarely use the traditional kind (dry) as a topping or coating ingredient anymore. I use panko crumbs instead.

    Progresso makes panko that's easy to find in the grocery store and works well.

- **Sugar:** White, brown, and confectioners sugar have a place in your pantry. I buy 2 pounds of white sugar about every year. When I want to counteract the tartness of tomatoes, I add a teaspoon of sugar to mellow the flavor. I use brown sugar in barbecue sauce and occasionally in a dessert (I make very few desserts from scratch). Ditto confectioners' sugar for desserts.

Finding a Place for Everything in Your Pantry

How is your pantry arranged? If you don't have the luxury of ample pantry space (who does?), use what you have to your best advantage. Some stores give classes on the best use of space. The Container Store comes to mind. IKEA has great shelving for taking advantage of the space you have, too.

I've lived where the pantry was an afterthought and I had to make do with what was there. (Brace yourself for a chauvinist remark: It was probably designed by a man.) When we bought a loft-condo under construction, I had some say on how to design the space of the pantry and kitchen layout. I couldn't add space, just arrange it.

I had the good fortune of having a closet/cabinet planning company design the space in the panty with my needs in mind. It's a walk-in style. I have shelves designed for canned and staple goods, deeper shelves for some appliances, and pull-out baskets for bulky products such as noodles and items that don't fit well on shelves. That's the good news. The bad news is that smack dab in the middle of the pantry is a 21-inch-diameter, concrete column. You don't move a column; you work/walk around it — literally!

I organized the pantry by putting like items together, such as all canned tomatoes, tomato sauce, and tomato paste. All pasta, rice varieties, and other dried starches, such as barley, cornmeal, and bulgur, are grouped together. In another area are different broths — reduced-sodium beef, reduced-sodium chicken, and vegetable. Of course, I tried to put the most-used items at eye level. The main point to remember is to put items where you'll remember their location. About every six months or so, I give my pantry a checkup to catch those items that occasionally end up in illogical places.

Spices sit on a Lazy Susan (named for me) in alphabetical order (I'm not kidding). I still deny that I'm a Virgo.

Miscellaneous items are scattered where space is available. I have some deep shelves that hold the slow cooker in an easy-access space. The indoor grill is easy to reach; the pressure cooker, which I don't use as often as I should, and the rice cooker, which I rarely use, are on higher shelves. I swear I have no pans under the bed.

Your pantry needs to be convenient for you, that is, you know where everything is located because you always put replenishments in the same place. (You do that, don't you?) You keep all broth together, likewise beans, canned tomatoes, pasta, rice, and so forth. You get the idea. If shelves are extra-deep, put seldom-used items in the back.

Checking out your cabinets

In the kitchen, I do have quite a few cabinets that house the baking dishes I use often (9 x 13, 7 or 8 x 11 or 12, and 8 x 8 inches). They stand on their edges in a rack for easy access. These cabinets are retrofitted with pull-out wire drawers or baskets for colanders, extra baking dishes, and miscellaneous items. Another pull-out drawer stores microwave cookware. Finally, I found a storage pull-out drawer for lids (at The Container Store) after years of saying bad words while accessing them. (I know two.)

In the upper cabinets are the most-used dishes and glasses for everyday meals.

To handle other pans, I have an over-the-sink hanging rack that takes care of a huge number of pans, skillets, and so on. If you have the space for one, save your money and install it. I do have to be careful removing some pans (because I'm rather short) for fear of dropping one and losing my front teeth. (Yes, I do use a stool when the Virgo isn't here; I'm not stupid.)

Drawers hold cooking utensils, flatware hot pads, and junk.

By no means is my kitchen perfect, but it does get better as I strive for improved organization. After all, I spend a great deal of time in the kitchen!

Making Use of Your Fridge and Freezer

Back in the olden days, people rarely had anything but preserved, "salted" meats and home-canned foods during the winter because of the scarcity of ways to safely store anything else. Of course, in the summer there were gardens, and when butchering time came, there was "fresh" meat.

We've come a long way, baby, since then. We can safely store so many more foods since the days of the root cellar, home-delivered ice, and salted meats. Thank goodness!

Here are my suggestions for the staples you should always have on hand in your refrigerator and freezer to make meal preparation faster.

In the refrigerator — I wish I had two

In the refrigerator, my dairy recommendations play the starring role:

- ✓ **Butter and soft, trans-fat-free margarines spreads:** I keep a minimal amount of butter refrigerated and freeze the rest because I don't use it as fast as the healthy, trans-fat-free "spread" I put on my bread.

  Use butter sparingly, when you can really tell the difference in the final product. When mashing potatoes, I put a teaspoon or two on top of the completed dish and let it melt so that everyone can take a scoop and get some butter with each serving.

✔ **Eggs:** Lower-cholesterol eggs are available in stores now, as are hard-cooked eggs. Reduce cholesterol (and saturated fat) in the diet by reducing your use of egg yolks.

✔ **Milk:** Skim or 1-percent milk and fat-free half-and-half are staples. Once in a while I use whipping cream, but not too often. When I do, I eat it all before I get it into the recipe.

✔ **Sour cream:** Choose low-fat or fat-free. I prefer low-fat for cooking because it has a creamier texture. For toppings, I use the fat-free version. Some people use plain yogurt instead of sour cream. It's a healthy thing to do.

✔ **Cheddar cheese:** Fifty-percent-lower-fat sharp cheddar and cheddar with jalapeño peppers are staples. I use Cabot as a first choice when I need cheddar, jalapeño cheddar, and pepper Jack cheeses. Otherwise, I look for low-fat versions of other types of cheese.

When grating cheese with a box grater, coat both sides of the section you're using with cooking spray for easy cleaning. And grate cheese on wax paper for quick cleanup.

✔ **Parmesan:** This is another staple. Buy the best you can afford. I can't afford the best because it's about $20 per pound. I'd lie awake at night wondering whether it was molding. I buy a mid-priced brand and sleep better.

In the freezer

Frozen vegetables are great when fresh ones aren't available or in season, or you're looking for a vegetable side dish. Most of the "unprocessed" varieties have no salt or sugar added to them. Watch out for the "sauced" ones. They're not in people's best interest because of additions like butter and salt.

If you can't have fresh vegetables, look for a frozen variety. If you have to use canned, go for the no-salt-added variety.

✔ **Chopped onions:** I keep these on hand for emergencies, as I discuss earlier.

✔ **Green beans:** These are a staple. I use them when I'm out of fresh vegetables; they're a satisfactory substitute. We like the smaller, thinner ones called *haricot vert.*

✔ **Corn:** While not a vegetable (but a starch), corn kernels are a staple.

✔ **Peas:** Tiny or petite green peas are a starch, too, but are also a staple because I like them. Feel free to substitute your own favorites (carrots, broccoli, Brussels sprouts) in place of mine. Love those Brussels sprouts!

Keep some protein on hand too. Then when you forget to buy ground beef, chicken breasts, or another protein that you planned for dinner, you can go to your freezer and thaw what you need. When your freezer is well-stocked with staples, you won't be grouchy because you have to run to the grocery store before you can get dinner on the table.

- **Lean ground beef (93- to 95-percent-lean):** Lower levels of fat cut the amount of saturated fats you eat (the ones that are harmful to your heart). You also waste less.

- **Individually wrapped, boneless, skinless chicken cutlets:** *Cutlets* are just chicken breasts that have been sliced thinner; I like them for their more even cooking and lower weight per portion. Often chicken breasts these days can weigh up to 8 ounces, when we should only be eating 4 ounces most of the time. Sometimes I buy the bigger ones and butterfly them myself. That's a cost-cutting maneuver.

To reduce your sodium/salt intake, read the label and avoid chicken that has been "enhanced" with salt, sodium, broth, or brine, as indicated on the label. Some companies like to "plump" their chickens. Plumping causes plumper profits and more water to cook out of the chicken.

Finally, keep some desserts and nuts in your freezer:

- **No-sugar-added Fudgsicles:** These are a quick fix for a sweet tooth.

- **Nuts:** Walnuts, almonds (whole, slivered, and sliced), pine nuts, and pecans last longer in the freezer because of their fat content. They can become rancid on the shelf, and I feel they're too expensive to take that chance.

Roasting nuts intensifies their flavor. To roast, spread them on a rimmed baking sheet. Bake 5 to 8 minutes at 350 degrees or until slightly browned and aromatic. Watch them carefully — they'll burn in a New York minute (I love to say that). I have no idea what a New York minute really is, but it sounds like it must be about 5 seconds. When I sprinkle nuts on dishes about to go into the oven, I don't roast them in advance.

The Tools of the Trade: Cookware and Appliances

Buy the best cookware and appliances you can afford to do the jobs you want them to do. Do I sound like a broken record? I have some really good cookware and some marginal pots and pans. The ones I use the most often (almost daily) cost more, but I use them more. I use the mid-sized skillet I own, which is a lower-end brand, only occasionally (every three months or so).

Think about shoes (which I do a lot). If you're going hiking, you want the best because of the terrain and the abuse you inflict on your feet (just like you want the best skillet). Women going to a dress-up social function might be less inclined to buy the best, brand-name, killer heels to wear for two hours (the equivalent of the every-three-month skillet). Guys, by the way, don't understand the shoe thing and never will. Virgo thinks I should wear only comfortable (in other words, ugly) shoes for every function. He asks silly questions like "Are those shoes comfortable?" "Of course not, but they sure look good," I reply. I ignore him like any self-respecting woman. He doesn't say silly things like this regarding cookware.

Because my stove and dishwasher came with our condo, I didn't have a lot of options without spending a fortune. When I upgrade, I'll pay more and get a higher-quality replacement. We bought the refrigerator and got a nice one.

 Try not to buy a dishwasher or garbage disposal that scares your pet. We always apologize to our kitties when we run the disposal because it's so loud it scares the poor babies. Our dishwasher is rather quiet — not like a helicopter hovering overhead. If noise is an issue, make sure you check it out before you pay for it.

If you have a choice, install an outside vent for your stove. A recirculating fan makes noise, but that type of fan does essentially nothing when it comes to venting. It takes the steam, odors, and so forth from the cooktop and blows them out into your face (or above your head). There's some sort of charcoal filter that's supposed to remove cooking odors. You want the odors and excess heat to be vented *outside*. If you're buying a new place (house, condo, or otherwise) put in your contract that your kitchen stove requires an outside vent. We did and were glad because somewhere along the line from promises to execution, the builder eliminated outside venting for all units as a cost-saving measure. Just because the salesperson "says" there will be outside venting doesn't mean that it will happen. A signed contract does.

Must-have pots and pans

Remember the analogy about riding a horse without a horse, which I related to ingredients? The same principle applies to pots and pans. How can you cook (unless you live in a cave) without pots and pans? Buy the best you can afford, and they just may last forever (if they don't, you may be able to use the limited lifetime guarantee). I'm still using some All-Clad that I bought in the late '90s and Calphalon from earlier than that.

Answer these questions before you decide what to buy:

- ✔ What size pots and skillets do you need for your family?
- ✔ What do you cook?
- ✔ How many mouths are you feeding?
- ✔ How often do you use each pot or pan?

Here are the pots and pans that help make meal prep a snap:

- ✔ **An 8- to 12-quart pot with a lid:** Buy All-Clad or Calphalon if you can afford it. Other quality brands exist; I just don't have any experience with them.

- ✔ **Twelve-inch and 8- or 9-inch nonstick skillets:** I use the larger one at least four times a week.

- ✔ **Heavy-bottomed small, medium, and large saucepans (with lids):** They keep food from sticking and cook food more evenly.

- ✔ **A heavy, rimmed baking sheet and rack:** Set the rack in the baking sheet to elevate food so that fat can drip into the baking sheet.

- ✔ **Glass baking dishes:** Buy 9-x-13-inch, 7- or 8-x-11- or 12-inch, and 8-x-8-inch sizes. They're mostly used for casseroles, but they're also good for baking meats and fish.

- ✔ **Pie plates:** These are handy for recipes other than those that require ice cream . . . such as pies.

Stirring things up with utensils

Unless you want to stir with your hands or fingers, you'll need some utensils. That piece of wood you got when you bought paint is not considered a cooking utensil. Choose utensils according to the dishes you prepare and how often you cook that recipe. If you never eat meat, you don't need a meat fork — except as a weapon.

- ✔ **Good-quality knives:** Eight-inch chef's and paring knives are essential. Buy the best knives you can afford. Serrated knives come in handy for foods likely to tear, such as bread and some cakes.

  Keep your knives sharp. Cutting is safer and takes less time when the knife is at its best. Also, use the proper one for the job (slicing, chopping, dicing, and so on).

- ✔ **Cutting boards:** I have at least five different sizes; all but one can go in the dishwasher. I find that two larger ones are needed when I'm attending to both meat and vegetables — one for trimming the fat from the meat or poultry, and one for chopping the vegetables.

  Never use the same cutting board for both types of food without sanitizing the board between uses.

- ✔ **Rubber spatulas:** These seem to disappear on a regular basis; therefore, keep several on hand and toss them when they become hard as rocks or show melted areas.

✔ **A cook's spoon for stirring:** This spoon is larger than a serving spoon and has a longer handle. I use ones that are safe for nonstick pans/skillets.

✔ **Wire whisks:** Whisks are useful for smooth blending and whipping eggs.

✔ **Utensils for your expensive nonstick pans:** You don't want to destroy the coating, so use utensils that are especially made for nonstick cookware.

✔ **A potato/vegetable peeler:** Many of them rust; when one does, throw it out and buy another one.

✔ **A wine opener:** Need I say more? Having a wine opener is better than cracking the bottle on the side of the sink.

✔ **A can opener:** Either an electric or manual one will work. It's important to keep it sanitized.

✔ **A meat fork:** This stabilizes meat when you carve it.

✔ **Kitchen shears:** These are useful for everything from cutting string to snipping fresh herbs.

✔ **Tongs:** These come in handy for placing items in a skillet and turning them.

✔ **A colander:** Use this bowl-shaped, perforated device for draining solid foods. If the food is "fine," use a sieve.

✔ **A food scale:** This helps you avoid portion distortion and make better choices. Some are digital; the less expensive ones are not.

✔ **Measuring spoons:** Should you buy metal or plastic spoons? I buy metal, and I have several sets. I don't use plastic ones. Round or oval ones? The round metal ones cost the least, but I like the oval-shaped metal spoons because they fit into spice jars more easily. To measuring spoon companies: Make all metal measuring spoons like this!

✔ **Measuring cups:** I use metal measuring cups exclusively. I consider them to be more accurate, too.

✔ **Thermometers:** Cooking foods to safe temperatures is a must, especially when you're cooking meats and reheating leftovers. Some thermometers remain in the food while it's in the oven. Others, such as a digital, instant-read thermometer, give a quick read but don't stay in the food while it's cooking.

Be food-safe when reheating cooked leftovers by bringing the temperature up to a minimum of 140 degrees. The food safety zone is below 40 degrees for cold foods and above 140 degrees for hot foods. At danger zone temperatures, bacteria can double their numbers every 20 to 30 minutes.

Never leave food unrefrigerated for more than two hours — one hour if the temperature is above 90 degrees. A thermometer is the only way to know whether the food is at the right temperature. This is serious business. My mantra is "When in doubt, throw it out."

Using a thermometer to test meat doneness

The absolute best way to determine the doneness of meat is with an instant-read or a digital thermometer. You'll prevent food-borne illness and overcooking, and hold foods at a safe temperature — responsibilities of all cooks. Hot foods should be held at 140 degrees or higher; cold foods should be held at 40 degrees or lower.

Follow the USDA's recommended safe minimum internal temperatures to make sure your meats are properly cooked:

✔ **Steaks and roasts:** 145 degrees

✔ **Fish:** 145 degrees

✔ **Pork:** 160 degrees

✔ **Ground beef:** 160 degrees

✔ **Egg dishes:** 160 degrees

✔ **Chicken breasts:** 165 degrees

✔ **Whole poultry:** 165 degrees

✔ **Leftovers:** 165 degrees

Thermometer placement is key. Place it in the thickest part of the meat, not near bone.

Making prep work easier with small appliances

Eons ago, a must-have "appliance" for the home cook was a butter churn. Then there was the cabbage slicer (for sauerkraut), the bread bowl (a place for rising yeast bread dough), and the apple peeler (for prepping apples to make apple butter). The list goes on. Today, we're all about plugging an appliance into the wall to make life easier for the cook. All but one of the following aids are electric:

✔ **Electric stand mixer:** Buy a Kitchen Aid if you can afford it. Look for sales, or buy a refurbished one. They have a more powerful motor, and you can operate one hands-free. I use it for cake batter and mashed potatoes, which I whip into a cloud-like frenzy.

✔ **Hand mixer:** This is useful at times when you don't want or need the power of a stand mixer. The hand mixer is good for mixing softened cream cheese and smaller quantities, and for instances when the mixing time is shorter. Don't plan to go anywhere while you're using it, because you're the mixer's "stand." Be sure to keep the beaters in the bowl when the mixer is turned on.

✔ **Slow cooker:** Get one with digital controls. The size depends on the size of your family and whether you want leftovers. I have a 6-quart one. A slow cooker is a sure winner for weeknight meals. You can even prepare the meal the night before, refrigerate the ceramic container, and start heating it in the morning for dinner that night. I'm crazy about the slow cooker, and my recipes and menus reflect that.

If you have a smooth cooktop, don't turn it on if you plan to use the cooktop surface as the slow cooker's cooking spot. Virgo did that when we were having company, and it was another of those cooking disasters that involve bad smells.

Use slow-cooker liners to simplify cleanup. They're expensive (there's no competition right now), but worth it to me. Reynolds makes them.

- **Microwave:** I have one regular microwave, plus a microwave-convection oven because I have only one conventional oven. Because I used to own a microwave store with a cooking school and taught microwave cooking classes, I'm very tuned into microwave cooking. The microwave is grossly underused. I maintain that the reason is that there's no one to teach classes anymore, and I don't have time to teach the whole world myself.

Buy a microwave that allows you to fit a 9-x-13-inch dish in it. Both of mine do, with the option of turning off the turntable to accommodate the larger dish.

- **Immersion blender:** Although an immersion blender is less powerful than a traditional blender, sometimes it's much more convenient. (I recommend having both — I contend that a traditional blender's main purpose is for making margaritas and daiquiris.) The Virgo uses the immersion blender all the time to make protein shakes. You could call it an "electric stick." It's about a foot long, with an enclosed blade on one end and the electric cord at the other end. You can use it with one hand wherever you have an outlet. I often use it if I'm making bean soup and I want to thicken it without adding flour or cornstarch. I place the blade end in the mixture in the pan, turn it on and whirl it for a few seconds, and voilà! Thicker soup. Cleanup is easy: Run hot water over the part that was in the food, and allow to dry.

- **Food processor:** Both regular-size and mini processors can come in handy. I don't use the larger processor nearly as much as I could because I don't have a convenient place to store it, but I do use it. The mini processor is great for making fresh breadcrumbs. It's also light-weight and easy to handle. I use it the most.

- **Indoor grill (if you can't cook outdoors):** Outdoor cooking is possible where we live but not too practical (an elevator is involved), so I use an electric indoor grill. I have a Cuisinart that holds three or four chicken breasts or four burgers and has removable plates for cleaning. The first one we had was a small George Foreman, but we outgrew it as we used it more. Either one is good.

✔ **Stovetop grill:** This fits over two burners and is useful when you have larger pieces of meat you want to grill, such as a flank steak or a whole grill-full of vegetables.

✔ **Rice-cooker:** Some cooks swear by them; I do better using my microwave for cooking rice (except for one time). My experience with an electric rice cooker hasn't been all that great. I'm sure it's just me because others think it's a wonderful appliance.

✔ **Pressure cooker:** I like it when I use it, but I don't use it often enough to make it worthwhile. Yes, my mother had one when I was a child, and it was a great mystery to me. She made a lot of great dishes in it. She was a brave woman.

Part II

A Year's Worth of Weekly Menu Plans

In this part . . .

*I*f Part I is the appetizer to *7-Day Menu Planner For Dummies,* Part II is the entree. You find 52 weeks' worth of dinner menus with something to please everybody — that's 365 days of no-stress menu planning. And as logical as it would be to start with Week 1, I recommend that you figure out what week of the year it is and then turn to that week for recipes that take advantage of seasonal foods. (Here's a hint: Week 26 is mid-year, and Week 51 is Christmas. You can go from there.) You'll get better-tasting meals and the most savings by choosing foods in season.

Week 1

Sunday *Family*

Prepare prize-winning **Beef Steak with Curried Onion and Plum Sauce** (see recipe) from a past National Beef Cook-Off. Accompany it with **jasmine rice, broccoli, mixed greens,** and **sourdough bread.** Buy a **carrot cake** for dessert. ***Plan ahead:*** Save enough cake for Wednesday.

Monday *Meatless*

You're in for a treat with **Rockin' Rainbow Pasta** (see recipe). Serve the multicolored pasta and bean dish with a **spinach salad** and **crusty rolls.** Enjoy **peaches** for a light dessert. ***Plan ahead:*** Save enough pasta for Tuesday.

Tuesday *Heat and Eat*

You can afford to relax and read the newspaper before dinner because all you have to do is heat the leftover **pasta.** Serve it with a **red-tipped lettuce salad** and **whole-grain rolls.** Sliced **kiwifruit** is a good dessert.

Wednesday *Budget*

Keep costs down with **turkey burgers.** To boost the flavor, cook some sliced onions and mushrooms in a little canola oil until lightly browned. Spoon over the burgers. Serve with a **romaine salad.** Slice the leftover **carrot cake** for dessert.

Thursday *Kids*

Kids will love **Tostada Bake.** Heat oven to 375 degrees. In a large nonstick skillet, cook 1 pound lean ground beef on medium; drain. Add ½ cup tomato sauce (from a 15-ounce can) and 1 packet reduced-sodium taco seasoning mix. Blend well. Place 2½ cups coarsely crushed baked corn chips in an 8-x-8-inch baking dish coated with cooking spray. Combine remaining tomato sauce and 1 15-ounce can rinsed pinto beans. Spread beef over chips, then spoon bean mixture over beef. Bake about 25 minutes or until bubbly. Sprinkle ¼ cup shredded 50-percent-reduced-fat cheddar cheese and ½ cup more crushed corn chips on top; bake 5 more minutes to melt cheese. Serve with **chopped lettuce** and extra **chips.** For dessert, how about **plums?**

Friday *Express*

Try one of **Simply Asia's Stir-Fry Meals** (or substitute another brand). Add your own favorite protein such as beef, chicken, or pork, and the meal will be on the table in no time. Stir in some extra vegetables for a delicious meal. Serve with a packaged **green salad** and **breadsticks.** For dessert, fresh **pineapple** is refreshing.

Saturday *Easy Entertaining*

Spicy Basque-Style Chicken (see recipe) is packed with flavor. Serve it over **yellow rice** tossed with frozen tiny **green peas.** Add an **arugula salad** and **baguettes.** Finish your meal with **fruit tarts.**

Beef Steak with Curried Onion and Plum Sauce

Prep time: 10 min • **Cook time:** 11–15 min • **Yield:** 4 servings

Ingredients	*Directions*
2 tablespoons olive oil	*1* Heat oil on medium until hot. Place steaks in skillet; cook top blade steaks 11 to 15 minutes (chuck eye steaks 9 to 11 minutes) for medium-rare to medium doneness, turning occasionally. Season with salt and pepper to taste.
4 beef shoulder top blade (flatiron) steaks, 4 to 6 ounces each, or 4 boneless beef chuck eye steaks (¾ inch thick)	
Salt and pepper to taste	*2* Remove steaks to platter; keep warm.
2 green onions with tops, sliced diagonally	*3* Add onions to skillet; cook and stir 1 to 2 minutes or until golden.
⅓ cup plum or blackberry all-fruit spread	
2 tablespoons mango chutney (such as Major Grey)	*4* Stir in preserves, chutney, and curry powder. Add water; cook and stir until sauce is hot.
¾ teaspoon curry powder	
¼ cup water	*5* Stir in lime juice and remove from heat.
1 tablespoon fresh lime juice	*6* Spoon sauce over steaks; garnish with peanuts.
¼ cup roasted chopped peanuts	

Per serving: 391 calories, 24g protein, 23g fat (53 percent calories from fat), 6g saturated fat, 22g carbohydrate, 75mg cholesterol, 89mg sodium, 1g fiber.

Rockin' Rainbow Pasta

Prep time: 20 min • **Cook time:** About 10 min, plus pasta • **Yield:** 8 servings

MEATLESS

Ingredients	Directions

Ingredients

1 tablespoon olive oil

3 tablespoons minced garlic

1 19-ounce can cannellini beans, rinsed

1 1-pound package frozen bell peppers and onions

1 pound penne pasta

¼ cup sliced pepperoncinis

¼ cup chopped black olives

¼ cup chopped fresh Italian parsley

¼ cup fresh lemon juice

¼ cup freshly grated parmesan cheese

Directions

1 In a large nonstick skillet, heat oil on medium heat. Add garlic; cook 3 minutes.

2 Increase heat to medium-high; add beans and peppers and onions. Cook 5 minutes.

3 Meanwhile, cook pasta according to directions; drain, reserving ½ cup pasta water.

4 To pasta pot, add peppers and onions and bean mixture, plus pepperoncinis, olives, parsley, and lemon juice; mix well.

5 Add pasta to pot; toss to mix.

6 Spoon into a large serving bowl. Sprinkle parmesan on top and serve.

Per serving: 315 calories, 11g protein, 4g fat (12 percent calories from fat), 0.9g saturated fat, 58g carbohydrate, 2mg cholesterol, 284mg sodium, 5g fiber.

Spicy Basque-Style Chicken

Prep time: 10 min • **Cook time:** About 15 min • **Yield:** 4 servings

Ingredients

- 1 teaspoon smoked paprika
- ¼ teaspoon pepper
- 1 pound boneless chicken breast tenders
- 2 teaspoons olive oil
- 2 teaspoons minced garlic
- ¼ cup sliced green olives
- 2 10-ounce cans mild diced tomatoes and green chilies
- 2 tablespoons crumbled bacon or finely chopped prosciutto
- 2 tablespoons chopped fresh parsley

Directions

1 Combine paprika and pepper, and sprinkle over chicken.

2 Heat oil in a large nonstick skillet on medium-high. Add chicken; cook 4 minutes.

3 Add garlic; cook 30 seconds.

4 Turn chicken. Add olives and tomatoes and chilies; bring to boil. Reduce heat and simmer 6 minutes.

5 Remove chicken from pan. Increase heat to medium-high; cook sauce 2 minutes more, stirring occasionally.

6 Sprinkle sauce with bacon and parsley. Serve chicken with sauce.

Per serving: 200 calories, 29g protein, 7g fat (30 percent calories from fat), 1.3g saturated fat, 6g carbohydrate, 69mg cholesterol, 975mg sodium, 2g fiber.

Adapted from Cooking Light *magazine.*

Week 2

Sunday *Family*

Take it easy by using a cooking bag to prepare a **baked turkey breast** for the family. To accompany the turkey, make **Baked Corn Pudding** (see recipe). Add fresh **broccoli** and **dinner rolls.** For dessert, buy a **cherry pie** and top with fat-free **vanilla ice cream.** *Plan ahead:* Save enough turkey for Monday and enough pie for Tuesday. Save enough corn pudding for Wednesday and some ice cream for Thursday.

Monday *Heat and Eat*

Use the leftover turkey for an easy **Turkey Pot Pie** (see recipe). Serve it with a **spinach salad.** Enjoy **pears** for dessert.

Tuesday *Budget*

Some would call it cheap, but I say frugal when I save money with dishes like **Taco Soup** (see recipe). Serve the stew-like, slow-cooker soup with a **sliced avocado salad.** Add **baked tortilla chips.** Slice the leftover **cherry pie** for dessert and top it with light **whipped cream.**

Wednesday *Express*

Choose any flavor **rotisserie chicken** for a quick meal. Accompany it with leftover **Baked Corn Pudding.** Add a packaged **green salad** and **biscuits.** Fresh **tropical fruits** make a simple dessert.

Thursday *Meatless*

For an easy and quick no-meat dinner, **ravioli and pesto** fills the bill. Cook 2 13-ounce packages frozen light cheese ravioli and toss with refrigerated pesto. Serve with a **romaine salad** and **garlic bread.** A little leftover **ice cream** is all the dessert you need.

Friday *Kids*

Make it **cheeseburger** night for the kids, using any burger. Add frozen **oven fries** and **carrot salad.** For dessert, **fudgsicles** are messy but fun.

Saturday *Easy Entertaining*

Serve your guests **Orange-Thyme Broiled Salmon.** In a resealable plastic bag, combine ⅓ cup orange juice, 1 tablespoon olive oil, 1 teaspoon each dried thyme and ground mustard, and ¼ teaspoon each garlic powder, salt, and pepper. Add 1 pound salmon fillets and coat. Refrigerate 20 minutes, turning once to coat. Remove salmon; discard marinade, and broil fish 10 minutes or until it flakes with a fork. Serve with **jasmine rice, green beans,** a **Boston lettuce salad,** and **crusty bread.** For dessert, **coconut cake** makes a festive finish.

FAMILY

Baked Corn Pudding

Prep time: 15 min • **Cook time:** About 1 hr, plus standing time • **Yield:** 8 servings

Ingredients	*Directions*
2 tablespoons butter or margarine	*1* Heat oven to 350 degrees. Coat an 8-x-8-inch baking dish with cooking spray.
2 tablespoons chopped onion	
¼ cup flour	*2* In a Dutch oven, melt butter on medium heat. Add onion; cook 3 to 4 minutes, stirring frequently, until tender.
¼ teaspoon salt	
½ teaspoon pepper	
2 cups 1-percent milk	*3* Stir in flour, salt, and pepper until well blended. Stir in milk. Cook 4 or 5 minutes, stirring constantly until thickened.
2 eggs, slightly beaten	
2 egg whites, slightly beaten	
1 cup shredded 50-percent-reduced-fat cheddar cheese	*4* Gradually stir in eggs, egg whites, and cheese. Stir in corn and parsley.
1 16-ounce package frozen whole-kernel corn, thawed	*5* Pour into baking dish. Sprinkle bread crumbs over corn mixture. Coat crumbs with cooking spray.
¼ cup chopped fresh parsley	
2 tablespoons plain bread crumbs	*6* Bake, uncovered, 50 to 60 minutes or until mixture is set and knife inserted in center comes out clean. Let stand 5 to 10 minutes before serving.

Per serving: 188 calories, 11g protein, 8g fat (34 percent calories from fat), 4.2g saturated fat, 22g carbohydrate, 72mg cholesterol, 258mg sodium, 2g fiber.

HEAT AND EAT

Turkey Pot Pie

Prep time: 10 min • **Cook time:** About 30 min • **Yield:** 6 servings

Ingredients	*Directions*
2 0.87-ounce packages turkey or chicken gravy mix	*1* Heat oven to 375 degrees.
½ teaspoon poultry seasoning **1½ cups 1-percent milk** **1 cup water** **2 tablespoons butter**	*2* In a large skillet, mix gravy mix, poultry seasoning, milk, water, and butter. Bring to boil on medium, stirring frequently.
3 cups chopped, cooked (leftover) turkey (see Note)	*3* Stir in turkey and vegetables. Return to boil; reduce heat and simmer 5 minutes.
2 cups frozen mixed vegetables **1 5.2- to 7.5-ounce refrigerated layered biscuits**	*4* Spoon into a 2-quart baking dish coated with cooking spray. Split biscuits and place on top of turkey mixture.
	5 Bake 15 minutes or until biscuits are golden brown.

Per serving: 292 calories, 25g protein, 11g fat (34 percent calories from fat), 4.3g saturated fat, 23g carbohydrate, 67mg cholesterol, 681mg sodium, 1g fiber.

Note: *Chicken may be substituted for turkey.*

BUDGET

Taco Soup

Prep time: About 20 min • **Cook time:** About 8 hr • **Yield:** 14 cups

Ingredients	*Directions*
1 pound lean ground beef	**1** Heat a medium nonstick skillet on medium. Cook beef and onion 7 minutes or until beef is no longer pink and onion is softened; drain.
1 medium onion, chopped	
1 16-ounce can chili beans	
1 15-ounce can kidney beans	**2** Place mixture in a 4-quart or larger slow cooker, along with all beans, corn, tomato sauce, water, tomatoes, chilies, and taco seasoning mix. Stir to blend.
1 15-ounce can less-sodium, whole-kernel corn	
1 8-ounce can no-salt tomato sauce	
1 cup water	**3** Cover and cook on low 8 hours.
2 14½-ounce cans no-salt, diced tomatoes	
1 4-ounce can diced green chilies, drained	
1 1.25-ounce package 30-percent-less-sodium taco seasoning mix	

Per cup: 172 calories, 11g protein, 4g fat (21 percent calories from fat), 1.3g saturated fat, 22g carbohydrate, 19mg cholesterol, 431mg sodium, 5g fiber.

Week 3

 Sunday *Family*

Celebrate family day with **Rosemary-Lemon Roast Chicken**. Heat oven to 350 degrees. Remove giblets from a 5- to 7-pound roaster; discard. Combine ¼ cup olive oil, 4 cloves peeled garlic, salt and pepper to taste, and ½ teaspoon crushed red pepper in a mini food processor. Pulse several times. Rub roaster inside and out with oil mixture. Place 1 bunch fresh rosemary and 1 halved lemon in body cavity. Place roaster, breast side up, in a shallow roasting pan. Roast 2 to 2½ hours or until thermometer inserted in thickest part of thigh registers 180 degrees. Remove from oven; let stand 10 minutes. Slice, remove skin, and serve. Serve the bird with **mashed potatoes, gravy,** frozen **tiny green peas,** and **dinner rolls.** For dessert, buy **apple crisp.** *Plan ahead:* Save enough chicken for Monday; save enough apple crisp for Tuesday.

 Monday *Heat and Eat*

Make **chicken sandwiches** for an easy meal. Brush slices of focaccia with olive oil. Top with sliced leftover chicken, roasted red pepper strips (from a jar), and red-tip lettuce. Serve with **pesto potato salad** (stir pesto and diced pimentos into deli potato salad). Finish with **peaches** for dessert.

 Tuesday *Meatless*

For a special, no-meat dinner, make **Lentil-Stuffed Peppers** (see recipe). Serve the peppers with steamed **baby carrots,** a **spinach salad,** and **whole-grain rolls.** Top leftover, warmed **apple crisp** with fat-free **vanilla ice cream.** *Plan ahead:* Save enough ice cream for Thursday.

 Wednesday *Budget*

Tuna Noodle Casserole is always welcomed as a stand-by budget chopper. Heat oven to 400 degrees. Coat a 1½-quart dish with cooking spray. In a large bowl, combine 1 10¾-ounce can condensed, 98-percent-fat-free cream of mushroom soup; ½ cup skim milk; 2 tablespoons diced pimento; 1 cup frozen green peas (thawed); 12 ounces canned light tuna (drained and flaked); and 2 cups hot, cooked, medium no-yolk noodles. Mix well. Spoon into prepared dish; bake uncovered 20 minutes or until hot. Top with ½ cup 50-percent-reduced-fat shredded cheddar cheese; bake 5 more minutes or until cheese melts. Serve with a **lettuce wedge** and **whole-grain rolls.** Enjoy **kiwifruit** for dessert.

 Thursday *Kids*

The kids are bound to like **Mediterranean Pasta and Pesto** (see recipe). Serve with **celery sticks** and **soft rolls.** Scoop the leftover **ice cream** and top it with light **chocolate sauce** for dessert.

 Friday *Express*

For a speedy meal, **Beef with Cabbage** won't let you down. Cook ¾ pound lean ground beef on medium about 6 minutes or until no longer pink; drain. Reduce heat to low; stir in 1 10- to 16-ounce package angel-hair coleslaw mix and ½ teaspoon celery seeds. Cover and cook 6 to 7 minutes or until cabbage is tender. Stir in 1 tablespoon white wine vinegar and 1 teaspoon sugar, and heat through. (Adapted from *The 15-Minute Chef,* by Patricia Mack [HP Books].) Serve with **parsley buttered potatoes** and **pumpernickel bread. Plums** are your dessert.

 Saturday *Easy Entertaining*

Invite friends for delicious **Sautéed Pork Loin with Mustard Grape Sauce** (see recipe). Serve the pork with **rice, sugar snap peas,** a **bibb lettuce salad,** and **baguettes.** Dessert is **sorbet** and **almond cookies.**

MEATLESS

Lentil-Stuffed Peppers

Prep time: 10 min • **Cook time:** About 25 min • **Yield:** 8 servings

Ingredients	*Directions*

4 large bell peppers (red, green, yellow, or orange)

1 14-ounce can vegetable broth

6 ounces water

¼ teaspoon salt

½ teaspoon freshly ground black pepper

2 cups dried brown lentils, picked over and rinsed

3 tablespoons tomato paste

¾ teaspoon turmeric

¾ teaspoon cumin

¾ teaspoon lemon pepper

4 ounces crumbled low-fat feta cheese

1 Halve peppers through stem end. Remove seeds and white membranes. Place cut side down in a baking dish; cover and microwave on high (100-percent power) 4 to 6 minutes or until slightly softened; drain. Allow peppers to cool.

2 Meanwhile, heat broth and water in large saucepan on medium-high heat. Add salt and pepper.

3 When liquid comes to a full boil, add lentils and reduce heat to low. Cover and simmer about 20 minutes or until soft but not mushy; drain any liquid.

4 Stir in tomato paste, turmeric, cumin, and lemon pepper.

5 Divide the lentils evenly among the peppers, filling each so that it mounds slightly. Top evenly with feta cheese. Serve warm or at room temperature.

Per serving: 228 calories, 18g protein, 2g fat (7 percent calories from fat), 1.1g saturated fat, 38g carbohydrate, 5mg cholesterol, 544mg sodium, 8g fiber.

Adapted from Stuff It! *by Lora Brody and Max Brody (William Morrow).*

KIDS

Mediterranean Pasta and Pesto

Prep time: 10 min • **Cook time:** About 20 min, plus pasta • **Yield:** 4 servings

Ingredients	*Directions*
8 ounces wagon wheel or bow-tie pasta	*1* Cook pasta according to directions.
1 slice bacon	*2* Heat a medium saucepan on medium heat; cook bacon 3 minutes or until crispy.
½ teaspoon minced garlic	
1 teaspoon dried thyme	*3* Reduce heat to low; add garlic and thyme. Cook 2 minutes. Add onion; cook 3 to 4 minutes or until softened. Add tomatoes and cook 2 minutes. Add cannellini beans with liquid and pepper. Bring to simmer; cook 5 minutes.
½ cup chopped onion	
½ cup no-salt-added diced tomatoes, drained	
1 15.5-ounce can cannellini beans	
1 pinch black pepper	*4* Drain pasta; combine with sauce. Just before serving, stir in pesto.
1 tablespoon pesto	

Per serving: 362 calories, 13g protein, 7g fat (17 percent calories from fat), 1.7g saturated fat, 61g carbohydrate, 5mg cholesterol, 318mg sodium, 7g fiber.

Sautéed Pork Loin with Mustard Grape Sauce

Prep time: 20 min • **Cook time:** About 25 min • **Yield:** 8 servings

Ingredients

8 slices (each ¼-inch thick) boneless pork loin (about 1½ pounds)

½ cup flour

¼ teaspoon kosher salt

½ teaspoon freshly ground black pepper

2 tablespoons canola oil, divided

1 cup red or green seedless grapes, halved

1 small onion, chopped

½ cup dry white wine

1 14-ounce can fat-free chicken broth

1 teaspoon packed dark brown sugar

1½ tablespoons Dijon mustard

Per serving: 203 calories, 18g protein, 10g fat (43 percent calories from fat), 2.4g saturated fat, 9g carbohydrate, 48mg cholesterol, 202mg sodium, 1g fiber.

Note: Deglaze means to add liquid to a pan in which meat has been roasted or sauteed, usually to make a sauce that incorporates the cooking juices.

Directions

1 Sprinkle a small amount of water on a large sheet of plastic wrap. Place two of the pork slices on wrap and sprinkle again with water. Cover with another sheet of wrap and press with the heel of your hand until ¼-inch thick.

2 Repeat Step 1 with remaining pork.

3 Mix flour, salt, and pepper in a pie plate. Heat half the oil in a large nonstick skillet on medium-high until hot.

4 Working in two batches, place pork in flour mixture; turn to coat. Shake off excess flour and add to skillet. Cook 2 minutes per side until browned. Transfer to a plate; cover loosely with foil. Repeat with remaining oil and pork.

5 Add grapes and onion to skillet. Reduce heat to medium and cook 5 minutes, stirring often, until onions are slightly softened.

6 Increase heat to medium-high, add wine, and bring to a boil. Cook rapidly to deglaze skillet (see Note) until liquid is reduced to 2 tablespoons. Add broth and sugar, and boil until reduced by half.

7 Reduce heat to medium and return pork to skillet with any accumulated juices. Simmer gently 3 minutes or until heated through. Transfer pork to large heated platter.

8 Remove skillet from heat, whisk in mustard, and season the sauce with salt and pepper. Pour sauce over pork and serve hot.

Week 4

Sunday *Family*

No matter which team you root for on Super Bowl Sunday, **Winner's Chili** (see recipe) is a touchdown kind of meal. Serve it topped with chopped **onions**, shredded **cheese** (50-percent-reduced-fat cheddar) and low-fat **sour cream**. Alongside, add **coleslaw** and **cornbread** (from a mix). For dessert, whether your team wins or loses, **brownies** will be a hit. *Plan ahead:* Save enough chili and coleslaw for Monday. Save enough brownies for Tuesday.

Monday *Heat and Eat*

Chili Spuds make good use of the leftover chili. Top hot, split baked potatoes with the heated chili. Garnish with sliced green onions. Add the leftover **coleslaw** and **whole-grain rolls** to the meal. Try fresh **pineapple** for dessert.

Tuesday *Budget*

Low cost and high flavor make **Mexican Chicken Soup** (see recipe) an excellent choice for dinner. Serve with **mixed greens** and **baked tortilla chips**. Offer the leftover **brownies** for dessert.

Wednesday *Meatless*

Comfort food without meat makes **Baked Manicotti** a perfect meal. Heat oven to 450 degrees. In a 9-x-13-inch baking dish coated with cooking spray, spread half of a 26-ounce jar of pasta sauce; top with 8 refrigerated manicotti. Pour remaining pasta sauce over manicotti and sprinkle with some freshly grated parmesan cheese. Bake, covered, 20 minutes. Remove cover and continue baking 5 minutes or until heated through. Serve with a **spinach salad** with **red onion rings** and **orange sections**. **Sugar cookies** are dessert.

Thursday *Express*

Make it quick tonight with **Tomato Basil Soup.** Heat 3 14½-ounce cans diced tomatoes with basil, garlic, and oregano over low heat until bubbling. Add 8 ounces low-fat cream cheese, diced. Simmer until most of the cheese is melted. Remove from heat. Use a handheld blender to puree. Serve with deli **egg salad** and **lettuce** on toasted, whole-grain **English muffins.** Make instant **butterscotch pudding** with 1-percent milk for dessert.

Friday *Kids*

Make the little angels happy tonight with a kid-favorite, **Meatball Mac and Cheese**. Cook packaged macaroni and cheese as directed. Stir in refrigerated, fully cooked, turkey mini meatballs that have been heated (or use thawed frozen meatballs). Serve with **green beans.** For something really fun, make **blue "cocoa."** Save the juice from canned blueberries. Mix the juice and 1-percent milk in a mug; warm in the microwave. Top with a few miniature marshmallows.

Saturday *Easy Entertaining*

Butterflied Leg of Lamb with Asian Seasonings (see recipe) is worthy of any guest. Serve with **jasmine rice, steamed carrots,** a **romaine salad,** and **sourdough bread.** Buy a **lemon meringue pie** for dessert.

FAMILY

Winner's Chili

Prep time: About 10 min • **Cook time:** 8 hr • **Yield:** About 10 cups

Ingredients

1 pound lean ground beef

1 medium onion, chopped

2 jalapeño peppers, seeded and finely chopped

1 15-ounce can chili beans

1 15-ounce can kidney beans

1 15-ounce can pinto beans

2 8-ounce cans no-salt-added tomato sauce

2 to 3 teaspoons chili powder

1 teaspoon cumin

¼ teaspoon salt

½ teaspoon pepper

¼ cup low-sodium beef broth

Directions

1 Combine all ingredients in a 4-quart or larger slow cooker.

2 Cook on low 8 hours and serve.

Per cup: _223 calories, 17g protein, 6g fat (31 percent calories from fat), 1.8g saturated fat, 25g carbohydrate, 26mg cholesterol, 429mg sodium, 8g fiber._

Mexican Chicken Soup

Prep time: 10 min • **Cook time:** About 10 min • **Yield:** 6 servings

BUDGET

Ingredients	_Directions_

2 14-ounce cans fat-free chicken broth

1 zucchini, diced

½ teaspoon minced garlic

½ teaspoon cumin

1 cup frozen corn

1 15-ounce can black beans, rinsed

2 cups shredded cooked chicken

½ cup salsa

½ cup chopped fresh cilantro

Crushed baked tortilla chips

Lime wedges

_1_ Combine broth, zucchini, garlic, and cumin in a large saucepan, and bring to a boil.

_2_ Stir in corn and beans. Simmer 2 minutes or until corn and zucchini are tender.

_3_ Stir in chicken, salsa, and cilantro. Heat through.

_4_ Top each serving with tortilla chips; serve lime wedges on the side.

**Per serving:** _186 calories, 21g protein, 3g fat (13 percent calories from fat), 0.6g saturated fat, 19g carbohydrate, 40mg cholesterol, 544mg sodium, 6g fiber._

EASY ENTERTAINING

Butterflied Leg of Lamb with Asian Seasonings

Prep time: 15 min • **Cook time:** 1–2¼ hr, plus standing time • **Yield:** 10–15 servings

Ingredients

2 teaspoons cinnamon

2 teaspoons ground ginger

2 teaspoons brown sugar

1 teaspoon anise seeds

½ teaspoon cayenne pepper

1 large clove minced garlic

2 tablespoons peanut oil

1 teaspoon sesame oil

1 3- to 4½-pound boneless leg of lamb, butterflied and trimmed of fat (see Note)

Directions

1 Heat oven to 325 degrees.

2 In a small bowl, combine cinnamon, ginger, sugar, anise, cayenne pepper, garlic, and oils; mix well. Rub mixture on all sides of lamb. Place on a rack in a roasting pan.

3 Bake 20 to 25 minutes per pound for medium-rare or until temperature reaches 145 degrees, or 25 to 30 minutes or 160 degrees for medium doneness.

4 Remove from oven; cover loosely with foil, and let stand 5 to 10 minutes. Slice and serve.

Per serving: 203 calories, 25g protein, 10g fat (46 percent calories from fat), 3g saturated fat, 2g carbohydrate, 78mg cholesterol, 60mg sodium, no fiber.

Note: *Ask the meat cutter to bone and butterfly the lamb for you.*

Week 5

 ## Sunday *Family*

Call the family for an extra-special meal of **Pork Chops with Sweet Mustard Sauce** (see recipe). Serve with **mashed potatoes**, fresh **broccoli florets**, a **mixed green salad**, and **whole-grain rolls**. Buy a **yellow layer cake** for dessert. *Plan ahead:* Save enough cake for Tuesday.

 ## Monday *Meatless*

Skip meat for a meal of **Italian vegetable stew.** In a Dutch oven, heat 1 tablespoon olive oil on medium. Add 4 medium zucchini, halved lengthwise and thinly sliced; 2 medium chopped eggplant; 1 large, thinly sliced onion; and ¼ teaspoon pepper. Cook 15 minutes or until vegetables are golden. Stir in 2 26-ounce jars red pasta sauce and ⅓ cup freshly grated parmesan cheese. Bring to a boil; reduce heat to low, and simmer, covered, 10 minutes. Serve over **couscous**. Add a **lettuce wedge** and **garlic bread**. For dessert, enjoy **pears**. *Plan ahead:* Save enough stew for Tuesday.

 ## Tuesday *Heat and Eat*

Take the night off and enjoy leftover **stew** served over **brown rice.** Add a **spinach salad** and **bread-sticks.** For dessert, slice some leftover **cake.**

 ## Wednesday *Kids*

Any way you prepare **Oven-Fried Chicken Tenders,** the kids always like them. Heat oven to 450 degrees. Coat chicken tenders with cooking spray; dredge in mashed potato flakes, and sprinkle with seasoned salt. Place on a baking sheet lined with nonstick foil, and bake 15 minutes, turning once. Serve with **hash-browned potatoes** (frozen), **baby carrots,** and **soft rolls.** For dessert, top fat-free **chocolate ice cream** with **marshmallow topping.** *Plan ahead:* Save enough ice cream for Saturday.

 ## Thursday *Express*

Make Valentine's Day special with **bacon-wrapped beef filet mignons** (refrigerated vacuum-packaged). Alongside, serve Bold American Catering's **gorgonzola macaroni and cheese.** Cook 8 ounces of any pasta according to directions. Meanwhile, heat 1 cup heavy cream on medium to a simmer; slowly add 4 ounces crumbled gorgonzola cheese to the cream, and stir until melted and smooth. Add pasta and salt and pepper to taste to the cream mixture, cooking and stirring over low heat until heated through. For some green, add a packaged **Caesar salad.** And to top it all off, **Dark Chocolate-Tangerine Truffles** (see recipe) will seal the deal. *Plan ahead:* You can make the truffles ahead and freeze them.

 ## Friday *Budget*

Tighten the purse strings with **ham steak with pineapple salsa** for dinner. For the salsa: Mix 1 cup drained pineapple tidbits with ½ cup salsa. Serve warm with the ham. Add **baked sweet potatoes**, a **spinach salad**, and **crusty rolls. Gingersnaps** are good for dessert.

 ## Saturday *Easy Entertaining*

Serve your guests grand-prize-winning **Maple-Glazed Chicken with Cranberry Arugula Rice** (see recipe) from a recent USA Rice cooking contest. Serve with **Brussels sprouts,** a **green salad,** and **baguettes.** For dessert, layer leftover chocolate ice cream with sliced bananas and toasted chopped walnuts for a **banana chocolate parfait.**

FAMILY

Pork Chops with Sweet Mustard Sauce

Prep time: About 15 min, plus marinating time • **Cook time:** About 10 min • **Yield:** 4 servings

Ingredients

¼ cup cider vinegar

¼ cup medium red onion, thinly sliced, plus ⅓ cup finely chopped

1 tablespoon olive oil

4 5-ounce, well-trimmed, boneless pork chops

½ teaspoon salt

¼ teaspoon pepper

⅓ cup low-fat sour cream

¼ cup Dijon mustard

2½ tablespoons peach or apricot jam

Directions

1 In a shallow dish, pour vinegar over sliced onions. Marinate 10 minutes or until ready to serve.

2 Meanwhile, heat oil in a large nonstick skillet on medium-high. Season pork with salt and pepper on both sides. Add to skillet and cook, turning once, 7 or 8 minutes or until browned and cooked through.

3 While pork cooks, mix sour cream, mustard, jam, and chopped onion until blended. Serve on pork and top with the pickled onions.

Per serving: 319 calories, 31g protein, 15g fat (43 percent calories from fat), 5.1g saturated fat, 14g carbohydrate, 94mg cholesterol, 672mg sodium, 1g fiber.

Adapted from Woman's Day *magazine.*

Dark Chocolate-Tangerine Truffles

EXPRESS

Prep time: 15 min, plus refrigeration time • **Cook time:** About 5 min • **Yield:** 24 truffles

Ingredients	*Directions*
⅓ cup dark chocolate chips or 3 ounces chopped dark chocolate	**1** Microwave chocolate in a medium bowl on high (100-percent power) 1 minute or until almost melted, stirring until smooth. Cool.
4 ounces neufchatal cheese, room temperature	**2** Add cheese, and beat with an electric mixer on medium until smooth. Add sugar and zest and beat until well-blended.
1⅓ cups powdered sugar, sifted	
Zest of one tangerine or half an orange	**3** Spread mixture into a small baking pan lined with plastic wrap; cover mixture with more wrap and refrigerate 1 to 24 hours.
1½ cups roasted sliced almonds, chopped	**4** Pull chocolate from pan by the plastic wrap corners. Cut into 24 pieces. Roll into balls, then roll each ball in chopped almonds.

Per truffle: *89 calories, 2g protein, 5g fat (49 percent calories from fat), 1.5g saturated fat, 10g carbohydrate, 3mg cholesterol, 22mg sodium, 1g fiber.*

Note: *The truffles freeze well if stored airtight in a single layer.*

EASY ENTERTAINING

Maple-Glazed Chicken with Cranberry Arugula Rice

Prep time: 15 min • **Cook time:** About 5 min, plus rice • **Yield:** 4 servings

Ingredients

2 tablespoons butter

¼ cup maple syrup

½ cup dried cranberries

2 cups grilled, sliced chicken breast (see Note)

½ teaspoon salt

½ teaspoon pepper

3 cups cooked brown rice

1 6-ounce package (5 to 6 cups) fresh baby arugula or spinach

½ cup gorgonzola cheese, crumbled

Directions

1 Melt butter in a large nonstick skillet on medium. Stir in syrup and cranberries; cook 1 minute. Add chicken, salt, and pepper. Cook 1 minute or until hot; remove chicken using slotted spoon and set aside.

2 Add rice and toss to coat; remove from heat.

3 Toss in arugula; spoon rice mixture onto platter. Top with chicken and cheese. Serve immediately.

Per serving: 491 calories, 30g protein, 14g fat (25 percent calories from fat), 7.6g saturated fat, 62g carbohydrate, 87mg cholesterol, 594mg sodium, 5g fiber.

Note: Packaged, refrigerated, grilled chicken strips may be used.

Week 6

 ## Sunday *Family*

Treat the family to the wonderful flavors of **Mexicali Round Steak** (see recipe). Serve it with **rice**, a sliced **grapefruit salad,** and **corn tortillas**. Make **flan** (from a mix) for dessert. *Plan ahead:* Save enough steak and rice for Monday.

 ## Monday *Heat and Eat*

Use the leftover steak and rice for **Steak Tortillas**. Slice the steak and heat with some of the sauce along with the rice. Combine, spoon onto fat-free flour tortillas, and roll. Top with **salsa**, low-fat **sour cream** and sliced **green onions**. Serve with a **chopped lettuce and tomato salad**. Enjoy **tropical fruits** for a light dessert.

 ## Tuesday *Budget*

Creamy Fettuccine is delicious on a cold winter's night. Cook 8 ounces fettuccine according to directions; drain. Meanwhile, mix together 1 tablespoon flour and ¼ teaspoon each salt, pepper, and nutmeg in a large saucepan. Whisk in 1 cup 1-percent milk and ¼ cup fat-free chicken broth until well-blended and smooth; cook 6 minutes over medium-high heat, stirring constantly until boiling and thickened. Stir in hot fettuccine, 1 cup tiny frozen peas (thawed), ¼ cup chopped cooked bacon, 1½ tablespoons freshly grated parmesan cheese and ¼ cup chopped basil. Heat through. Toss to mix, and serve. Add a **lettuce wedge** and **garlic bread**. For dessert, **kiwifruit** is all you need.

 ## Wednesday *Kids*

Kids can't eat enough **Sloppy Joes.** Use a mix and serve on hamburger buns. Add **baked chips** and **stuffed celery sticks** (fat-free cream cheese garnished with raisins). For dessert, how about **orange sections?**

 ## Thursday *Express*

Make **Black Bean Soup** for a quick meal. Add cumin to canned black bean soup while it's heating. Serve over quick-cooking **brown rice;** garnish with low-fat sour cream and chopped onion. Add a packaged **green salad** and **crackers**. Make instant **banana pudding** (from a mix) with 1-percent milk for dessert.

 ## Friday *Meatless*

Packed with flavor (and vitamin A), **Bow-Tie Pasta with Winter Squash and Walnuts** (see recipe) is a unique no-meat entree. Serve with a **spinach salad** and **whole-grain bread**. **Peaches** are an easy dessert.

 ## Saturday *Easy Entertaining*

Serve your guests **Baked Scallops** (see recipe) over **angel hair pasta** that's been tossed with freshly grated **parmesan cheese**. Serve with **snow peas, Bibb lettuce,** and **sourdough bread**. Buy **fruit tarts** for dessert.

FAMILY

Mexicali Round Steak

Prep time: 15 min • **Cook time:** 8–9 hr • **Yield:** 6 servings

Ingredients

1½ pounds boneless round or sirloin tip steak

1 cup frozen corn, thawed

1 cup chopped fresh cilantro

½ cup low-sodium beef broth

2 medium celery ribs, thinly sliced

1 large onion, sliced

2½ cups salsa

1 15-ounce can black beans, rinsed

1 cup shredded Monterey Jack cheese with jalapeño peppers

Directions

1 Remove fat from beef; divide beef into 6 portions. Place beef in a 4-quart or larger slow cooker.

2 In a large bowl, mix remaining ingredients (except cheese); pour over beef. Cover and cook on low 8 to 9 hours.

3 Spoon beef and sauce onto a warm platter; top with cheese.

Per serving: 351 calories, 35g protein, 10g fat (28 percent calories from fat), 5.3g saturated fat, 26g carbohydrate, 80mg cholesterol, 766mg sodium, 6g fiber.

MEATLESS

Bow-Tie Pasta with Winter Squash and Walnuts

Prep time: 15 min, plus standing time • **Cook time:** 7 min, plus pasta • **Yield:** 6 servings

Ingredients	*Directions*
1 pound winter squash (such as butternut, acorn, or kabocha), peeled, seeded, and cubed	*1* Microwave cubed squash with a little water on high (100-percent power) for 5 or 6 minutes or until almost tender; let stand covered 3 minutes. Drain and mash.
1 pound bow-tie pasta	
1 tablespoon extra-virgin olive oil	*2* Meanwhile, cook pasta according to directions; drain.
2 cloves minced garlic	
3 tablespoons minced fresh parsley	*3* Heat oil in a large nonstick skillet on medium. Add garlic and cook 30 seconds. Add mashed squash, the parsley, and salt and pepper to taste.
Salt and pepper to taste	
2 tablespoons walnuts, chopped	*4* Toss the drained pasta with squash mixture, and serve topped with walnuts and parmesan cheese.
¼ cup freshly grated parmesan cheese	

Per serving: 356 calories, 12g protein, 6g fat (15 percent calories from fat), 1.2g saturated fat, 63g carbohydrate, 3mg cholesterol, 59mg sodium, 3g fiber.

EASY ENTERTAINING

Baked Scallops

Prep time: About 10 min • **Cook time:** 10–15 min • **Yield:** 4 servings

Ingredients

1 pound sea scallops

⅔ cup Japanese (panko) bread crumbs

2 tablespoons melted butter

2 tablespoons fresh lemon juice

2 small cloves minced garlic

¼ teaspoon salt

¼ teaspoon freshly ground pepper

Directions

1 Heat oven to 425 degrees. Place scallops in a 2-quart baking dish coated with cooking spray.

2 In a small bowl, combine bread crumbs, butter, lemon juice, garlic, salt, and pepper. Sprinkle over scallops.

3 Bake 10 to 15 minutes or until scallops are opaque and topping is golden.

Per serving: 188 calories, 20g protein, 7g fat (32 percent calories from fat), 3.7g saturated fat, 11g carbohydrate, 53mg cholesterol, 384mg sodium, no fiber.

Adapted from Coastal Living _magazine._

Week 7

Sunday *Family*

Go all out for the family and prepare your own recipe for **roasted chicken** today. Serve the juicy bird with **Parsley Buttered Linguine** (toss hot, cooked linguine with chopped fresh parsley, butter, freshly grated parmesan, and cooked tiny green peas). Add a **spinach salad** and **dinner rolls.** For dessert, buy a **coconut pie.** *Plan ahead:* Save enough chicken for Monday. Save enough pie for Tuesday.

Monday *Budget*

A good way to save money is to prepare **Chicken Tetrazzini** (see recipe) for dinner. Serve it with **mixed greens** and **garlic bread.** For a simple dessert, try **plums.** *Plan ahead:* Save enough tetrazzini for Tuesday.

Tuesday *Heat and Eat*

Take a break from yesterday's cooking. All you have to do tonight is reheat Monday's **Chicken Tetrazzini** and serve it with a **romaine salad.** Add **whole-grain rolls.** Dessert is leftover **pie.**

Wednesday *Express*

Make it quick with **Reuben Wraps.** Spread burrito-size flour tortillas with low-fat Russian dressing. Top with deli coleslaw, sliced corn beef, and low-fat Swiss cheese. Roll tightly and cut in half crosswise. Serve with **pickled beets** and deli **German potato salad.** For dessert, enjoy **chunky applesauce.**

Thursday *Kids*

We know kids will like **Baja Chipotle Fish Tacos** (see recipe). Serve them with **oven fries** (frozen) and **green beans.** Instant **butterscotch pudding** made with 1-percent milk is a good dessert.

Friday *Meatless*

Egg salad sandwiches are delicious as well as being low-cost. Make your own "salad" and reduce the fat and cholesterol by using more cooked egg whites than yolks along with low-fat mayonnaise and salt and pepper to taste. I always add a little sweet pickle relish, too. Spread the salad on toasted, whole-grain English muffins, and top with lettuce and sliced tomatoes. Add canned **navy bean soup** for an easy soup-and-sandwich meal. Fat-free **strawberry ice cream** is good for dessert. *Plan ahead:* Save enough ice cream for Saturday.

Saturday *Easy Entertaining*

Prepare **Broiled Balsamic Filet Mignons** (see recipe) for your guests. Keep it simple and serve the filets with **baked potatoes** with low-fat **sour cream** and chopped **chives.** Add a packaged **Caesar salad.** For dessert, top **angel food cake** with leftover **ice cream** and **strawberries.**

BUDGET

Chicken Tetrazzini

Prep time: 25 min • **Cook time:** 20–25 min, plus pasta • **Yield:** 8 servings

Ingredients

8 ounces spaghetti

1 8-ounce package sliced fresh mushrooms

½ cup sliced green onions

1 tablespoon butter or margarine

¼ cup flour

⅛ teaspoon pepper

⅛ teaspoon nutmeg

1¼ cups fat-free chicken broth

1¼ cups half-and-half

2 cups chopped cooked chicken breast

2 tablespoons dry sherry, if desired

¼ cup freshly grated parmesan cheese, divided

¼ cup toasted, sliced almonds

Directions

1 Heat oven to 350 degrees. Cook spaghetti according to directions; drain.

2 Meanwhile, in a large saucepan, cook mushrooms and green onions in hot butter for 5 minutes or until tender. Stir in flour, pepper, and nutmeg. Add broth and half-and-half all at once. Cook and stir until thickened and bubbly.

3 Stir in chicken, sherry if desired, and half the parmesan cheese. Add cooked spaghetti; stir gently to coat.

4 Transfer mixture to a 9-x-13-inch baking dish coated with cooking spray. Sprinkle with remaining cheese and almonds.

5 Bake, uncovered, 15 to 20 minutes or until heated through.

Per serving: 281 calories, 19g protein, 10g fat (33 percent calories from fat), 4.7g saturated fat, 28g carbohydrate, 50mg cholesterol, 157mg sodium, 2g fiber.

Adapted from Better Homes and Gardens Cookbook, *12th Edition, Jennifer Darling, Editor (Meredith Books).*

Baja Chipotle Fish Tacos

KIDS

Prep time: 15 min, plus marinating time • **Cook time:** 15 min • **Yield:** 6 servings

Ingredients

½ cup plus 2 to 4 tablespoons Baja Chipotle Marinade with Lime Juice (such as Lawry's or another brand)

1½ pounds cod or other firm, white fish fillets

¼ cup low-fat mayonnaise

¼ cup low-fat sour cream

12 corn tortillas, warmed

2 cups shredded green cabbage

Directions

1 In a resealable plastic bag, combine ½ cup marinade and fish; turn to coat. Marinate in refrigerator for 30 minutes. Remove fish; discard marinade.

2 Broil fish 15 minutes. Meanwhile, in a small bowl, combine mayonnaise, sour cream, and remaining 2 to 4 tablespoons marinade.

3 To serve, arrange fish in 2 stacked tortillas (for each taco), top with cabbage and drizzle with sauce. Serve immediately.

Per serving: 196 calories, 20g protein, 4g fat (19 percent calories from fat), 1.4g saturated fat, 19g carbohydrate, 48mg cholesterol, 656mg sodium, 2g fiber.

Broiled Balsamic Filet Mignons

Prep time: 5 min • **Cook time:** About 15 min • **Yield:** 4 servings

Ingredients	Directions

Ingredients

2 tablespoons molasses

2 teaspoons balsamic vinegar

4 4-ounce beef tenderloin steaks, about 1 inch thick

¾ teaspoon salt

¾ teaspoon pepper

Directions

1 Heat broiler.

2 In a medium bowl, whisk together molasses and vinegar. Add steaks, turning to coat.

3 Place steaks on baking sheet coated with cooking spray. Sprinkle with salt and pepper.

4 Broil 6 minutes; turn. Broil an additional 5 minutes or until desired degree of doneness. Serve immediately.

Per serving: 196 calories, 24g protein, 7g fat (32 percent calories from fat), 2.5g saturated fat, 9g carbohydrate, 67mg cholesterol, 490mg sodium, no fiber.

Week 8

Sunday *Family*

Chili Cumin Pork Tenderloin makes a great family meal. Heat oven to 425 degrees. In a small bowl, mix 1 tablespoon chili powder, 1½ teaspoons each cumin, garlic powder, and dried oregano, 1 teaspoon reduced-sodium seasoned salt, ½ teaspoon coarse-grind pepper, and ¼ teaspoon cinnamon. Rub seasonings all over 2 1-pound pork tenderloins. Refrigerate 30 minutes to 4 hours. Place in a shallow pan, and bake 20 to 30 minutes or until internal temperature is 150 degrees. Remove from oven; let stand 5 minutes. Slice and serve. Add packaged **long-grain and wild rice,** steamed **carrots, mixed greens,** and **crusty bread.** Buy a **blueberry pie** for dessert. *Plan ahead:* Save enough pork, rice, and pie for Monday.

Monday *Heat and Eat*

Pork Wraps are easy to prepare. Spread vegetarian refried beans on warm, fat-free flour tortillas. Top with heated chopped pork, shredded lettuce, guacamole, and low-fat sour cream. Roll and enjoy. Add leftover **rice** on the side. Slice the leftover **pie** for dessert.

Tuesday *Budget*

You can turn lower-cost steaks into delicious **Parmesan-Crusted Cubed Steaks** (see recipe) with just a few ingredients. Serve the budget-friendly beef with **mashed potatoes** and steamed, sliced **zucchini.** Add a **lettuce wedge** and **whole-grain rolls.** Fresh **pineapple** is a simple dessert to finish a fine meal.

Wednesday *Express*

Try **Buffalo Drumsticks** for a quick meal. Heat oven to 350 degrees. Stir 2 teaspoons hot pepper sauce into 2 tablespoons melted butter. Brush on skinless drumsticks, and bake 30 minutes or until cooked through. Serve with **corn on the cob** and **carrot and cucumber sticks** with **blue cheese dressing** for dipping. Make **cornbread muffins** from a mix. **Pears** are your dessert. *Plan ahead:* Save enough carrot sticks for Thursday.

Thursday *Kids*

Buy frozen **burritos** for a meal kids will love. Serve with canned **pinto beans** and leftover **carrot sticks.** Bring out fat-free **vanilla ice cream** with **chocolate sprinkles** for dessert.

Friday *Meatless*

Lentil Chili Soup (see recipe) is perfect for a no-meat dinner. Serve it with a **spinach salad** and **hard-cooked egg wedges.** Add **whole-grain rolls.** Buy a **carrot cake** for dessert. *Plan ahead:* Save enough cake for Saturday.

Saturday *Easy Entertaining*

Put **Tarragon Chicken** (see recipe) on your favorites list and invite guests to enjoy it, too. Serve it over **rice.** Add a **Boston lettuce salad** and **baguettes.** Serve the leftover **cake** for dessert.

BUDGET

Parmesan-Crusted Cubed Steaks

Prep time: 5 min • **Cook time:** 10–12 min • **Yield:** 4 servings

Ingredients	*Directions*
⅓ **cup water**	*1* Pour water into shallow dish. Combine bread crumbs and cheese in a second shallow dish. Dip each steak in water and then crumb mixture, turning to coat both sides.
⅔ **cup seasoned dry bread crumbs**	
⅓ **cup freshly grated parmesan cheese**	*2* In a large nonstick skillet, heat 1 tablespoon oil on medium-high until hot. Cook 2 steaks 5 to 6 minutes until no longer pink in the center, turning once. Remove steaks; keep warm.
4 **4-ounce beef cubed steaks**	
2 **tablespoons canola oil, divided**	*3* Repeat with remaining oil, reducing heat to medium to avoid overbrowning.
	4 Serve immediately.

Per serving: 308 calories, 31g protein, 14g fat (40 percent calories from fat), 3.1g saturated fat, 14g carbohydrate, 70mg cholesterol, 486mg sodium, 1g fiber.

Lentil Chili Soup

Prep time: 15 min • **Cook time:** 40–45 min • **Yield:** 11 cups

MEATLESS

Ingredients	*Directions*
1½ teaspoons canola oil	**1** Heat oil in a large Dutch oven on medium-high. Add garlic and onion; cook 2 to 3 minutes or until golden.
1 tablespoon minced garlic	
2 cups chopped onion	
1 16-ounce package frozen crinkle-cut carrots	**2** Add remaining ingredients; mix well. Bring to boil, and then lower heat to low and simmer, uncovered, 35 to 40 minutes or until the lentils are tender.
12 ounces lentils (1½ cups), rinsed and picked over	
4 cups low-sodium or regular mixed-vegetable juice (such as V-8)	**3** Season with salt, pepper, and hot sauce.
1 14-ounce can vegetable broth	
3 cups water	
½ to 1 teaspoon chili powder	
½ teaspoon cumin	
1 teaspoon dried oregano	
Salt and pepper to taste	
Hot pepper sauce as desired	

Per cup: 155 calories, 9g protein, 1g fat (5 percent calories from fat), no saturated fat, 29g carbohydrate, no cholesterol, 255mg sodium, 6g fiber.

EASY ENTERTAINING

Tarragon Chicken

Prep time: 15 min • **Cook time:** 7 hr, 25 min • **Yield:** 6 servings

Ingredients

6 well-trimmed, bone-in, skinless chicken thighs

2 well-trimmed, bone-in, skinless chicken legs

1 medium onion, thinly sliced

4 cloves garlic, thinly sliced

2 plum tomatoes, seeded and diced

⅓ cup tarragon vinegar

2 teaspoons dried tarragon

1 tablespoon Dijon mustard

½ teaspoon salt

½ teaspoon pepper

½ cup half-and-half

2 tablespoons flour

Directions

1 Place chicken in a 4-quart or larger slow cooker. Add onion, garlic, tomatoes, vinegar, tarragon, mustard, salt, and pepper. Cover and cook on low for 7 hours or until chicken is cooked through and onions are softened.

2 Whisk half-and-half and flour in a small bowl until smooth. Stir in some hot liquid from cooker; then stir the mixture into cooker.

3 Cover and cook on high 25 minutes or until liquid thickens.

Per serving: 225 calories, 24g protein, 11g fat (44 percent calories from fat), 3.7g saturated fat, 7g carbohydrate, 87mg cholesterol, 330mg sodium, 1g fiber.

Adapted from Woman's Day *magazine.*

Week 9

Sunday · *Family*

For today's family feast, prepare **Lemon-Garlic Marinated Lamb Chops** (see recipe). For an unusual side, serve **grilled romaine.** Heat grill or grill pan on medium-high. Cut romaine hearts in half lengthwise, leaving ends intact to hold them together. Cut off any bruised tips. Brush romaine with olive oil, and grill about 6 minutes or until charred and slightly wilted, turning a few times. Season with salt and pepper; serve immediately. (Adapted from *The Food You Crave* by Ellie Krieger [Taunton Press].) Add steamed, fresh **baby carrots** and **sourdough bread.** End the meal with a **berry cobbler.** *Plan ahead:* Save enough lamb for Monday and enough cobbler for Tuesday.

Monday · *Heat and Eat*

Warm the leftover **lamb chops** and serve with **couscous** cooked with golden raisins (add raisins to boiling water before adding couscous). Add fresh **broccoli spears** seasoned with a little butter to brighten the plate. Alongside, add a **spinach salad** and **flatbread. Tropical fruit** is good for dessert.

Tuesday · *Express*

With a few store-bought ingredients, you can have **Grilled Chicken Salad** in no time. Heat packaged grilled chicken strips in a skillet with a little butter, and sprinkle with McCormick's Grill Mates Montreal Chicken Seasoning. Serve the chicken with a packaged **green salad** and **garlic toast.** Warm the leftover **cobbler** and top it with fat-free **vanilla ice cream** for dessert. *Plan ahead:* Save enough ice cream for Thursday and Saturday.

Wednesday · *Kids*

The kids won't mind having chicken two nights in a row if the second meal is **Baked Chicken Fingers.** Heat oven to 450 degrees. Dip chicken tenders in beaten egg and then crushed potato chips. Bake on a nonstick, foil-lined pan for 10 minutes or until cooked through. Serve with **tater tots,** frozen **peas and carrots,** and **soft rolls.** How about **peaches** for dessert?

Thursday · *Budget*

Egg and Bacon Quesadillas are a delicious way to save a little money. Heat oven to 425 degrees. Coat a baking sheet with cooking spray. Place 4 fat-free flour tortillas on it. Sprinkle them with some shredded pepperjack cheese. Drain an 11-ounce can of Mexican-style canned corn and divide among tortillas. Cook and crumble 4 slices bacon to sprinkle on top of the corn, along with 4 sliced, hard-cooked eggs, sliced green onions, and some more cheese. Top with another tortilla. Lightly coat tortillas with cooking spray. Bake 6 minutes; press down, then turn and bake 6 more minutes or until lightly browned and crisp. Cut into wedges and serve with salsa. Add **multigrain chips** and **deli coleslaw.** Leftover **ice cream** is for dessert.

Friday · *Meatless*

"Good flavor and simple" are part of my recipe-testing notes for no-meat **Mushroom and Brown Rice Soup** (see recipe). Serve the soup with **mixed greens** and **cheese toast** (shredded cheese on toasted whole-grain English muffins). Enjoy **red and green grapes** for dessert.

Saturday · *Easy Entertaining*

Cajun seasoning livens up this **Buttery Cajun Shrimp** (see recipe). Serve the shrimp with **rice, sugar snap peas,** a **Bibb lettuce salad,** and **whole-grain rolls.** For dessert, top the leftover **ice cream** with **strawberries.**

FAMILY

Lemon-Garlic Marinated Lamb Chops

Prep time: 15 min, plus marinating time   •   **Cook time:** About 10 min   •   **Yield:** 8 servings

Ingredients

2 tablespoons olive oil

2 tablespoons fresh lemon juice

1 teaspoon lemon zest

1 tablespoon plus 1 teaspoon dried oregano

3 tablespoons minced garlic

¾ teaspoon salt

½ teaspoon freshly ground black pepper

16 4-ounce lamb loin chops, trimmed of all visible fat

Directions

1   In a small bowl, stir together the oil, lemon juice and zest, oregano, garlic, salt, and pepper.

2   Put chops in a resealable plastic bag; add marinade, and turn to coat. Seal and marinate for 20 minutes to 1 hour at room temperature, turning occasionally.

3   Heat broiler, grill, or grill pan over medium heat. Remove chops and discard marinade.

4   Grill or broil 4 to 5 minutes per side for medium-rare or to desired doneness.

Per serving: 215 calories, 29g protein, 10g fat (44 percent calories from fat), 3.4g saturated fat, no carbohydrate, 91mg cholesterol, 226mg sodium, no fiber.

Adapted from The Food You Crave, *Ellie Krieger, RD (Taunton Press).*

Mushroom and Brown Rice Soup

Prep time: 10 min • **Cook time:** About 20 min • **Yield:** 9 cups

MEATLESS

Ingredients	Directions
1 tablespoon olive oil	**1** Heat oil in a 4-quart or larger pan on medium-high heat. Add onion; cook 5 minutes, stirring occasionally.
1 medium onion, finely chopped	
1 8-ounce package sliced white mushrooms	**2** Add mushrooms and carrots, and cook 8 to 10 minutes or until golden and tender; stir occasionally.
1 4-ounce package assorted sliced wild or crimini mushrooms	
1 cup shredded carrots	**3** Add garlic, salt, thyme, and pepper; cook 1 minute, stirring.
1 clove pressed garlic	
¼ teaspoon salt	**4** Add broth, rice, and water; cover and heat to boiling on medium-high. Reduce heat to medium; cook, partially covered, 5 minutes or until rice is tender.
¼ teaspoon dried thyme	
⅛ teaspoon ground pepper	
4 cups vegetable broth	
¾ cup quick-cooking brown rice	
2 cups water	

Per cup: 64 calories, 2g protein, 2g fat (24 percent calories from fat), 0.2g saturated fat, 11g carbohydrate, 0mg cholesterol, 496mg sodium, 1g fiber.

EASY ENTERTAINING

Buttery Cajun Shrimp

Prep time: 10 min • **Cook time:** 10–12 min • **Yield:** 4 servings

Ingredients

2 tablespoons fresh lemon juice

1 teaspoon Cajun seasoning

1 tablespoon minced fresh parsley

⅛ teaspoon cayenne pepper

1 pound medium, peeled and deveined shrimp

2 tablespoons butter, cut into small pieces

Directions

1 Heat oven to 425 degrees. Combine lemon juice, Cajun seasoning, parsley, and cayenne pepper in a medium bowl; mix well. Add shrimp and toss to coat.

2 Arrange shrimp in a single layer in a 9-x-13-inch baking dish coated with cooking spray. Dot with butter.

3 Bake 10 to 12 minutes or just until the shrimp turn pink.

Per serving: 140 calories, 18g protein, 7g fat (44 percent calories from fat), 3.8g saturated fat, 1g carbohydrate, 183mg cholesterol, 353mg sodium, no fiber.

Week 10

Sunday   *Family*

Celebrate St. Patrick's Day with **Home-Style Corned Beef and Dilled Cabbage** (see recipe). Serve the traditional dish with deli **German potato salad, pickled beets,** and **rye bread.** For dessert, buy an **apple pie.** *Plan ahead:* Save enough corned beef, potato salad, beets, and bread for Monday; save enough pie for Tuesday.

Monday   *Heat and Eat*

Really celebrate "the green" with **corned beef sandwiches on rye.** Slather the bread with spicy hot mustard and add some horseradish; pile on the leftover corned beef. Don't forget the leftover **potato salad** and **pickled beets** as accompaniments. For a green dessert, try **lime sherbet.**

Tuesday   *Meatless*

Serve this slow-cooker version of **Vegetable Chili** (see recipe) with a **lettuce wedge** and **whole-grain rolls.** Slice the leftover **pie** for dessert.

Wednesday   *Express*

Make it fast tonight with **tortellini** for dinner. Cook a 16-ounce package of frozen cheese tortellini according to directions. Meanwhile, heat your favorite red pasta sauce. Drain tortellini, toss with some of the sauce and ½ cup drained black olives. Spoon into serving bowls; garnish with freshly grated parmesan cheese. Pass the remaining sauce at the table. Serve with a packaged **romaine salad** and **garlic bread.** Dessert is fresh **pineapple.**

Thursday   *Kids*

No kid could resist a dish called **Porcupine Meatballs.** Heat oven to 350 degrees. In a large bowl, lightly beat one egg. Add a heaping tablespoon from 1 10¾-ounce can condensed tomato soup and mix lightly. Mix in ¼ cup each quick-cooking rice and chopped onion, 1 tablespoon chopped fresh parsley, ½ teaspoon onion salt, and a little black pepper. Lightly mix in 1 pound 95-percent-lean ground beef. From the mixture, make 1½-inch meatballs. Place in a baking dish; bake 20 to 25 minutes. Combine remaining soup plus another can of tomato soup with 2 (or more) tablespoons Worcestershire sauce; mix until smooth and heat in the microwave. Spoon over meatballs. Serve the meatballs and sauce over **spaghetti.** Add **chopped lettuce** and **breadsticks.** Slice **kiwifruit** for dessert.

Friday   *Budget*

Crab Bisque sounds expensive, but this version isn't. In a large pan, mix together 2 14¾-ounce cans creamed corn; 2 cups fat-free half-and-half, 2 cups frozen O'Brien potatoes (thawed), ¾ teaspoon dried thyme, ¼ teaspoon salt, and ½ teaspoon pepper. Simmer, uncovered, on medium for 10 to 12 minutes. Stir in ½ pound coarsely chopped imitation crab meat (surimi); simmer 2 minutes or until soup is heated throughout. (Adapted from *Woman's Day* magazine.) Serve with a **spinach salad** and **crackers. Orange and grapefruit sections** make a good dessert.

Saturday   *Easy Entertaining*

Impress your guests with **Tuscan Roasted Chicken and Vegetables** (see recipe). Serve the combo with a **romaine salad** and **crusty rolls.** For dessert, buy a **cheesecake.**

FAMILY

Home-Style Corned Beef and Dilled Cabbage

Prep time: 25 min • **Cook time:** 2½–3½ hr • **Yield:** About 10 servings

Ingredients

For the corned beef:

2½ to 3½ pounds boneless, corned beef brisket

2 cups water

¼ cup honey

1 tablespoon Dijon mustard

For the cabbage:

1 2-pound head cabbage, cut into 8 wedges

3 tablespoons butter, softened

1 tablespoon Dijon mustard

1½ teaspoons chopped fresh dill

Directions

1 Heat oven to 350 degrees. Place brisket and water in Dutch oven. Bring just to simmer; do not boil. Cover, place in oven, and cook 2½ to 3½ hours or until fork-tender.

2 About 10 minutes before brisket is done, cover and microwave cabbage 10 minutes on high (100-percent power) or until tender; let stand 3 minutes.

3 Remove brisket from water; trim fat. Place on rack in broiler pan so surface of beef is 4 inches from heat. Combine honey and 1 tablespoon mustard, and brush top of brisket; broil 3 minutes. Brush with remaining glaze; broil 2 more minutes.

4 Combine butter, 1 tablespoon mustard, and dill; spread on hot cabbage.

5 Carve brisket diagonally across grain. Serve with cabbage.

Per serving (brisket): 255 calories, 17g protein, 17g fat (62 percent calories from fat), 5.8g saturated fat, 8g carbohydrate, 89mg cholesterol, 1,061mg sodium, no fiber.

Per serving (cabbage): 55 calories, 1g protein, 4g fat (55 percent calories from fat), 2.2g saturated fat, 6g carbohydrate, 9mg cholesterol, 71mg sodium, 2g fiber.

MEATLESS

Vegetable Chili

Prep time: 15 min • **Cook time:** 8 hr • **Yield:** 12 cups

Ingredients	*Directions*
½ cup shredded or sliced carrots	*1* Combine all ingredients in a 4-quart or larger slow cooker.
1 rib celery, sliced	
1 small sweet onion, chopped	*2* Cover and cook on low 8 hours.
1 8-ounce package sliced fresh crimini mushrooms	
1 medium zucchini, diced into ¾-inch cubes	
1 medium yellow squash, diced into ¾-inch cubes	
1½ teaspoons chili powder	
½ teaspoon dried basil	
1 teaspoon pepper	
½ cup vegetable broth	
1½ cups tomato juice	
1 14½-ounce can no-salt-added diced tomatoes	
2 15-ounce cans canned pinto, black, white, or kidney beans, rinsed	
½ cup frozen corn	

Per cup: 98 calories, 6g protein, 1g fat (7 percent calories from fat), no saturated fat, 18g carbohydrate, no cholesterol, 296mg sodium, 6g fiber.

EASY ENTERTAINING

Tuscan Roasted Chicken and Vegetables

Prep time: 15 min • **Cook time:** About 1 hr • **Yield:** 4 servings

Ingredients

3 medium zucchini (about 1½ pounds)

1 bulb fennel

6 plum tomatoes, cut into quarters and seeded

3 tablespoons olive oil, divided

¾ teaspoon salt, divided

4 bone-in, skinless chicken breasts (about 2½ pounds)

4 teaspoons minced garlic

1 teaspoon lemon zest

1 tablespoon fresh lemon juice

Freshly ground black pepper

1 tablespoon chopped fresh rosemary

Directions

1 Heat oven to 375 degrees. Halve zucchini crosswise, then lengthwise. Cut each quarter into even wedges.

2 Remove outermost layer of fennel bulb; discard. Cut bulb in half to retain part of stem end. Cut each half into 8 thin wedges so each wedge is held together by a small piece of stem.

3 Place zucchini, fennel, and tomatoes in a roasting pan. Toss with 2 tablespoons of the oil and ¼ teaspoon salt. Arrange chicken beside vegetables.

4 In a small bowl, combine remaining oil and salt, the garlic, and lemon zest and juice. Rub mixture into chicken. Season with pepper.

5 Roast 30 minutes; remove from oven. Sprinkle vegetables with rosemary and stir.

6 Increase oven temperature to 425 degrees. Return pan to oven and roast 20 to 30 more minutes or until chicken registers 170 degrees and vegetables are tender and beginning to brown.

Per serving: 284 calories, 31g protein, 12g fat (38 percent calories from fat), 1.9g saturated fat, 14g carbohydrate, 68mg cholesterol, 563mg sodium, 5g fiber.

Adapted from The Food You Crave *by Ellie Krieger (Taunton Press).*

Week 11

 Sunday *Family*

Celebrate Easter with the family and enjoy a **Baked Ham with Honey Apricot Glaze** (see recipe). Serve with **baked sweet potatoes,** fresh **asparagus,** and **dinner rolls.** For dessert, buy an **Easter bunny cake.** *Plan ahead:* Save enough ham for Monday and Wednesday; save enough cake for Monday.

 Monday *Heat and Eat*

Ham Pasta Salad makes good use of leftovers. Cook 8 ounces spiral pasta according to directions; drain and return to pot. Stir in 2 cups diced leftover ham; ⅓ cup low-fat Italian dressing; 1 14-ounce can drained, water-packed, quartered artichokes; and 1 7½-ounce jar drained, roasted red peppers, coarsely chopped. Toss to mix. Serve with a **lettuce wedge** and **breadsticks.** Slice the leftover **cake** for dessert.

 Tuesday *Budget*

Tasty and easy on the budget, **Broccoli Chicken Parmesan** is an excellent choice for dinner. Heat 1 tablespoon vegetable oil in a nonstick skillet on medium. Add 1 pound sliced, ¼-inch-thick red potatoes. Cover and cook 10 minutes; stir occasionally. Stir in 1 10- to 12-ounce can drained chicken breast (or 2 cups chopped cooked chicken) and 2 cups fresh broccoli florets. In a small bowl, mix together 1 10¾-ounce can 98-percent-fat-free broccoli cheese soup, ½ cup 1-percent milk, and ¼ teaspoon garlic powder; add to skillet. Sprinkle with ¼ cup freshly grated parmesan cheese. Heat to boil. Cover and cook on low for 5 minutes or until heated through. Serve with **mixed greens** and **crusty bread. Plums** are dessert.

 Wednesday *Kids*

Kids like **Ham and Swiss Potato Bake.** Heat oven to 400 degrees. Mix together 1 4.6-ounce package dehydrated julienne potatoes and sauce mix and 2½ cups boiling water in a 2-quart baking dish. Stir in ⅔ cup 1-percent milk, 1½ cups diced ham, and ⅔ cup shredded, low-fat Swiss cheese. Bake, uncovered, 50 minutes; sprinkle with ¼ cup plain dry bread crumbs. Bake 10 to 14 minutes more or until golden. Add **carrot sticks** and **cornbread muffins** (from a mix). Serve fresh **fruit** for dessert. *Plan ahead:* Cook brown rice for Thursday.

 Thursday *Meatless*

Try this **Rice-Nut Loaf** (see recipe) for a slice of flavor. Serve with **spaghetti, peas and carrots** (frozen), and **sourdough bread.** Fresh **pineapple** is dessert.

 Friday *Express*

Take it easy tonight and serve a frozen **vegetable lasagna.** Add a packaged **Italian salad** and **garlic bread.** Buy **tapioca pudding** for dessert.

 Saturday *Easy Entertaining*

Your guests will enjoy **Mediterranean Cod** (see recipe). Serve with **roasted red potatoes,** a **romaine salad,** and **baguettes.** Serve **Cappuccino Ice Cream Pie** for dessert. In a mixing bowl, combine 1.4-ounce sugar-free, instant chocolate pudding mix; 1 to 2 teaspoons instant coffee granules; 1 cup 2-percent milk; and 1 cup fat-free vanilla ice cream. Beat 2 minutes. Stir in 2 cups thawed whipped topping and pour into a low-fat graham cracker crust. Chill 30 minutes or until firm. Slice and serve with additional topping.

FAMILY

Baked Ham with Honey Apricot Glaze

Prep time: 10 min • **Cook time:** 1¾–2¼ hr, plus standing time • **Yield:** 4 servings per pound

Ingredients

1 5- to 7-pound spiral-sliced, fully cooked smoked ham

½ cup honey

3 ounces orange juice concentrate, thawed

3 tablespoons reduced-sodium soy sauce

3 tablespoons apricot jam

¼ teaspoon nutmeg

⅛ teaspoon ground cloves

Directions

1 Heat oven to 325 degrees. Place ham on rack in shallow roasting pan. In a medium bowl, mix together remaining ingredients; set aside.

2 Bake ham 30 minutes; pour glaze over ham and continue to bake 1 hour 15 minutes to 1 hour 45 minutes (15 to 18 minutes per pound) or until internal temperature reaches 140 degrees.

3 Remove from oven; let stand 5 minutes, and serve.

Per serving: 165 calories, 22g protein, 4g fat (20 percent calories from fat), 1.2g saturated fat, 11g carbohydrate, 65mg cholesterol, 1,107mg sodium, no fiber.

Rice-Nut Loaf

Prep time: 20 min • **Cook time:** 50–60 min, plus rice, plus standing time • **Yield:** 8 servings

MEATLESS

Ingredients

3 cups cooked brown rice

2 cups shredded 50-percent-reduced-fat cheddar cheese

4 lightly beaten eggs, or
2 whole eggs and 4 egg whites

1 medium onion, chopped

1 cup shredded carrots

½ cup Italian-style bread crumbs

¼ cup chopped walnuts

¼ cup chopped sunflower kernels

¼ cup sesame seeds

½ teaspoon salt

¼ teaspoon freshly ground black pepper

2 cups red pasta sauce

Directions

1 Heat oven to 350 degrees. Combine rice, cheese, eggs, onion, carrots, bread crumbs, walnuts, sunflower kernels, sesame seeds, salt, and pepper; pack into a 9-inch loaf pan coated with cooking spray.

2 Bake 50 to 60 minutes or until firm. Let cool in pan 10 minutes. Meanwhile, heat pasta sauce.

3 Unmold loaf; slice and serve with pasta sauce.

Per serving: 330 calories, 18g protein, 15g fat (40 percent calories from fat), 4.8g saturated fat, 33g carbohydrate, 121mg cholesterol, 705mg sodium, 4g fiber.

EASY ENTERTAINING

Mediterranean Cod

Prep time: 10 min • **Cook time:** About 5 min • **Yield:** 4 servings

Ingredients

4 4- to 6-ounce cod fillets, ½ inch thick

Salt and pepper to taste

2 tablespoons olive oil, divided

4 plum tomatoes, diced

¼ cup sliced kalamata olives

Pinch crushed, dried thyme

1 teaspoon dried basil

Directions

1 Sprinkle cod with salt and pepper to taste. Heat 1 tablespoon oil in a large nonstick skillet over medium-high until hot. Add cod and cook 30 seconds, turning once.

2 Sprinkle cod with tomatoes, olives, and thyme. Reduce heat; cover and cook 2 minutes.

3 Add basil and remaining oil. Cook, covered, 1 to 2 minutes or until cod is opaque throughout.

Per serving: 187 calories, 21g protein, 10g fat (47 percent calories from fat), 1.3g saturated fat, 4g carbohydrate, 49mg cholesterol, 183mg sodium, 1g fiber.

Week 12

 Sunday *Family*

Treat the family to your own special recipe for **leg of lamb.** Accompany it with flavor-packed **Potatoes Florentine:** In a medium saucepan, cook 4 teaspoons pine nuts and 2 cloves minced garlic in 2 teaspoons olive oil for 1 minute or until nuts are golden. Add 2 cups fresh spinach leaves; cook 30 seconds or until wilted. Split and fluff 4 hot baked potatoes, and season the inside of each with salt and pepper. Spoon spinach mixture into potatoes. Add a **mixed green salad** and **sourdough bread.** Buy a **blueberry pie** for dessert. *Plan ahead:* Save enough lamb and pie for Monday.

 Monday *Heat and Eat*

Chop some of the leftover lamb, mix with some couscous, moisten with plain yogurt, and make **stuffed pitas** using whole-grain pita bread lined with a lettuce leaf. Serve with **baked vegetable chips.** Munch on **baby carrots** and **sliced cucumbers** on the side. The leftover **pie** is dessert.

 Tuesday *Budget*

Meaty Mushroom Chili (see recipe) is another great economical chili recipe. Serve it with a **lettuce wedge** and baked **tortilla chips. Peaches** are a simple dessert.

 Wednesday *Express*

How about **Egg, Beef, and Pepper Sandwiches** for a quick meal? Heat a large nonstick skillet on medium-high. Add 1 16-ounce package frozen pepper strips with onions, and cook 4 minutes or until vegetables are thawed and hot. Add 3 ounces deli roast beef (cut into strips). Drizzle cut sides of four warmed sandwich rolls with low-fat Italian dressing. Arrange one sliced, hard-cooked egg on one side of each roll. Top with pepper mixture, lettuce leaves, and the other half of the roll. Serve with frozen **oven fries.** Buy **brownies** for dessert. *Plan ahead:* Save enough brownies for Friday.

 Thursday *Kids*

Keep the kids happy with **Taco Pie** (see recipe). Add **carrot sticks** on the side. Make **butterscotch pudding** (from a mix) with 1-percent milk for dessert.

 Friday *Meatless*

Keep it simple with **Sweet Onion Vegetable Soup.** In a Dutch oven, combine 2 medium chopped sweet onions, 3 diced carrots, 3 ribs sliced celery, 2 cloves minced garlic, 1 tablespoon finely chopped fresh rosemary, and 2 tablespoons extra-virgin olive oil. Cook on medium 6 to 8 minutes to soften vegetables. Add 6 cups vegetable broth, 1 14½-ounce can fire-roasted diced tomatoes, 3 cups shredded cabbage, and 2 15-ounce cans rinsed cannellini beans. Bring to a boil; reduce heat, and simmer, partially covered, 30 minutes or until cabbage is tender and soup is slightly thickened. Alongside, add **egg salad sandwiches** with **sliced tomatoes** and **lettuce** on **whole-grain toast.** Serve leftover **brownies** for dessert.

 Saturday *Easy Entertaining*

Quinoa Pilaf with Salmon and Asparagus (see recipe) is a delicious and fitting meal for guests. Serve the combo dinner with a **red-tipped lettuce salad** and **baguettes.** Top **angel food cake** with **lemon curd** (store-bought) for a special dessert. *Tip:* Look for quinoa with the rice and other grains.

BUDGET

Meaty Mushroom Chili

Prep time: 10 min • **Cook time:** About 30 min • **Yield:** About 8 cups

Ingredients

½ pound 95-percent-lean ground beef

1 medium onion, chopped

1 tablespoon chili powder

1 teaspoon cumin

1 pound sliced fresh white mushrooms

1 14½-ounce can diced tomatoes with jalapeño peppers

1 8-ounce can no-salt-added tomato sauce

1 15-ounce can chili beans

1 15-ounce can red beans, rinsed

2 teaspoons minced garlic

⅛ teaspoon salt

Shredded 50-percent-reduced-fat sharp cheddar cheese

Sliced green onions

Directions

1 In a Dutch oven, cook beef and onion on medium-high 6 minutes or until beef is no longer pink and onion is softened; drain.

2 Add chili powder and cumin; cook 30 seconds. Add mushrooms, tomatoes, tomato sauce, both beans, garlic, and salt. Reduce heat to low and simmer, uncovered, stirring occasionally, 15 minutes or until vegetables are done.

3 Ladle into bowls; garnish with cheese and onions.

Per cup: 181 calories, 15g protein, 3g fat (14 percent calories from fat), 0.8g saturated fat, 25g carbohydrate, 16mg cholesterol, 583mg sodium, 8g fiber.

Taco Pie

Prep time: 10 min • **Cook time:** About 45 min, plus cooling time • **Yield:** 6 servings

KIDS

Ingredients

1 pound 95-percent-lean ground beef

½ medium onion, finely chopped

1 1.25-ounce envelope 30-percent-less-sodium taco seasoning mix

1 4-ounce can chopped green chilies, drained

1 cup 1-percent milk

2 eggs

½ cup low-fat all-purpose baking mix (such as Bisquick)

¾ cup shredded Monterey Jack cheese

Salsa

Low-fat sour cream

Shredded lettuce

Chopped tomatoes

Directions

1 Heat oven to 400 degrees. Coat a 9-inch pie plate with cooking spray. Cook ground beef and onion in a large, nonstick skillet on medium, stirring occasionally, 6 minutes or until beef is no longer pink and onion is tender; drain.

2 Stir in seasoning mix. Spoon mixture into pie plate; top with chilies.

3 In a medium bowl, mix together milk, eggs, and baking mix. Pour into pie plate.

4 Bake 25 minutes or until knife inserted into center comes out clean. Sprinkle with cheese. Bake 8 to 10 minutes longer. Cool 5 minutes. Serve with salsa, sour cream, lettuce, and tomatoes.

Per serving: 256 calories, 24g protein, 11g fat (38 percent calories from fat), 4.9g saturated fat, 14g carbohydrate, 127mg cholesterol, 678mg sodium, 1g fiber.

EASY ENTERTAINING

Quinoa Pilaf with Salmon and Asparagus

Prep time: 25 min • **Cook time:** About 20 min, plus quinoa • **Yield:** 4 servings

Ingredients

1 cup uncooked quinoa

2 14-ounce cans fat-free chicken broth plus ½ cup, divided

2½ cups water, divided

1 pound salmon fillets

2 tablespoons butter or margarine

1 pound fresh asparagus, cut diagonally into 2-inch pieces

4 medium green onions, sliced

1 cup frozen tiny green peas, thawed

½ cup halved grape tomatoes

1 teaspoon no-salt lemon pepper seasoning

2 teaspoons chopped fresh dill or ½ teaspoon dried

Directions

1 Rinse quinoa thoroughly in a fine-mesh strainer, holding under cold water until water is clear; drain well.

2 In a 2-quart saucepan, heat 1 can broth and ¼ cup water to boiling on medium-high heat. Add quinoa; reduce heat to low. Cover; simmer 10 to 12 minutes or until liquid is absorbed.

3 Meanwhile, in a large skillet, heat the remaining 2¼ cups water and the second can of fat-free chicken broth to boiling on high.

4 Add salmon, skin side up; reduce heat to low. Cover; simmer 10 to 12 minutes or until fish flakes easily with fork.

5 Remove salmon with slotted spoon to plate; let cool. Discard cooking liquid and skin from salmon; break salmon into large pieces. Rinse and dry the skillet.

6 Melt butter in skillet on medium heat. Add asparagus; cook 5 minutes, stirring frequently. Stir in onions; cook 1 minute, stirring frequently. Stir in peas, tomatoes, and the ½ cup broth; cook 1 minute.

7 Gently stir quinoa, salmon, lemon pepper seasoning, and dill into asparagus mixture. Cover; cook about 2 minutes or until thoroughly heated.

Per serving: 422 calories, 34g protein, 13g fat (27 percent calories from fat), 4.6g saturated fat, 43g carbohydrate, 74mg cholesterol, 381mg sodium, 8g fiber.

Adapted from Betty Crocker Whole Grains, Easy Everyday Recipes by Cheri Olerud (Wiley).

Week 13

 ### Sunday *Family*

Make **Balsamic-Marinated Flank Steak** for family day. Place 1 1½-pound flank steak in a resealable plastic bag with ½ cup balsamic salad dressing; turn to coat. Refrigerate 6 to 24 hours. Remove steak; discard marinade. Grill, uncovered, 17 to 21 minutes for medium-rare to medium. Carve crosswise into thin slices and serve. Alongside, add **Bean and Barley Salad** (see recipe), steamed fresh **broccoli**, and **crusty rolls**. Buy a **lemon meringue pie** for dessert. ***Plan ahead:*** Save enough pie for Monday.

 ### Monday *Budget*

Try something new and be frugal at the same time with **Peruvian Quinoa Pork Stew** (see recipe). Serve this unusual stew with a **spinach salad** and **whole-grain bread**. Slice the leftover **pie** for dessert. ***Plan ahead:*** Save enough stew for Tuesday.

 ### Tuesday *Heat and Eat*

Heat the leftover **stew,** and serve it over **couscous** for an easy meal. Add a **romaine salad** and **breadsticks**. Make instant **butterscotch pudding** for dessert, using 1-percent milk.

 ### Wednesday *Express*

Make it quick tonight with deli **chicken salad sandwiches** on whole-grain bread. Add any **bean soup** and a **lettuce and tomato salad.** For dessert, enjoy sliced **mango.**

 ### Thursday *Kids*

Make their day and serve the kids **pizza** (frozen). Top it off with any extra vegetables on hand. Add a **chopped lettuce and cherry tomato halves salad.** Munch on **peanut butter cookies** for dessert.

 ### Friday *Meatless*

Pasta Mexican-Style with Tomatoes and Avocado is as easy to prepare as it gets. In a large saucepan, combine 1 14½-ounce can undrained diced tomatoes with jalapeno peppers, 1 14-ounce can vegetable broth, and 1 cup water; bring to a boil. Add 8 ounces angel hair pasta; cook 5 minutes or until tender. Stir in one ripened, diced avocado. Serve immediately with **mixed greens** and **garlic bread.** For dessert, fat-free **strawberry ice cream** tastes good. ***Plan ahead:*** Save enough ice cream for Saturday.

 ### Saturday *Easy Entertaining*

Treat your lucky guests to **Spicy Chicken in Peanut Sauce** (see recipe). Serve it over **couscous** and add a **Boston lettuce salad.** Top leftover **ice cream** with warm **fudge sauce** for a divine dessert.

Bean and Barley Salad

Prep time: 20 min • **Cook time:** For the barley • **Yield:** About 8½ cups

Ingredients

1 cup quick-cooking barley

2 cups canned navy beans, rinsed

¼ cup chopped fresh cilantro leaves

2 tomatoes, diced

2 onions, thinly sliced green

1 11-ounce can corn, rinsed

1 avocado, diced

½ cup thinly sliced celery

⅓ cup coarsely chopped toasted walnuts

For the dressing:

1 tablespoon walnut or olive oil

2 tablespoons red wine vinegar

1 tablespoon fresh lemon juice

Directions

1 Cook barley according to directions. Drain and rinse under cold water; allow to cool.

2 In a large bowl, combine the barley, beans, cilantro, tomatoes, onions, corn, avocado, celery, and walnuts.

3 In a small bowl, whisk together the oil, vinegar and juice; pour over salad. Toss to coat.

Per cup: 263 calories, 9g protein, 10g fat (32 percent calories from fat), 1.2g saturated fat, 37g carbohydrate, 0mg cholesterol, 388mg sodium, 9g fiber.

BUDGET

Peruvian Quinoa Pork Stew

Prep time: 20 min • **Cook time:** About 50 min • **Yield:** 8 servings

Ingredients

1½ cups quinoa

2 teaspoons olive oil

1 pound well-trimmed boneless pork loin, cut into ¾-inch pieces

¼ teaspoon salt

½ teaspoon pepper

1 medium red bell pepper, sliced into ¼-inch slices

1 tablespoon minced garlic

2 teaspoons paprika

2 teaspoons cumin

5 cups fat-free chicken broth

1¼ cups diced plum tomatoes (remove seeds)

¼ cup dry sherry

⅓ cup ripe olives, rinsed and halved

½ cup chopped fresh basil

Finely chopped unsalted peanuts for garnish

Directions

1 Rinse quinoa in a fine sieve for 2 minutes under cold water; set aside.

2 Heat oil in a Dutch oven on medium-high; add pork, salt, and pepper. Cook 4 to 5 minutes or until browned, stirring occasionally.

3 Add bell pepper and continue cooking 2 to 3 minutes or until softened. Stir in garlic, paprika, and cumin; cook for one more minute. Add broth, tomatoes, and sherry, and bring to a boil. Reduce heat to low; simmer, covered, 20 minutes.

4 Uncover; stir in olives, quinoa, and basil. Cover and cook 15 to 20 minutes more. Garnish with peanuts. Serve immediately.

Per serving: 249 calories, 18g protein, 8g fat (28 percent calories from fat), 1.9g saturated fat, 26g carbohydrate, 32mg cholesterol, 397mg sodium, 4g fiber.

EASY ENTERTAINING

Spicy Chicken in Peanut Sauce

Prep time: 20 min • **Cook time:** 7–8 hr • **Yield:** 6 servings

Ingredients

1 large onion, chopped

2 10-ounce cans diced tomatoes with chilies

1 14½-ounce can no-salt-added diced tomatoes

2 tablespoons honey

1½ teaspoons cumin

1 teaspoon cinnamon

8 bone-in, skinless chicken thighs (about 3 pounds), trimmed of visible fat

⅓ cup creamy low-fat peanut butter

Directions

1 In a 4-quart or larger slow cooker, combine onion, all the tomatoes, honey, cumin, and cinnamon; mix well. Add chicken; spoon mixture over chicken.

2 Cover and cook on low for 7 to 8 hours.

3 Stir in peanut butter until melted and well-blended. Serve chicken with sauce.

Per serving: 295 calories, 23g protein, 13g fat (39 percent calories from fat), 3.2g saturated fat, 23g carbohydrate, 66mg cholesterol, 581mg sodium, 4g fiber.

Adapted from the Betty Crocker Cookbook, Heart Health Edition *(Wiley).*

Week 14

Sunday *Family*

It's easy to cook a **turkey breast** for the family if you use a cooking bag and follow the simple directions. On the side, **Baked Macaroni and Pimento Cheese** (see recipe) will be a hit. Add fresh **asparagus** and **whole-grain rolls**. For dessert, buy a **Boston cream pie**. *Plan ahead:* Save enough turkey for Monday and Tuesday; save enough macaroni and cheese and pie for Monday.

Monday *Heat and Eat*

Use some of the leftover turkey for **turkey sandwiches** on **whole-grain bread**. Spread the bread with Dijon mustard and peach preserves and top the turkey with **lettuce and tomatoes**. Heat the leftover **macaroni and cheese**. Slice the leftover **pie** for dessert.

Tuesday *Kids*

Call the kids for **Turkey Dagwoods.** Cut a 1-pound loaf French bread in half, lengthwise; then cut into 4 pieces crosswise. Brush cut sides of bread with honey-mustard salad dressing. Layer bottom half with thin slices of deli ham, thinly sliced (leftover) turkey, 50-percent-reduced-fat cheddar cheese slices, sliced tomatoes, and shredded lettuce. Top with remaining bread. Secure with toothpicks, cut in half, and serve. Add deli **carrot salad** and **veggie chips** on the side. For dessert, make instant **chocolate pudding** with 1-percent milk and stir in sliced **bananas.**

Wednesday *Express*

Make it quick tonight with deli **seafood salad** over packaged **greens**. Start the meal with **vegetarian vegetable soup** and **crackers**. Finish with fresh **pineapple**.

Thursday *Budget*

For low cost and high flavor, try **Fettuccine with Bacon and Roasted Red Peppers** (see recipe). Serve with **mixed greens** and **garlic bread**. **Peaches** are your dessert.

Friday *Meatless*

Spice up the traditional and serve **Grilled Cheese with Pear Slices.** For each sandwich, lay two slices of whole-grain bread on a flat surface, spread spicy mustard to taste, layer slices of pear and 50-percent-reduced-fat sharp cheddar cheese, then top with other slice of bread before grilling. Serve with **oven fries** (frozen) and a **spinach salad**. Make or buy **brownies** for dessert. *Plan ahead:* Save enough brownies for Saturday.

Saturday *Easy Entertaining*

You might want to add company-worthy **Chinese Barbeque Pork Tenderloin** (see recipe) to your favorites file, as I did. Serve it with **rice** and **Cranberry Walnut Coleslaw.** For the coleslaw dressing, combine ⅓ cup each cider vinegar, canola oil, and sugar and 1 teaspoon celery seeds; set aside. In a large bowl, combine 1 cup each coarsely chopped walnuts and dried cranberries, 2 cups each finely sliced red and green cabbages, and ¼ cup thinly sliced red onion. Pour dressing over mixture; toss to coat. Cover and refrigerate 3 hours before serving. Stir salad and drain liquid just before serving. Add **baguettes**. For dessert, top the leftover **brownies** with fat-free **vanilla ice cream** and drizzle with **strawberry sauce**.

FAMILY

Baked Macaroni and Pimento Cheese

Prep time: 20 min • **Cook time:** About 20–25 min, plus pasta • **Yield:** 12 servings

Ingredients

8 ounces elbow macaroni

3 tablespoons butter

¼ cup flour

2 cups skim milk

½ teaspoon salt

¼ teaspoon cayenne pepper

⅛ teaspoon garlic powder

8 ounces shredded 50-percent-reduced-fat sharp cheddar cheese (such as Cabot)

1 4-ounce jar diced pimentos, drained

⅓ cup fine dry bread crumbs

⅓ cup freshly grated parmesan cheese

Directions

1 Cook macaroni according to directions; drain. Heat oven to 350 degrees.

2 Meanwhile, in a large skillet, melt butter on medium. Gradually whisk in flour until smooth; cook, whisking constantly 1 minute.

3 Gradually whisk in milk, salt, cayenne pepper, and garlic powder. Cook, whisking constantly, 3 to 5 minutes or until thickened.

4 Stir in cheddar cheese and pimentos and cook until cheese is melted and sauce is smooth. Remove from heat. Stir in pasta. Spoon mixture into a 9-x-13-inch baking dish coated with cooking spray.

5 Stir together bread crumbs and parmesan cheese in a shallow dish or pie plate. Sprinkle over mixture.

6 Bake 15 to 20 minutes or until golden and bubbly.

Per serving: 189 calories, 11g protein, 7g fat (33 percent calories from fat), 4.3g saturated fat, 22g carbohydrate, 20mg cholesterol, 306mg sodium, 1g fiber.

Adapted from Southern Living *magazine.*

BUDGET

Fettuccine with Bacon and Roasted Red Peppers

Prep time: 15 min • **Cook time:** About 5 min, plus fettuccine • **Yield:** 4 servings

Ingredients	Directions
8 ounces fettuccine	*1* Cook fettuccine according to directions; drain.
1 7-ounce jar roasted red peppers, drained	*2* Cut peppers into ¼-inch-wide strips; set aside.
2 slices bacon, chopped	
1 cup sliced onion	*3* Cook bacon in a large Dutch oven 2 minutes on medium-high or until crisp. Add onion and garlic; cook 1 minute. Add peppers, peas, and broth; simmer 1 minute.
3 cloves minced garlic	
1 cup frozen tiny green peas	
¼ cup fat-free chicken broth	
2 tablespoons freshly grated parmesan cheese	*4* Stir in fettuccine, cheese, salt, and pepper; mix well and serve.
¼ teaspoon salt	
¼ teaspoon black pepper	

Per serving: 296 calories, 12g protein, 3g fat (10 percent calories from fat), 1g saturated fat, 54g carbohydrate, 6mg cholesterol, 426mg sodium, 4g fiber.

EASY ENTERTAINING

Chinese Barbeque Pork Tenderloin

Prep time: 10 min • **Cook time:** 20–25 min, plus standing time • **Yield:** 4 servings

Ingredients

1 1-pound pork tenderloin

2 teaspoons brown sugar

½ teaspoon five-spice powder

¼ teaspoon salt

⅛ teaspoon cayenne pepper

1 tablespoon hoisin sauce

1 tablespoon orange juice

½ teaspoon dark (toasted) sesame oil

Directions

1 Heat oven to 400 degrees. Trim fat from pork. Combine sugar, five-spice powder, salt, and cayenne pepper. Rub pork with spice mixture.

2 Place pork on a rack coated with cooking spray in a foil-lined broiling pan. Bake 10 minutes.

3 Meanwhile, combine hoisin sauce, juice, and oil; brush all over tenderloin. Bake 10 to 15 more minutes or until thermometer registers 155 degrees.

4 Remove from oven; tent with foil and let stand 5 minutes before slicing.

Per serving: 153 calories, 23g protein, 5g fat (27 percent calories from fat), 1.4g saturated fat, 4g carbohydrate, 63mg cholesterol, 211mg sodium, no fiber.

Adapted from Cooking Light *magazine.*

Week 15

Sunday *Family*

Have a picnic with your own **grilled chicken.** Accompany it with a recipe from the 42nd Pillsbury Bake-Off, **You Won't Know It's Not Potato Salad** (see recipe). Add **baked beans** (canned) and **whole-grain rolls.** Buy a **coconut cake** for dessert. *Plan ahead:* Prepare enough chicken for Monday; save enough potato salad and cake for Tuesday.

Monday *Heat and Eat*

With some of the leftover chicken, make **Creamed Chicken** (see recipe) and serve it over **rice.** On the side, add a **spinach salad** and **biscuits.** For dessert, try **pears.**

Tuesday *Express*

Turn deli tuna into **Mediterranean Tuna** by stirring in some capers and lemon juice. Spread a little butter and some hummus on whole-grain bread; top with lettuce, tomato, and the tuna mixture. Serve with left-over **"potato salad," baked chips,** and **pickles.** Slice some leftover **cake** for dessert.

Wednesday *Kids*

Sing "Happy Trails" as you prepare **Cowboy Tacos** for the kids. In a shallow bowl, combine 1 pound bone-less pork loin cut into 1-x-1-x-¼-inch strips and 1 1.25-ounce package reduced-sodium taco seasoning mix; toss to coat. Heat 1 tablespoon canola oil in a large nonstick skillet on medium-high until hot. Add pork; cook and stir 3 to 5 minutes. Stir in 1 cup drained chunky salsa, 1 cup undrained chili beans, and ¼ cup apricot preserves. Reduce heat to low; simmer 10 to 12 minutes, stirring occasionally. Meanwhile, heat 6 taco shells as directed. To serve, spoon ⅓ cup pork mixture into each taco shell. Top with low-fat **sour cream.** Serve with **guacamole** and **shredded lettuce.** For dessert, a **homemade root beer float** is extra-special. Combine ¾ cup sugar and 1 cup boiling water; stir until dissolved. Add 1½ teaspoons root beer concentrate. Chill. When ready to serve, combine root beer mixture with 1 quart club soda. Stir slowly to mix. Place 2 scoops fat-free vanilla ice cream in a tall glass. Slowly pour root beer between ice cream and side of glass. Serve immediately. *Plan ahead:* Save enough taco mixture and guacamole for Thursday.

Thursday *Budget*

Make **Taco Cornbread** by heating the leftover pork taco mixture and spooning over squares of **cornbread** (from a mix). Serve with steamed **carrots** and leftover **guacamole.** Make **flan** (from a mix) for dessert.

Friday *Meatless*

Fusilli with Broccoli and Potatoes (see recipe) is an easy, no-meat dinner. Serve with **mixed greens** and **garlic bread.** For dessert, try **red and green grapes.**

Saturday *Easy Entertaining*

It's quick, it's flavorful, and it's perfect for guests, so **Parmesan Herb Shrimp** is on the menu tonight. Melt 2 tablespoons butter in a large skillet on low. Add 1 pound uncooked, large, peeled and deveined shrimp; cook and stir on medium heat 5 minutes or just until shrimp turn pink. Stir in 2 tablespoons parmesan herb seasoning blend, 2 tablespoons dry white wine, and 1 teaspoon finely chopped fresh parsley. Serve over **rice.** On the side, add **sugar snap peas,** a **Bibb lettuce salad,** and **baguettes.** Buy **fruit tarts** for dessert.

FAMILY

You Won't Know It's Not Potato Salad

Prep time: 20 min; chilling time, 30 min • **Cook time:** 20–30 min • **Yield:** 12 servings

Ingredients

4 hard-cooked eggs

2 1-pound packages frozen cauliflower florets

1 10-ounce package frozen peas and carrots

1¾ cups low-fat mayonnaise

1 teaspoon sugar

1 teaspoon salt

¼ teaspoon pepper

¼ teaspoon paprika

1 tablespoon cider vinegar

1 teaspoon yellow mustard

1 cup sliced celery

⅔ cup minced onion

Directions

1 Chop eggs; set aside. In a large bowl, microwave cauliflower and peas and carrots according to directions. Drain in colander; rinse with cold water. Place colander in bowl and cool in refrigerator for 30 minutes minimum.

2 In a small bowl, mix mayonnaise, sugar, salt, pepper, ⅛ teaspoon paprika, vinegar, and mustard; set aside.

3 Remove vegetables from refrigerator; discard any liquid in bowl. Pat drained vegetables dry with paper towels. Chop any large cauliflower pieces into ¾-inch chunks.

4 Place vegetables back in bowl. Add celery, onion, and eggs.

5 Pour mayonnaise mixture over salad; stir until vegetables and eggs are well-coated. Sprinkle with remaining paprika. Chill before serving.

Per serving: 125 calories, 5g protein, 7g fat (45 percent calories from fat), 1.7g saturated fat, 13g carbohydrate, 71mg cholesterol, 576mg sodium, 3g fiber.

HEAT AND EAT

Creamed Chicken

Prep time: 10 min • **Cook time:** About 10 min • **Yield:** 4 servings

Ingredients	*Directions*

½ **cup flour**

2¼ **cups 2-percent milk, divided**

1 cup frozen tiny green peas, thawed

1 teaspoon dried sage

1 teaspoon butter

2 cups leftover cooked diced chicken

1 4-ounce jar diced pimentos, drained

1 tablespoon fresh lemon juice

¼ **teaspoon freshly ground black pepper**

1 In a large saucepan on medium, whisk flour and ½ cup milk together until smooth. Stir in remaining milk. Cook 5 minutes or until mixture is thick, stirring constantly with a whisk.

2 Add peas, sage, butter, chicken, and pimentos, stirring to combine. Cook 2 minutes or until thoroughly heated.

3 Remove from heat; stir in juice and pepper.

Per serving: 291 calories, 30g protein, 7g fat (23 percent calories from fat), 3.3g saturated fat, 25g carbohydrate, 73mg cholesterol, 162mg sodium, 3g fiber.

Adapted from Cooking Light *magazine.*

MEATLESS

Fusilli with Broccoli and Potatoes

Prep time: 15 min • **Cook time:** About 20 min • **Yield:** 6 servings

Ingredients

- 8 ounces fusilli pasta
- 1 cup vegetable broth
- 1½ tablespoons extra-virgin olive oil
- ½ teaspoon crushed red pepper
- ⅛ teaspoon black pepper
- 3 cloves minced garlic
- 2 cups cubed red potatoes (about 1 pound)
- 2 pounds broccoli florets
- ½ cup freshly grated parmesan cheese

Directions

1 Cook pasta according to directions; drain.

2 In a large bowl, combine broth, oil, red pepper, black pepper, and garlic.

3 Cook potatoes in boiling water about 7 minutes or until tender; drain.

4 Cover and microwave broccoli 10 minutes on high (100-percent power); drain well and cool.

5 To broth mixture, add potatoes, broccoli, and pasta. Toss, sprinkle with cheese, and serve.

Per serving: 285 calories, 13g protein, 7g fat (20 percent calories from fat), 1.8g saturated fat, 46g carbohydrate, 6mg cholesterol, 214mg sodium, 7g fiber.

Week 16

Sunday *Family*

Apple Mustard-Glazed Pork Chops make a delicious family meal. Season 4 boneless, center-cut pork chops (about 1 pound total) with pepper. Heat 1 teaspoon canola oil in a large nonstick skillet on medium-high; cook chops 1 minute or until browned. Turn, stir in ¼ cup apple juice and 2 tablespoons each apple jelly and Dijon mustard. Reduce heat to low; cover and cook 8 minutes. Serve with **baked sweet potatoes,** fresh **asparagus,** and **sourdough bread.** Buy a **berry cobbler** for dessert. *Plan ahead:* Prepare enough pork and sweet potatoes and save enough cobbler for Monday.

Monday *Heat and Eat*

Remodel the leftover pork into **pork sandwiches on whole-grain toast.** Spread 1 to 2 teaspoons honey-mustard on each slice of bread. Top 4 slices with thinly sliced cooked (leftover) pork chops, 4 thin slices Swiss cheese, and Boston lettuce. Serve with leftover **baked sweet potatoes** cut into wedges. Warm the leftover **cobbler** and top it with fat-free **vanilla ice cream.** *Plan ahead:* Save enough ice cream for Thursday.

Tuesday *Express*

Make it quick tonight with **Chicken Kaisers Supreme.** Top split kaiser roll halves with grainy mustard, slices of cooked chicken breast and provolone cheese, a pineapple ring, and sliced mushrooms. Add lettuce, sprinkle with fat-free Italian dressing, and top with remaining roll halves. Serve with **veggie chips,** and have **kiwifruit** for dessert.

Wednesday *Budget*

Bow-Tie Pasta with Mushrooms and Sausage has great flavor. Cook 8 ounces pasta according to directions; drain. Meanwhile, cut 12 ounces sweet Italian chicken sausage links into 1-inch pieces, and cook in a large nonstick skillet on medium heat 10 minutes or until browned and cooked through. Remove sausage; set aside. In skillet, heat 1 tablespoon olive oil on medium. Add 12 ounces fresh sliced mushrooms, 1 medium coarsely chopped green bell pepper, and 1 medium chopped onion; cook and stir 8 minutes or until softened. Add cooked sausage and 2 cups marinara sauce. Cook 5 minutes or until heated through. Ladle sauce over hot pasta; sprinkle with freshly grated parmesan cheese. Serve with a **romaine salad** and **garlic bread.** Enjoy tropical **sliced mangoes** for dessert.

Thursday *Kids*

My Meatloaf (see recipe) is a hit with kids. Serve with **mashed potatoes, green beans,** and **soft rolls.** For dessert, kids can decorate their own **cupcakes** and enjoy leftover **ice cream** on the side.

Friday *Meatless*

Make your no-meat dinner fun with **Mushroom Primavera with Spaghetti Squash** (see recipe). Serve the flavorful combo with a **spinach salad** and **whole-grain rolls.** For dessert, make **vanilla mousse** (from a mix).

Saturday *Easy Entertaining*

Invite guests for **Roasted Chicken Thighs with Sherried Grapes and Watercress** (see recipe). Start your meal with **tomato broth** (heat tomato juice plus fat-free chicken broth) and a **Caesar salad.** Add **whole-grain bread.** Buy a **cheesecake** for dessert.

My Meatloaf

Prep time: 10 min • **Cook time:** 25 min, plus standing time • **Yield:** 4 servings

Ingredients

½ cup ketchup

1½ tablespoons Dijon mustard

1 pound 95-percent-lean ground beef

½ cup finely chopped carrots

¼ cup finely chopped onion

¼ cup seasoned bread crumbs

¼ teaspoon salt

½ teaspoon dried oregano

⅛ teaspoon pepper

1 egg, lightly beaten

Directions

1 Heat oven to 400 degrees. In a small bowl, blend ketchup and mustard with a whisk; reserve 2½ tablespoons.

2 In a medium bowl, combine remaining ketchup-mustard mixture, beef, carrots, onion, bread crumbs, salt, oregano, pepper, and egg.

3 Divide mixture into 4 equal portions. Shape each portion into a 4-x-2½-inch loaf; place on a baking pan lined with nonstick foil.

4 Spread about 2 teaspoons reserved ketchup mixture evenly over each loaf.

5 Bake 25 minutes or until internal temperature is 160 degrees. Remove from oven, let stand 2 minutes, and serve.

Per serving: 243 calories, 28g protein, 8g fat (29 percent calories from fat), 2.8g saturated fat, 16g carbohydrate, 115mg cholesterol, 841mg sodium, 1g fiber.

Adapted from Cooking Light *magazine.*

Mushroom Primavera with Spaghetti Squash

MEATLESS

Prep time: 15 min • **Cook time:** About 25 min • **Yield:** 4 servings

Ingredients	Directions
1 3-pound spaghetti squash	**1** Pierce squash 5 or 6 times through skin to center to vent. Place on paper towels in microwave and cook on high (100-percent power) 10 minutes or until squash has softened. Remove and cool until squash is easy to handle. Be careful removing squash; it will be very hot.
1 tablespoon olive oil	
1 pound sliced white button or crimini mushrooms	
1 cup chopped onion	
1 tablespoon minced garlic	**2** Cut lengthwise and remove seeds with a spoon. Remove the spaghetti-like strands of squash with a fork, and place them in a bowl; cover to keep warm and set aside.
1½ cups grape tomatoes, halved	
1 cup crumbled fat-free feta cheese	**3** Meanwhile, heat oil in a large nonstick skillet on medium-high. Add a single layer of mushrooms and cook without stirring about 5 minutes or until mushrooms become red-brown on one side.
2 tablespoons sliced kalamata olives	
½ cup chopped fresh basil, plus more for garnish	**4** Stir in onions and garlic; cook 5 more minutes or until onions are softened.
	5 Add tomatoes, cheese, and olives; cook 3 minutes longer or until mixture is hot and bubbling. Remove pan from heat and stir in basil.
	6 Reheat squash in the microwave (if necessary) and divide among 4 shallow bowls. Spoon sauce over squash and garnish with additional freshly chopped basil. Serve immediately.

Per serving: 221 calories, 15g protein, 6g fat (21 percent calories from fat), 0.9g saturated fat, 34g carbohydrate, no cholesterol, 725mg sodium, 7g fiber.

EASY ENTERTAINING

Roasted Chicken Thighs with Sherried Grapes and Watercress

Prep time: 20 min • **Cook time:** 30–35 min • **Yield:** 4 servings

Ingredients

8 bone-in skinless chicken thighs (about 2½ pounds)

2 cloves halved garlic

3 tablespoons extra-virgin olive oil, divided

1 teaspoon salt, divided

1 teaspoon pepper, divided

1 pound seedless red and green grapes, removed from stem

3 tablespoons sherry vinegar

1 tablespoon butter, melted

½ teaspoon sugar

2 bunches watercress, stems removed, or 6 cups baby spinach

Directions

1 Heat oven to 450 degrees. Rub each thigh all over with piece of garlic. Place thighs in a large bowl and toss with 2 tablespoons oil; season with ½ teaspoon of the salt and pepper.

2 Place chicken on one side of a large, rimmed baking dish lined with nonstick foil.

3 In a medium bowl, toss grapes with vinegar, butter, and sugar. Season mixture with remaining salt and pepper. Spread grapes on the other half of baking sheet.

4 Bake 30 to 35 minutes (to 180 degrees) or until juices run clear when pierced with a fork, stirring grapes occasionally.

5 In medium bowl, toss watercress or spinach with remaining oil. Arrange on a platter or on individual plates; place chicken on top. Spoon grapes over chicken and serve.

Per serving: 458 calories, 33g protein, 26g fat (51 percent calories from fat), 6.9g saturated fat, 23g carbohydrate, 122mg cholesterol, 732mg sodium, 1g fiber.

Week 17

 ## Sunday *Family*

Beef Loin Steaks with Grilled Red Onion Relish (see recipe) make a special meal for the family. Serve them with **roasted potatoes, a spinach salad,** and **dinner rolls.** Everyone will welcome **chocolate meringue pie** for dessert. ***Plan ahead:*** Save enough steak and vegetables, the reduced balsamic vinegar, and pie, and prepare extra potatoes for Monday.

 ## Monday *Heat and Eat*

Make good use of the leftovers and serve **Grilled Beef and Onion Salad** tonight. In a small bowl, whisk together ¼ cup olive oil, 2 tablespoons leftover reduced balsamic vinegar, 1 clove minced garlic, and salt and pepper to taste; set aside. Arrange 4 leftover grilled squash halves, cut into ¾-inch pieces, and leftover grilled onion wedges over 8 cups mixed salad greens. Carve the 2 leftover steaks into slices; arrange over salad. Drizzle vinaigrette over salad; toss. Alongside, add the leftover heated **potatoes** and add **whole-grain rolls.** Slice the leftover **pie** for dessert.

 ## Tuesday *Express*

For a quick meal, **Deviled Chicken Tenders** are easy to prepare. Heat oven to 425 degrees. Lightly coat chicken tenders with Dijon mustard. Roll in seasoned dry bread crumbs to coat. Coat chicken with cooking spray. Bake 20 minutes or until crisp. Serve with deli **pasta salad** and **biscuits. Plums** are your dessert.

 ## Wednesday *Kids*

Let the kids help prepare **chili dogs** (using fat-free hot dogs and vegetarian chili) served on whole-grain buns. Add **oven fries** (frozen) and deli **carrot salad. Peaches** are an easy dessert.

 ## Thursday *Meatless*

Think warmer weather and serve this delicious **Mediterranean Penne Salad** (see recipe). Serve with a **lettuce wedge** and **Italian bread.** Fresh **strawberries** make a wonderful dessert. ***Plan ahead:*** Save enough pasta for Friday.

 ## Friday *Budget*

Make **pasta-stuffed tomatoes** for dinner. Hollow out large tomatoes and fill them with leftover pasta. Garnish with freshly grated parmesan cheese. Serve with **green beans** and **whole-grain rolls.** Slice **mangoes** for dessert.

 ## Saturday *Easy Entertaining*

You're not likely to have leftovers when you serve **Shrimp with Pasta and Feta Cheese** (see recipe). Add an **arugula salad** and **garlic bread. Cherry Dream** is a company-worthy dessert. Cut 1 10-ounce angel food cake into cubes; sprinkle cubes on bottom of a 9-x-9-inch baking dish. In a medium bowl, fold 1⅓ cups frozen fat-free whipped topping (thawed) into 1 21-ounce can light cherry pie filling. Spoon mixture evenly over cake. Let chill, covered, several hours or overnight. Garnish each serving with a sprig of mint.

FAMILY

Beef Loin Steaks with Grilled Red Onion Relish

Prep time: 20 min • **Cook time:** 8–18 min • **Yield:** 8 servings

Ingredients

½ **cup balsamic vinegar**

4 teaspoons garlic-pepper seasoning, divided

4 boneless beef top loin (strip) steaks, cut ¾ inch thick (about 8 ounces each)

2 medium red onions, each cut into 12 wedges

2 medium yellow squash, cut lengthwise in half

2 medium zucchini squash, cut lengthwise in half

2 tablespoons olive oil

1 teaspoon chopped fresh oregano

Salt to taste

Directions

1 Bring vinegar to a boil in a small pan. Lower heat; simmer 6 to 8 minutes or until reduced by half; set aside.

2 Press 2 teaspoons garlic-pepper seasoning evenly onto steaks.

3 Thread onion wedges onto 4 10-inch metal skewers. Brush onions and cut sides of squash with oil; sprinkle with remaining 2 teaspoons garlic pepper.

4 Grill steaks, uncovered, 15 to 18 minutes for medium-rare to medium doneness, turning occasionally. Grill squash 8 to 12 minutes and onions 12 to 15 minutes or until tender, turning occasionally.

5 Remove onions from skewers; toss half the onions with 2 tablespoons of the reduced vinegar, oregano, and salt to taste.

6 Carve 2 steaks into slices. Serve with half of the onions and half of the squash.

Per serving: 216 calories, 26g protein, 8g fat (34 percent calories from fat), 2.3g saturated fat, 10g carbohydrate, 46mg cholesterol, 202mg sodium, 2g fiber.

Mediterranean Penne Salad

Prep time: 20 min • **Cook time:** For the pasta • **Yield:** 6 servings

MEATLESS

Ingredients

2½ cups penne pasta

⅔ cup hummus

3 tablespoons fresh lemon juice

2 tablespoons olive oil

1 cup red grape tomatoes, halved

½ cup chopped red onion

⅓ cup black or green pitted olives, halved

¼ cup crumbled fat-free feta cheese

¼ cup chopped fresh basil

1 tablespoon capers

¼ teaspoon salt

½ teaspoon black pepper

2 tablespoons toasted slivered almonds

Directions

1 Cook pasta according to directions; rinse in cold water and drain well. Place in a large bowl.

2 In a small bowl, combine hummus, juice, and oil; mix well and set aside.

3 To pasta, add tomatoes, onion, olives, feta cheese, basil, capers, salt, and pepper; gently toss to mix well.

4 Spoon hummus mixture over pasta; toss to coat. Cover and chill. Sprinkle with almonds just before serving.

Per serving: 236 calories, 9g protein, 10g fat (35 percent calories from fat), 1.2g saturated fat, 33g carbohydrate, no cholesterol, 414mg sodium, 5g fiber.

EASY ENTERTAINING

Shrimp with Pasta and Feta Cheese

Prep time: 15 min • **Cook time:** About 10 min, plus pasta • **Yield:** 4 servings

Ingredients

8 ounces pasta shells (about 3 cups)

1 tablespoon olive oil

½ cup chopped onion

1 tablespoon chopped fresh basil

1½ teaspoons fresh oregano

½ teaspoon minced garlic

1 14½-ounce can drained diced tomatoes with oregano, basil, and garlic

1 cup seeded and chopped plum tomatoes

1 pound uncooked shelled and deveined shrimp

¼ cup dry white wine

¼ teaspoon salt

¼ teaspoon pepper

¼ cup crumbled fat-free feta cheese for garnish

Directions

1 Cook pasta according to directions; drain.

2 Meanwhile, in a large skillet, heat oil on medium-high. Add onion, basil, oregano, and garlic; cook and stir 5 minutes or until onion is tender.

3 Add both tomatoes, shrimp, wine, salt, and pepper. Cook and stir 2 minutes or until shrimp are pink and tomatoes are heated through.

4 Spoon over pasta; garnish with feta cheese.

Per serving: 404 calories, 30g protein, 5g fat (12 percent calories from fat), 0.9g saturated fat, 56g carbohydrate, 168mg cholesterol, 1,027mg sodium, 3g fiber.

Week 18

 ## Sunday *Family*

Celebrate Mother's Day with flavorful and simple **Almond-Chocolate Baked French Toast** (see recipe). Serve it with **Canadian bacon** and **fresh fruit** sprinkled with toasted coconut.

 ## Monday *Budget*

Serve economical **Black Bean Chicken Chili** (see recipe) tonight. Add a **romaine salad** and **cornbread** (from a mix). **Pears** are good for dessert. *Plan ahead:* Save enough chili and cornbread for Tuesday.

 ## Tuesday *Heat and Eat*

The leftover **chili** is even better when the flavors have had more time to blend. Serve it over **brown rice** and garnish with fat-free sour cream. Add a **mixed green salad** and the leftover **cornbread**. Fresh **pineapple** makes an easy dessert.

 ## Wednesday *Express*

Chicken Satay is quick and full of flavor. Whisk ¼ cup each low-fat creamy peanut butter and water with 1 tablespoon each fresh lime juice, reduced-sodium soy sauce, grated ginger, and brown sugar until smooth. Skewer 1¼ pounds chicken tenders; brush with canola oil, then grill 5 minutes, turning once until cooked through. Serve the chicken with the sauce and lime wedges. (Adapted from *Woman's Day* magazine.) Add **corn on the cob** and **breadsticks**. Buy **tapioca pudding** for dessert.

 ## Thursday *Kids*

Call the kids for **Pizza Burgers** and let them take part in the cooking. Heat oven to 350 degrees. Brown 1 pound 93- to 95-percent-lean ground beef. Meanwhile, stir ½ teaspoon dried oregano and ¼ cup grated parmesan cheese into 1 to 1½ cups pizza sauce. Spoon beef and sauce over halves of whole-wheat English muffins. Top with shredded mozzarella cheese, and bake until the cheese bubbles. Add **baby carrots** to munch on. **Fudgesicles** make a dandy dessert.

 ## Friday *Meatless*

Forget meat and enjoy **Horseradish-Stuffed Potatoes** for an easy meal. For the sauce, in a medium bowl, combine 1 cup fat-free sour cream, ¼ cup prepared horseradish, 3 tablespoons 1-percent milk, 1 tablespoon snipped fresh chives, and ¼ teaspoon white pepper. Cut tops from 4 8-ounce baked potatoes. Scoop out pulp and mix with sauce and ¼ cup chopped red bell pepper. Spoon mixture back into potatoes, garnish with additional snipped chives, and serve. Add a **spinach salad** with **red onion rings** and **hard-cooked egg wedges,** and **whole-grain rolls.** For dessert, top fat-free **vanilla ice cream** with fresh **strawberries.** *Plan ahead:* Save enough ice cream for Saturday.

 ## Saturday *Easy Entertaining*

Pork Medallions with Red Onion Marmalade (see recipe) is a special meal for guests. Serve with **lemon rice.** (Stir some butter, fresh lemon juice, and lemon zest into hot cooked rice.) Add **snow peas,** a **Boston lettuce salad,** and **baguettes.** For dessert, make **caramel sundaes** with leftover vanilla ice cream and caramel sauce. Top the sundaes with light whipped cream.

FAMILY

Almond-Chocolate Baked French Toast

Prep time: 15 min • **Cook time:** 15–20 min • **Yield:** 6 servings

Ingredients

1 16-ounce unsliced loaf of bread (sourdough, Italian, or whole-grain)

1½ cups 1-percent milk

3 eggs

¼ cup sugar

1 teaspoon pure vanilla extract

½ teaspoon cinnamon

¼ teaspoon nutmeg

½ teaspoon orange zest (orange part only)

⅓ cup chocolate chips, roughly chopped

½ cup toasted sliced almonds

Directions

1 Heat oven to 400 degrees. Line a large rimmed baking sheet with nonstick foil.

2 With a serrated knife, cut bread into 1-inch-thick slices. Remove crusts. Cut each slice in half on a diagonal. Cut each half in half again so you have four triangles.

3 In a medium bowl, whisk together milk, eggs, sugar, vanilla, cinnamon, nutmeg, and zest. Dip both sides of bread into milk mixture; place on prepared baking sheet.

4 Spoon some of the remaining milk mixture over bread and sprinkle with chocolate pieces.

5 Bake 15 to 20 minutes or until golden. Top with almonds, and serve warm.

Per serving: 425 calories, 17g protein, 12g fat (25 percent calories from fat), 4.1g saturated fat, 64g carbohydrate, 110mg cholesterol, 559mg sodium, 4g fiber.

BUDGET

Black Bean Chicken Chili

Prep time: 15 min • **Cook time:** 25–35 min • **Yield:** About 8½ cups

Ingredients	*Directions*
1 tablespoon canola oil	*1* Heat oil in a large nonstick skillet or Dutch oven on medium. Add onion, garlic, chili powder, oregano, cumin, and salt. Cook 4 minutes or until vegetables are softened.
¾ cup chopped onion	
2 cloves minced garlic	
2 to 3 tablespoons chili powder	*2* Stir in chicken, tomatoes with liquid, and broth. Simmer, uncovered, 15 minutes.
1 tablespoon dried oregano	
2 teaspoons cumin	*3* Stir in corn and beans; cook 5 to 10 minutes or until slightly thickened.
¼ teaspoon salt	
3 cups chopped or shredded cooked chicken	*4* Garnish with cheese and sour cream as desired.
1 28-ounce can diced fire-roasted tomatoes	
2 cups fat-free chicken broth (see Note)	
1 10-ounce package frozen corn, thawed	
2 15-ounce cans black beans, rinsed	
Shredded 50-percent-reduced-fat sharp cheddar cheese	
Fat-free sour cream	

Per cup: *267 calories, 23g protein, 7g fat (21 percent calories from fat), 1.1g saturated fat, 31g carbohydrate, 40mg cholesterol, 736mg sodium, 9g fiber.*

Note: *If chili becomes too thick, add extra broth or water to desired consistency.*

EASY ENTERTAINING

Pork Medallions with Red Onion Marmalade

Prep time: 25 min • **Cook time:** About 30 min • **Yield:** 4 servings

Ingredients

2 teaspoons butter, divided

2 medium red onions, thinly sliced

3 tablespoons sugar

2 tablespoons fresh lemon juice

½ teaspoon salt, divided

1 1-pound, well-trimmed pork tenderloin

2 teaspoons lemon zest (yellow part only)

¼ teaspoon coarsely ground black pepper

Directions

1 In a large nonstick skillet, melt 1 teaspoon butter on medium. Add onions and cook about 15 minutes or until soft and golden, stirring occasionally.

2 Stir in sugar, lemon juice, and ¼ teaspoon salt. Reduce heat to low; simmer 5 minutes. Spoon mixture into small bowl; cover to keep warm.

3 Meanwhile, cut tenderloin lengthwise in half. Cut each half crosswise into 4 pieces.

4 Place pork pieces between 2 sheets plastic wrap. With the heel of your hand, flatten to a thickness of ½-inch.

5 In a small bowl, mix lemon zest with remaining salt and the pepper. Rub mixture on 1 side of each medallion.

6 In the skillet you used for Steps 1 and 2, melt remaining butter on medium. Add medallions, lemon side up. Cook 6 to 7 minutes or until pork is just barely pink throughout, turning once.

7 Serve with onion marmalade.

Per serving: 209 calories, 23g protein, 6g fat (25 percent calories from fat), 2.5g saturated fat, 16g carbohydrate, 68mg cholesterol, 352mg sodium, 2g fiber.

Week 19

Sunday *Family*

Buy a **smoked turkey breast** for an easy family meal. Accompany the flavorful bird with **Warm Dijonnaise Potato Salad** (see recipe), which gets a gold star at my house for its good taste. Alongside, add **grilled asparagus** and **whole-grain rolls.** For dessert, buy a **carrot cake.** *Plan ahead:* Save enough turkey and cake and prepare enough potato salad for Monday.

Monday *Heat and Eat*

Use the leftover turkey for **turkey and Swiss sandwiches** on **whole-grain bread.** Spread the bread with chutney and top the turkey and Swiss with shredded lettuce. Add leftover **potato salad** to the plate. Slice a piece of leftover **cake** for dessert.

Tuesday *Budget*

Save some money and make **Skillet Lasagne** (see recipe) for a low-cost meal. Serve it with a **romaine salad** and **garlic bread.** Enjoy **sliced mango** for dessert.

Wednesday *Meatless*

Any burger is a good burger to me. Tonight, opt for **veggie burgers** on **whole-grain buns.** Top with your favorites such as lettuce, tomato, pickles, onions, mustard, and low-fat mayonnaise. Serve with **corn on the cob.** Fresh **strawberries** make a great dessert.

Thursday *Express*

Make it quick tonight with **crab cakes** (frozen) for dinner. Top them with **Cilantro Tartar Sauce.** Mix ½ cup low-fat or regular tartar sauce with ½ cup chopped fresh cilantro and 1 tablespoon fresh lemon or lime juice; spread on the crab cakes. Serve with deli **coleslaw, hash-browned potatoes** (frozen), and **whole-grain bread.** Try **plums** and **oatmeal cookies** for dessert.

Friday *Kids*

The kids can make their own **Grilled Ham and Cheddar on Raisin Bread.** Coat the outside of the bread with cooking spray and grill until golden and cheese melts. Serve with **baby carrots.** Make a **Peanut Butter and Banana Smoothie** to go alongside. For one serving, blend 1 cup cold 1-percent milk, 1 cut-up frozen ripe banana, and 2 tablespoons creamy peanut butter in a blender until smooth.

Saturday *Easy Entertaining*

Salmon and Beet Salad (see recipe) is both pretty and delicious, which makes it great for guests. Serve **New England clam chowder** and **crackers** to start the meal. Finish with **angel food cake** topped with **lemon curd** for dessert.

FAMILY

Warm Dijonnaise Potato Salad

Prep time: 15 min • **Cook time:** About 15 min • **Yield:** 4 servings

Ingredients

¾ **pound small red potatoes, halved**

¾ **pound small Yukon gold potatoes, quartered**

2 thinly sliced green onions

1½ **tablespoons Dijonnaise**

1 tablespoon seasoned rice vinegar

1 tablespoon olive oil

1½ **teaspoons fresh, chopped tarragon**

½ **teaspoon coarse salt**

¼ **teaspoon pepper**

Directions

1 Place potatoes in a pot with cold water; cover and bring to boil. Reduce heat to medium and gently boil 10 to 12 minutes or until potatoes are just tender. Drain.

2 Place potatoes in a large bowl along with the onions. In a small bowl, whisk together the Dijonnaise, vinegar, oil, tarragon, salt, and pepper. Pour over potatoes and toss gently to coat.

3 Serve while still warm or at room temperature.

Per serving: 174 calories, 4g protein, 4g fat (20 percent calories from fat), 0.5g saturated fat, 32g carbohydrate, 0mg cholesterol, 368mg sodium, 5g fiber.

Adapted from Woman's Day *magazine.*

Skillet Lasagne

Prep time: 15 min   •   **Cook time:** About 15 min, plus pasta   •   **Yield:** 5 servings

BUDGET

Ingredients	*Directions*
6 ounces campanella or other small pasta	*1* Cook pasta according to directions; drain.
12 ounces Italian sausage links, casings removed	*2* In a large nonstick skillet, cook sausage, breaking the meat up with the back of a spoon, for 5 minutes or until no longer pink; drain if necessary.
2 14½-ounce cans diced tomatoes with basil, garlic, and oregano	
1 6-ounce can no-salt-added or regular tomato paste	*3* Stir in tomatoes and tomato paste. Simmer 5 minutes. Remove from pan; keep warm.
1 cup part-skim shredded mozzarella cheese	*4* Place half the cooked pasta in bottom of skillet. Pour half the tomato-meat mixture over pasta. Sprinkle with half the cheese; repeat layers.
	5 Cover and cook on medium 4 minutes or until heated through and cheese melts. Remove from heat, let stand 1 minute, and serve.

Per serving: 378 calories, 25g protein, 10g fat (24 percent calories from fat), 4.6g saturated fat, 48g carbohydrate, 35mg cholesterol, 1,412mg sodium, 4g fiber.

EASY ENTERTAINING

Salmon and Beet Salad

Prep time: 20 min, plus marinating time • **Cook time:** 10 min • **Yield:** 4 servings

Ingredients

For the salmon:

1 16-ounce jar whole pickled beets

1 pound salmon fillet with skin, cut into 4 equal pieces

1 5- to 6-ounce package (6 cups) mixed greens

8 ounces cooked fresh green beans

2 tablespoons crumbled cooked bacon

For the dressing:

3 tablespoons reserved liquid from pickled beets, divided

⅓ cup low-fat balsamic or raspberry dressing

1 tablespoon minced green onion

1½ teaspoons chopped fresh dill, plus additional dill for garnish

¼ teaspoon pepper

Directions

1 Drain beets; reserving 3 tablespoons juice (discard remaining juice). In a small bowl, combine beet juice with balsamic or raspberry dressing. Stir in green onion, dill, and pepper; set aside.

2 Place salmon in shallow dish and drizzle with ¼ cup dressing; turn to coat. Cover and marinate in refrigerator for 15 to 30 minutes. Reserve remaining dressing; set aside.

3 Cut beets in half. In a medium bowl, combine beets with 2 tablespoons reserved dressing; toss to coat and set aside.

4 Heat oven to 450 degrees. Place salmon, skin side down, on one half of rimmed baking sheet lined with nonstick foil. Place beets on other half of baking sheet.

5 Roast 8 to 10 minutes or until salmon is cooked through. Remove from oven; discard skin.

6 Divide greens among 4 individual plates. Top with equal amounts of green beans and beets. Place one portion of salmon on each salad. Sprinkle with bacon and additional dill.

7 Drizzle each serving with remaining dressing.

Per serving: 259 calories, 29g protein, 6g fat (20 percent calories from fat), 1.1g saturated fat, 25g carbohydrate, 70mg cholesterol, 380mg sodium, 5g fiber.

Note: *If desired, salmon and beets can be made up to 1 day in advance, refrigerated, and served cold.*

Week 20

Sunday *Family*

Pot Roast with Carrots and Potatoes (see recipe) makes a good family-friendly meal. Add a **mixed green salad** and **dinner rolls** to round it out. Spoon fresh **strawberries** over fat-free **strawberry ice cream** for dessert. *Plan ahead:* Save enough pot roast and some strawberries for Monday; save enough ice cream for Tuesday.

Monday *Heat and Eat*

Use some leftover beef and assemble a **sandwich platter** for an easy Memorial Day meal. Besides the leftover sliced beef, add deli sliced roast chicken or turkey, Swiss cheese, cheddar cheese, potato salad, coleslaw, lettuce, tomatoes, onions, pickles, olives, low-fat mayonnaise, and a variety of mustards. Arrange a basket with **assorted breads** such as whole-grain and rye. For dessert, offer **brownies** with leftover **strawberries.**

Tuesday *Express*

For a quick meal, make **Chicken Salad Nicoise.** Arrange one head Boston lettuce on a serving platter. Mound an 8- to 10-ounce package cooked, carved chicken breast in the center. Arrange 1 16-ounce can rinsed cut green beans, 1 16-ounce can drained sliced potatoes, 1 cup grape tomato halves, and ½ cup pitted whole black olives around the edges. Drizzle with ⅓ cup low-fat balsamic dressing. Serve with **baguettes.** Top leftover **ice cream** with **chocolate sauce.**

Wednesday *Meatless*

Enjoy **Pasta Primavera with Caramelized Onions** (see recipe) for a no-meat meal. Serve the vegetable-packed pasta with a **spinach salad** and **garlic bread.** For dessert, **peaches** garnished with low-fat ricotta cheese are simple.

Thursday *Budget*

Atlanta friend Charlotte Margolin suggests this **Chicken and Collards** recipe for an easy and inexpensive meal. In a 5-quart or larger slow cooker, place 2 to 3 pounds bone-in, skinless chicken thighs. Add 1 16-ounce package collard greens, 1 thinly sliced Vidalia onion, 2 minced garlic cloves, 2 ribs finely chopped celery, 1 cup pale dry sherry (or fat-free chicken broth), and 2 cups fat-free chicken broth. Using tongs, mix ingredients (except chicken). Cover and cook on low 9 or 10 hours. (Adapted from *American Pi, The Cookbook,* Paideia School [Wimmer Publishing].) To serve, spoon cooked **rice** into a shallow bowl or plate, top with collards, chicken (discard bones), and some juice. Add **cornbread** (from a mix). Fresh **pineapple** makes a light dessert.

Friday *Kids*

It's **Fish 'n' Chips** for the kids' dinner tonight. Cook frozen fish fillets as the package directs. Cut to size, and serve in toasted hot dog buns spread with **tartar sauce.** Serve with **oven fries** (frozen) and **baby carrots.** For dessert, dip **orange sections** in **chocolate pudding.**

Saturday *Easy Entertaining*

Serve your favorite guests **Walnut Chicken Sauté** (see recipe). Add **sugar snap peas, a red-tipped lettuce salad,** and **baguettes.** For dessert, buy a **lemon meringue pie.**

FAMILY

Pot Roast with Carrots and Potatoes

Prep time: 15 min • **Cook time:** 7–8 hr • **Yield:** 4–6 servings

Ingredients

1 2 ½- to 3-pound boneless well-trimmed shoulder or chuck roast

2 cups baby carrots

2 medium new potatoes, halved

1 large onion, sliced

1 rib celery, cut into 1-inch pieces

1 cup tomato juice mixed with ½ teaspoon hot sauce

½ cup water

1 envelope from 2.2-ounce box dry onion soup mix

3 tablespoons flour

¼ teaspoon pepper

Directions

1 Place roast in a 4-quart or larger slow cooker. Arrange carrots, potatoes, onion, and celery on and around roast.

2 In a medium bowl, combine tomato juice with hot sauce, water, onion soup mix, flour, and pepper; spoon over vegetables.

3 Cover and cook on low 7 to 8 hours or until roast and vegetables are tender.

4 Place roast and vegetables on a large platter; spoon sauce over all. Serve immediately.

Per serving (beef): 220 calories, 36g protein, 7g fat (31 percent calories from fat), 2.8g saturated fat, no carbohydrate, 72mg cholesterol, 58mg sodium, no fiber.

Per serving (vegetables/sauce): 148 calories, 4g protein, 1g fat (5 percent calories from fat), no saturated fat, 32g carbohydrate, no cholesterol, 935mg sodium, 4g fiber.

Pasta Primavera with Caramelized Onions

MEATLESS

Prep time: 15 min • **Cook time:** About 30 min, plus pasta • **Yield:** 5 servings

Ingredients	Directions
8 ounces penne pasta	**1** Cook pasta according to directions; drain.
2 tablespoons olive oil	
2 medium onions, halved and thinly sliced	**2** Meanwhile, heat oil in a large nonstick skillet on medium-low. Add onions; cook 15 minutes or until golden. Add both peppers and zucchini; cook 8 to 10 minutes or until softened.
1 medium red bell pepper, sliced into ¼-inch strips	
1 small green bell pepper, sliced into ¼-inch strips	**3** Return cooked pasta to pan; add vegetables and pesto sauce to pasta, and toss gently to coat.
2 large (7 inches long) zucchini, halved lengthwise and sliced ¼ inch thick	
⅓ cup basil pesto sauce	**4** Spoon into bowls and sprinkle cheese on top.
¼ cup freshly grated parmesan cheese	

Per serving: 324 calories, 10g protein, 14g fat (35 percent calories from fat), 2.4g saturated fat, 46g carbohydrate, 4mg cholesterol, 272mg sodium, 7g fiber.

EASY ENTERTAINING

Walnut Chicken Sauté

Prep time: 15 min • **Cook time:** About 30 min • **Yield:** 4 servings

Ingredients

1¼ pounds small red potatoes, cut into 1-inch pieces

1 teaspoon canola oil

4 boneless, skinless chicken breasts (about 1¼ pounds)

Salt and pepper to taste

8 ounces mushroom caps, halved or quartered

¼ cup dry white wine

½ cup fat-free chicken broth, divided

1½ teaspoons cornstarch

¼ cup chopped green onions

1 tablespoon chopped fresh rosemary leaves

½ cup chopped toasted walnuts

Parsley sprig for garnish if desired

Directions

1 Cover potatoes with cold water in a medium saucepan; cover pan, and bring to a boil. Cook 7 to 10 minutes or until barely tender. Drain well; set aside.

2 Heat oil in a large, nonstick skillet on medium. Season chicken with a little salt and pepper. Brown chicken 3 minutes on each side; remove and set aside.

3 To same skillet, add potatoes and mushrooms and cook, tossing and stirring frequently, 7 to 10 minutes or until lightly browned. Add wine and 1/4 cup broth; stir.

4 Place chicken on top of vegetables. Cover and simmer 5 minutes or until chicken is no longer pink and juices are clear.

5 Add cornstarch to remaining broth and blend until smooth. Add to skillet, along with green onions and rosemary. Push chicken aside, and stir and cook 1 minute or until sauce thickens. Stir in walnuts.

6 Arrange chicken and vegetables on a platter and garnish with parsley if desired.

Per serving: 403 calories, 40g protein, 13g fat (28 percent calories from fat), 1.5g saturated fat, 30g carbohydrate, 82mg cholesterol, 156mg sodium, 5g fiber.

Week 21

Sunday *Family*

Today, put **Gingered Roast Pork Tenderloin and Supersweet Corn** (see recipe) on the menu. Serve with **green beans**, a **romaine salad** and **sourdough bread**. Buy a **peach pie** for dessert. ***Plan ahead:*** Prepare an extra pork tenderloin for Monday; save enough pie for Tuesday.

Monday *Heat and Eat*

Whip up a quick **Pork Stir-Fry.** Use frozen stir-fry vegetables and a bottled stir-fry sauce. Toss the leftover pork (cut into ½ inch strips) into the mixture the last 2 minutes, and stir-fry until hot. Serve your creation over **rice** with **breadsticks** on the side. For dessert, **red and green grapes** always taste good.

Tuesday *Meatless*

Citrus Bean Salad makes a good no-meat dinner. In a large bowl, combine 1 15- to 16-ounce can each rinsed black beans and garbanzo beans, 1 11-ounce can drained Mandarin oranges (reserve 2 tablespoons juice), 1 small diced yellow bell pepper, ⅓ cup finely chopped fresh cilantro, ⅓ cup low-fat balsamic vinaigrette, the reserved orange juice, and ¾ teaspoon chili powder; toss to mix. Just before serving, add 1 chopped avocado; toss to mix. Serve with **vegetable soup** and **crusty rolls.** For dessert, slice the leftover **pie** and top it with fat-free **vanilla ice cream.** ***Plan ahead:*** Save enough ice cream for Thursday.

Wednesday *Kids*

You'll be a hero when you serve the kids **Taco Supper Skillet.** In a large nonstick skillet, cook 8 ounces 93- to 95-percent-lean ground beef on medium-high heat for 5 to 7 minutes or until no longer pink. Stir 1 1.25-ounce package 40-percent-less-sodium taco seasoning mix, 2¼ cups water, 1½ cups wagon wheel or other pasta, 1½ cups frozen corn, and 1 15-ounce can rinsed pinto beans into beef. Heat to boiling; stir. Reduce heat to medium-low. Cover; cook 10 to 15 minutes or until pasta is tender and most of the liquid has been absorbed. Stir in ½ cup low-fat sour cream. Remove from heat. Sprinkle with 1 cup shredded 50-percent-reduced-fat cheddar cheese, and serve. Add **celery sticks** and **cornbread muffins** (from a mix). Slice **kiwifruit** for dessert.

Thursday *Express*

Stop by the deli for **egg salad** and make sandwiches on whole-grain bread lined with lettuce. Add **tomato soup.** For dessert, top leftover **ice cream** with **chocolate sauce.**

Friday *Budget*

Enjoy this **Frittata with Onion, Basil, and Tomato** (see recipe). Alongside, add **hash-browned potatoes** (frozen), a **lettuce wedge**, and **whole-grain bread.** For dessert, it's time for fresh **plums.**

Saturday *Easy Entertaining*

Everyone is sure to like this simple **Lemon Dill Tilapia** (see recipe). Serve it with **parsley buttered rice** (toss cooked rice with a little butter and chopped fresh parsley), fresh **asparagus,** and **whole-grain rolls. Blueberry Lemon Tarts** are an easy dessert. Heat oven to 350 degrees. From a refrigerated package of low-fat biscuits, roll each biscuit into a 4-inch round. Line each of 8 large muffin cups with dough. Prick dough all over with fork to prevent it from rising too much. Bake about 10 minutes or until browned. Cool; remove shells from pan. Fill with instant lemon pudding made with 1-percent milk, and top with fresh blueberries.

FAMILY

Gingered Roast Pork Tenderloin and Supersweet Corn

Prep time: 20 min • **Cook time:** 25 min, plus standing time • **Yield:** 4 servings

Ingredients

1 cup orange juice, divided

2 tablespoons canola oil

3 to 4 teaspoons ground ginger

2 teaspoons minced garlic

¼ teaspoon salt

½ teaspoon pepper

1 pound well-trimmed pork tenderloin

4 ears corn on the cob, husks removed

1 teaspoon cornstarch

Sliced green onions, limes, and oranges for garnish

Directions

1 Place a shallow roasting pan in the upper third of the oven. Heat oven to 425 degrees.

2 In a small bowl, combine 2 tablespoons orange juice, the oil, ginger, garlic, salt, and pepper. Brush all sides of pork and corn, reserving 1 tablespoon orange-ginger mixture for later use.

3 Place pork in hot roasting pan. Roast 10 minutes. Add corn to pan; turn pork and roast 10 more minutes or until internal temperature reaches 155 degrees and some of the corn kernels are light brown.

4 Remove from oven and place pork and corn on a platter; cover with foil and let stand 5 minutes.

5 Meanwhile, add remaining orange juice to roasting pan; stir to loosen any browned bits. Transfer to a small saucepan; stir in cornstarch and reserved orange-ginger mixture. Cook and stir 5 minutes or until clear and thickened.

6 Cut pork into ½-inch slices. Serve with orange-ginger sauce. Garnish with sliced onions, and serve with lime and orange wedges if desired.

Per serving: 276 calories, 26g protein, 9g fat (27 percent calories from fat), 1.8g saturated fat, 26g carbohydrate, 63mg cholesterol, 205mg sodium, 3g fiber.

Frittata with Onion, Basil, and Tomato

BUDGET

Prep time: 20 min • **Cook time:** About 30 min • **Yield:** 4 wedges

Ingredients	Directions
1 medium onion **2 tablespoons olive oil, divided** **1 14½-ounce can diced fire-roasted tomatoes, drained** **½ cup chopped fresh basil, divided** **4 eggs** **4 egg whites** **¼ cup freshly grated parmesan cheese**	**1** Cut onion in half lengthwise. Cut each half into narrow wedges. In a large nonstick skillet, heat 1 tablespoon oil. Add onion and cook 10 to 12 minutes or until golden. **2** Remove about ⅓ of the onion from skillet and keep warm. Add tomatoes and all but 1 tablespoon of basil to skillet, and cook with onions 1 minute. **3** Place eggs and egg whites in medium bowl, and beat with a fork. Add onion-tomato-basil mixture to eggs, stirring just to combine. **4** Heat remaining 1 tablespoon oil in skillet on medium until hot. Pour egg mixture into hot skillet. Cover and cook on low 12 to 15 minutes or until set. **5** Top with reserved onions and basil; sprinkle with cheese. Let stand 2 minutes; cut into wedges, and serve warm.

Per wedge: 214 calories, 14g protein, 13g fat (54 percent calories from fat), 3.3g saturated fat, 12g carbohydrate, 216mg cholesterol, 457mg sodium, 3g fiber.

EASY ENTERTAINING

Lemon Dill Tilapia

Prep time: 10 min • **Cook time:** 18–22 min • **Yield:** 4 servings

Ingredients	*Directions*

Ingredients

4 5-ounce tilapia fillets

½ teaspoon salt

½ teaspoon pepper

2 sliced lemons, cut into 12 slices total

¼ cup shredded carrots

2 tablespoons chopped fresh dill

2 tablespoons chopped fresh parsley

4 teaspoons butter

Directions

1 Heat oven to 400 degrees. Sprinkle tilapia with salt and pepper.

2 Cut 4 pieces of parchment paper into 13-x-9-inch rectangles. Place three lemon slices crosswise in center of one rectangle. Top with one fillet. Repeat with remaining lemon slices, tilapia, and paper.

3 Sprinkle fillets evenly with carrots, dill, and parsley. Top each with 1 teaspoon butter.

4 Fold paper to make a packet; crease the folds. (Leave enough space to allow air to circulate in packet.)

5 Place on a baking sheet; bake 18 to 22 minutes or until fish is opaque throughout. Serve immediately.

Per serving: 174 calories, 29g protein, 6g fat (32 percent calories from fat), 3.2g saturated fat, 1g carbohydrate, 81mg cholesterol, 397mg sodium, no fiber.

Adapted from Cooking Light *magazine.*

Week 22

 ## Sunday *Family*

Celebrate family day by serving your own **grilled chicken**. Add **brown rice** on the side along with **Summer Squash Casserole** (see recipe), a **mixed greens salad**, and **whole-grain rolls. Apple cobbler** makes a tasty dessert. ***Plan ahead:*** Grill enough chicken and save enough cobbler for Monday.

 ## Monday *Heat and Eat*

With the leftover chicken, make delicious **Mexican Green Rice with Chicken and Avocado** (see recipe) for dinner. Serve with **corn tortillas**. Top the leftover **cobbler** with light **whipped cream** for dessert.

 ## Tuesday *Kids*

Serve the kids **Hamburger Steak with Gravy** (see recipe). Alongside, add **mashed potatoes, soft rolls,** and **carrot-raisin salad.** In a small bowl, combine 1 8-ounce container plain low-fat yogurt, 1 8- to 10-ounce bag shredded carrots, ½ cup raisins, and ⅛ teaspoon each cinnamon and salt; mix until well combined. For dessert, **creamsicles** are kid-friendly. ***Plan ahead:*** Save enough carrot-raisin salad for Wednesday.

 ## Wednesday *Budget*

Make budget-friendly **Tuna Melts** tonight. Spread deli tuna on rye bread; top with slices of 50-percent-reduced-fat cheddar cheese and another slice of bread. Brown in a covered nonstick skillet until cheese melts. Serve with **baked chips** and leftover **carrot raisin salad**. Dessert is **banana pudding.**

 ## Thursday *Meatless*

Penne Pasta with Creamy Tomato Sauce couldn't be easier. Cook 8 ounces penne pasta according to directions. Add 2 cups fresh broccoli florets the last 2 minutes of cook time; drain. Meanwhile, heat 1 tablespoon extra-virgin olive oil in a large saucepan. Add 1 cup marinara sauce, 1 teaspoon dried basil, and ½ teaspoon crushed red pepper. Simmer 2 minutes on medium. Stir in 1 cup 1-percent milk; heat gently on low. Remove from heat. Stir in ¾ cup freshly grated parmesan cheese. Toss with pasta and broccoli, and serve with a **romaine salad** and **garlic bread. Pears** are your dessert.

 ## Friday *Express*

For a fast meal, **Chicken Pizza** is the answer. Heat oven to 450 degrees. Place 1 12-inch ready-to-serve pizza crust on a rimmed cookie sheet. Spread 2 cups refrigerated Lloyd's Honey Hickory Barbecue Sauce with Shredded Chicken (or another brand) over crust. Arrange 1 cup shredded mozzarella cheese and 1 each thinly sliced onion and green bell pepper (separated into rings) on top of cheese. Bake 12 to 14 minutes or until cheese is bubbly and chicken is hot. Serve immediately. Add a salad of **sliced avocado** and **lettuce.** Enjoy fresh **blueberries** for a light dessert.

 ## Saturday *Easy Entertaining*

Invite special guests for **Grilled Lamb Chops**. In a small bowl, combine 2 teaspoons cracked black pepper, a pinch cayenne pepper, 2 tablespoons minced garlic, 2 tablespoons chopped fresh rosemary (1 tablespoon dried), 2 tablespoons fresh minced parsley, and ½ teaspoon salt. Pat 8 lamb loin chops dry with paper towels; roll in seasoning blend. Cover and refrigerate 30 minutes. Remove from refrigerator; warm to room temperature. In a skillet on medium-high heat, quickly sear chops in 2 tablespoons hot olive oil. Remove chops; place on heated grill. Grill 7 to 14 minutes for medium-rare to medium doneness. While the grill is hot, add some of your favorite **vegetables** to the grill. Serve **corn on the cob** and **crusty bread** to round out the meal. For dessert, **lemon sorbet** with **butter cookies** is easy and tastes good.

FAMILY

Summer Squash Casserole

Prep time: 15 min • **Cook time:** About 1 hr. • **Yield:** 10 servings

Ingredients

2¼ pounds summer squash, quartered lengthwise and thinly sliced crosswise (about 10 cups)

⅔ cup onion, finely chopped

1 4-ounce can chopped green chilies, drained

1 4-ounce can chopped jalapeños, drained

½ teaspoon salt

2 cups shredded 50-percent-reduced-fat sharp cheddar cheese, divided

¼ cup flour

¾ cup mild or medium salsa

Thinly sliced green onions for garnish

Directions

1 Heat oven to 400 degrees. Coat a 9-x-13-inch baking dish with cooking spray.

2 In a large bowl, combine squash, onion, chilies, jalapeños, salt, and half the cheese. Sprinkle with flour; toss to coat.

3 Spread mixture in the prepared dish. Cover with nonstick foil. Bake 35 to 40 minutes or until bubbly and squash is tender.

4 Remove from oven and remove foil. Spread salsa on top; sprinkle with remaining cheese. Bake, uncovered, 20 minutes or until golden and heated through.

5 Just before serving, garnish with green onions if desired.

Per serving: 99 calories, 8g protein, 4g fat (33 percent calories from fat), 2.5g saturated fat, 10g carbohydrate, 12mg cholesterol, 555mg sodium, 2g fiber.

Adapted from Eating Well *magazine.*

HEAT AND EAT

Mexican Green Rice with Chicken and Avocado

Prep time: 15 min • **Yield:** 4 servings

Ingredients	*Directions*
1½ cups cooked rice	*1* In a large bowl, combine rice, beans, tomato, lettuce, cilantro, and half the salad dressing; toss.
1 15-ounce can black beans, rinsed	
1 cup chopped tomato	*2* Arrange on a platter, lined with lettuce if desired.
1 cup shredded lettuce	
¼ cup chopped fresh cilantro	*3* In the same bowl, combine chicken, avocado, and remaining half of dressing. Spoon over rice salad.
3 tablespoons low-fat oil and vinegar salad dressing, divided	
1½ cups diced chicken	
1 ripe avocado, halved and cut into cubes	

Per serving: 372 calories, 25g protein, 13g fat (32 percent calories from fat), 2.2g saturated fat, 38g carbohydrate, 46mg cholesterol, 499mg sodium, 10g fiber.

KIDS

Hamburger Steak with Gravy

Prep time: 15 min • **Cook time:** About 15 min • **Yield:** 4 servings

Ingredients

2 honey-wheat or whole-wheat bread slices

1 pound ground round beef

1 egg, lightly beaten

2 cloves minced garlic

½ teaspoon salt

¼ teaspoon pepper

1 1.2-ounce envelope brown gravy mix

1½ cups water

1 tablespoon canola oil

Directions

1 Process bread slices in a food processor 10 seconds or until finely chopped. Place crumbs in a large bowl; add beef, egg, garlic, salt, and pepper. Gently combine until blended.

2 Shape mixture into 4 4-inch patties. Whisk together gravy mix and water; set aside.

3 In a large nonstick skillet, heat oil on medium-high. Cook patties 2 minutes on each side or just until browned. Remove from skillet.

4 Stir in prepared gravy and bring to a simmer. Return patties to skillet and spoon gravy over each patty.

5 Cover, reduce heat to low, and simmer 8 to 10 minutes or until cooked through.

Per serving: 337 calories, 27g protein, 18g fat (48 percent calories from fat), 5g saturated fat, 16g carbohydrate, 118mg cholesterol, 910mg sodium, 1g fiber.

Adapted from Southern Living *magazine.*

Week 23

 Sunday *Family*

Help Dad show off his cooking skills with **Santa Fe Grilled Steaks and Corn** (see recipe). Add **Spicy Black Bean Salad** alongside. In a medium bowl, combine 1 15-ounce can rinsed and drained black beans, 1 large peeled orange cut into ½-inch pieces, ⅓ cup thinly sliced green onions, ¼ cup fresh lime juice, and 2 table-spoons canola oil; mix gently. Serve with **crusty rolls.** For dessert, present Dad with your homemade **brownies.** While still warm, top with small pieces of peppermint patties and a little chocolate syrup. Garnish with light whipped cream. ***Plan ahead:*** Save enough steak and brownies for Monday.

 Monday *Heat and Eat*

Make **Steak Roll-Ups** for a quick meal. In a medium bowl, mix 1 cup chopped cooked steak, 3 cups torn fresh spinach leaves, 1 cup 50-percent-reduced-fat shredded jalapeño cheese, ½ medium red bell pepper cut into strips, and ¼ cup each sliced green onions and chopped fresh cilantro. Place 4 7- to 8-inch fat-free flour tortillas on a square of wax paper. Divide beef/spinach mixture, and spoon down center of each tortilla. Microwave each for 30 seconds on high (100-percent power). Roll; cut crosswise into quarters. Serve hot with **rice.** Serve the leftover **brownies** for dessert.

 Tuesday *Meatless*

Start your no-meat meal with canned **minestrone soup**. Follow the soup with **Tex-Mex Salad** (see recipe). Add **crackers.** For dessert, top **ice cream** with fat-free **butterscotch sauce.**

 Wednesday *Express*

For an easy meal, buy refrigerated **roasted chicken** and visit the deli for **tabbouleh** and some **carrot salad.** Add **flatbread.** Pick up some **banana pudding** for a homey dessert.

 Thursday *Budget*

Be budget-wise and try flavorful **Vegetable-Turkey Chili** (see recipe) to up your vegetables, fiber, folate, potassium, and vitamin C. Serve the nutrition-packed dish with **brown rice,** a **lettuce wedge,** and **cornbread** (from a mix). Fresh **strawberries** with light whipped cream make a great dessert. ***Plan ahead:*** Save enough chili for Friday.

 Friday *Kids*

Make **Turkey Chili Tacos** for the kids. Warm the leftover chili, and spoon into warmed taco shells. Top with shredded 50-percent-reduced-fat cheddar cheese, mild salsa, and fat-free sour cream. Add vegetarian **refried beans** to the plate. Dip **jicama sticks** into ranch dressing for some crunch. The kids will like **popsicles** for dessert.

 Saturday *Easy Entertaining*

Treat guests to zesty **Flounder with Asian Glaze.** Heat broiler. Coat one side of 4 6-ounce flounder fillets with cooking spray. Place coated side down on rack in broiler pan. Combine ¼ cup low-fat mayonnaise, 1 tablespoon light soy sauce, 2 teaspoons peeled and grated fresh ginger, and 1 seeded and minced jalapeño pepper. Spread mixture over flounder; broil 4 minutes or until mayonnaise mixture is lightly browned and fish flakes easily. Serve with **rice** and steamed fresh **asparagus.** Add a **Boston lettuce salad** and **baguettes.** For dessert, **Blueberry-Mango Colada** is refreshing. In a large bowl, combine 2 cups fresh blueberries, 2 mangoes (peeled, seeded, and sliced), and ¼ cup frozen concentrated piña colada mix (thawed). Spoon mixture into stemmed dessert dishes. Garnish with blueberries, mango slices, and thin lime slices threaded onto long wooden picks, if desired.

FAMILY

Santa Fe Grilled Steaks and Corn

Prep time: 5 min, plus soaking time • **Cook time:** 25–30 min • **Yield:** 4 servings

Ingredients

4 ears corn on the cob in husks

½ cup steak sauce

2 cloves minced garlic

1½ teaspoons chili powder

½ teaspoon cumin

3 beef porterhouse steaks, cut 1-inch thick

2 tablespoons butter

Directions

1 Peel corn, leaving husks attached at base; remove silk. Rewrap corn in husks; tie closed. Soak in cold water 30 minutes.

2 Meanwhile, in a small bowl, combine steak sauce, garlic, chili powder, and cumin; reserve ¼ cup glaze. Heat grill.

3 Drain corn; place on medium-hot grill. Grill, uncovered, 20 to 30 minutes, turning frequently.

4 After 10 minutes, place steaks on grill with corn. Grill, uncovered, 14 to 16 minutes for medium-rare to medium doneness, turning occasionally and brushing with glaze during last 5 minutes.

5 Combine reserved ¼ cup glaze with butter in a 2-cup measuring cup. Microwave on medium (50-percent power) 3 to 4 minutes or until butter is melted. Carefully peel corn; brush with chili butter.

6 Reserve 1 steak for Monday. Divide remaining 2 steaks into 4 portions; serve with remaining chili butter.

Per serving: 385 calories, 33g protein, 20g fat (45 percent calories from fat), 8.3g saturated fat, 20g carbohydrate, 86mg cholesterol, 367mg sodium, 3g fiber.

MEATLESS

Tex-Mex Salad

Prep time: 15 min • **Yield:** 4 servings

Ingredients

1 15- to 16-ounce can each black and garbanzo beans (chickpeas), rinsed and drained

1 peeled orange with white pith removed, quartered lengthwise and sliced

1 small yellow bell pepper, diced

⅓ cup finely chopped fresh cilantro

½ cup bottled orange vinaigrette or other fruit vinaigrette

¾ teaspoon chili powder

6 red radishes

1 avocado

2 hard-cooked sliced eggs for garnish

Directions

1 In a large bowl, combine beans, orange, bell pepper, cilantro, vinaigrette, and chili powder; toss to mix and coat.

2 Before serving, thinly slice radishes, and peel and dice avocado. Add both to bean mixture; toss to mix and coat. Garnish with sliced eggs. Serve immediately.

Per serving: *374 calories, 16g protein, 16g fat (38 percent calories from fat), 2.6g saturated fat, 43g carbohydrate, 106mg cholesterol, 889mg sodium, 15g fiber.*

BUDGET

Vegetable-Turkey Chili

Prep time: 15 min • **Cook time:** About 35 min • **Yield:** 6 servings

Ingredients	Directions

Ingredients

2 teaspoons canola oil

1 pound ground turkey breast

1 large onion, chopped

1 green bell pepper, chopped

2 tablespoons chili powder

1 teaspoon each cumin, garlic powder, and black pepper

1 14½-ounce can stewed tomatoes

1 14-ounce can fat-free chicken broth

¾ cup tomato-vegetable juice cocktail (such as V-8)

1 15-ounce can pinto beans, rinsed and drained

1 cup frozen corn

1 small red onion, chopped

Directions

1 Heat oil in a large pot on medium. Add turkey and cook 5 minutes or until no longer pink.

2 Add onion and cook 6 minutes or until softened.

3 Add green pepper, chili powder, cumin, garlic powder, and black pepper. Cook 4 minutes or until green pepper is softened and spices are fragrant.

4 Stir in tomatoes with juice, broth, tomato-vegetable juice, beans, and corn; cover and simmer 15 to 20 minutes, stirring occasionally.

5 Garnish with red onion, and serve immediately.

**Per serving:** 253 calories, 25g protein, 3g fat (12 percent calories from fat), 0.5g saturated fat, 31g carbohydrate, 51mg cholesterol, 641mg sodium, 7g fiber.

Adapted from a National Cancer Institute recipe.

Week 24

Sunday *Family*

Liven up family day with **Cajun Roast Pork Loin** (see recipe). Serve it with **Creole potato salad** by doctoring your favorite potato salad with some diced red and green bell pepper, diced onion, and diced celery. Season with spicy brown mustard and a dash of hot pepper sauce. Add **sliced tomatoes** and **baguettes** on the side. For dessert, **Spiced Tapioca with Fruit Salsa** makes a sweet statement. Combine 4 cups store-bought tapioca pudding with ¼ teaspoon allspice and 1 tablespoon fresh lime juice. Separately, combine 1½ cups fresh diced strawberries, 1 diced kiwifruit, ¼ teaspoon allspice, and 2 teaspoons lime juice; toss to mix. Spoon pudding into 8 stemmed dessert dishes and top with salsa. *Plan ahead:* Save enough pork and dessert for Monday.

Monday *Heat and Eat*

Use some of the leftover pork for **Pork Sub Sandwiches.** Cut a 1-pound loaf French bread in half horizontally. Spread bottom half with fat-free cream cheese; layer with sliced pork, sliced provolone cheese, and canned drained sliced mushrooms. Replace top. Cut loaf in half; wrap in paper towels. Microwave on high 45 seconds. Remove top; add shredded lettuce, sliced tomatoes, sliced onion, and thinly sliced banana peppers. Replace top; cut into serving portions. Serve with **baked chips** and **pickles.** Present the leftover **tapioca** for dessert.

Tuesday *Budget*

You could buy one, but why not prepare this **Tuscan Pizza?** Heat oven to 425 degrees. Thinly slice ½ pound spicy Italian turkey sausage and cook in a large nonstick skillet about 3 minutes. Remove from skillet; set aside. To skillet, add 2 medium onions, cut into thin wedges, and 1 each red and green bell pepper, cut into thin strips; cook on medium about 10 minutes or until softened. Spread 1½ cups pasta sauce on a ready-to-bake pizza crust. Sprinkle with 1 cup shredded mixed cheeses. Top cheese with sausage, onion, and pepper mixture. Sprinkle with 1 more cup cheese and 1 teaspoon dried oregano. Bake 20 minutes or until cheese is melted and crust is golden. Serve with a **spinach salad.** For dessert, **oatmeal cookies** are a favorite.

Wednesday *Meatless*

Skip meat tonight and enjoy **Vegetable Curry** (see recipe). Serve over **basmati rice** and add a **lettuce wedge** and **flatbread** alongside. Enjoy **pears** for dessert.

Thursday *Kids*

The adults might want to eat out tonight while the children make their own **peanut butter and sliced apple sandwiches** (sprinkle the apples with cinnamon). Add **carrot salad** to the plate. Dessert is **chocolate pudding** with fresh **strawberries** and light **whipped cream.**

Friday *Express*

For a quick meal, **grilled mozzarella and tomato sandwiches on Italian bread** are a twist on an old favorite. Serve with **minestrone soup.** Fresh **pineapple** is a summery dessert.

Saturday *Easy Entertaining*

Chicken Paprika (see recipe) is a great meal for guests. Serve the easy, flavor-packed dish over **no-yolk noodles.** Add a **bibb lettuce salad** and **whole-grain rolls.** Buy a **carrot cake** for dessert.

FAMILY

Cajun Roast Pork Loin

Prep time: About 10 min • **Cook time:** 40–50 min, plus standing time • **Yield:** 8–10 servings

Ingredients

1 2- to 2½-pound boneless pork loin roast, well-trimmed

3 tablespoons paprika

½ teaspoon cayenne pepper

1 tablespoon garlic powder

2 teaspoons dried oregano

2 teaspoons dried thyme

½ teaspoon salt

½ teaspoon white pepper

½ teaspoon cumin

¼ teaspoon nutmeg

Directions

1 Heat oven to 350 degrees. Combine all seasonings and rub over all surfaces of roast.

2 Place on a rack in a shallow roasting pan lined with foil. Roast 20 minutes per pound or until internal temperature reaches 150 degrees.

3 Remove from oven; tent with foil and let stand 10 minutes. Slice and serve.

Per serving: 173 calories, 23g protein, 8g fat (40 percent calories from fat), 2.7g saturated fat, 3g carbohydrate, 63mg cholesterol, 200mg sodium, 1g fiber.

Ring in the New Year with this Parmesan-Crusted Tenderloin with Savory Mushroom Sauce. Find it in Week 52.

This Chickpea and Tomato Curry will make you forget about meat for a night. Turn to Week 42 for the recipe.

Impress your sweetie with Dark Chocolate-Tangerine Truffles for Valentine's Day! See the recipe in Week 5.

This Walnut Chicken Sauté is sure to please. Flip to Week 20 for the recipe.

Spicy Linguine with Shrimp will delight any seafood lover. Find the recipe in Week 49.

Celebrate Easter with the family and enjoy Baked Ham with Honey Apricot Glaze. Turn to Week 11 for the recipe.

Make your mom proud and prepare Almond-Chocolate Baked French Toast on Mother's Day. See the recipe in Week 18.

This Fresh and Fruity Salad includes spinach, beets, peaches, blueberries, and almonds. Head to Week 36 for the recipe.

Try Grilled Lime Chicken with Avocado Salsa for a flavor sensation. Check out the recipe in Week 34.

Serve your guests Orange-Thyme Broiled Salmon for a special meal. Find the recipe in Week 2's menu.

With leftover chicken and some avocado, make delicious Mexican Green Rice. Turn to Week 22 for the recipe.

Linguine with Spinach-Almond Pesto is knock-your-socks-off delicious! See the recipe in Week 32.

McCormick In

Avocados from Mexico

This flavorful Pork and Supersweet Corn combo is a pretty and scrumptious one-dish meal. See the recipe in Week 33.

Add Cranberry Walnut Co
your favorite recipes file.
Week 14's menu for the re

Desserts like this Star-Spangled Blueberry Parfait are a part of the 7-Day Menu Planner. Flip to Week 25 for the recipe.

For a change from the routine family meal, put Gingered Roast Pork Tenderloin and Supersweet Corn on the menu. Flip to Week 21 for the recipe.

Make family night special with Turkey and Vegetable Skewers with Walnut Lime Curry Sauce. Turn to Week 28 for the recipe

This Blueberry-Mango Colada makes a refreshing dessert. Find the recipe in the menu for Week 23.

You'll love these mouthwatering Roasted Chicken Thighs with Sherried Grapes and Watercress. See Week 16 for the recipe.

Parmesan-Crusted Cubed Steaks make the perfect meal on a frosty winter night. Check out the recipe in Week 8.

For a special family meal, try Mediterranean Pork Kebabs served with couscous and chopped kalamata olives. See Week 47 for the recipe.

Colorful and healthy, a Salmon and Beet Salad is perfect to serve to guests. Turn to Week 19 for the recipe.

Surprise the family with these Moroccan-Style Beef Kebabs with Spiced Bulgur. Find the recipe in Week 48.

This Tuscan Pizza is made with spicy Italian turkey sausage and is budget-friendly. Check out Week 24's menu for the recipe.

Vegetable Curry

Prep time: 15 min • **Cook time:** 6–7 hr • **Yield:** 9 cups

MEATLESS

Ingredients

1 large onion, chopped

1½ pounds Yukon gold potatoes, quartered

4 cups butternut squash, cut into 1½-inch pieces

4 cups cauliflower florets

1 15-ounce can chickpeas, rinsed

1 medium red bell pepper, cut into 1-inch pieces

1 14-ounce can light coconut milk

¼ cup flour

2 to 3 teaspoons red curry paste (see Note)

1 cup frozen green peas

Fat-free sour cream for garnish

Chopped fresh cilantro for garnish

Directions

1 In a 4-quart or larger slow cooker, place onion, potatoes, squash, cauliflower, chickpeas, and bell pepper; mix well.

2 In a medium bowl, whisk together the coconut milk, flour, and curry paste. Pour over vegetables.

3 Cover and cook on low 6 to 7 hours or until vegetables are tender.

4 Stir in peas; cover and let stand 5 minutes.

5 Garnish with sour cream and cilantro.

Per cup: 199 calories, 7g protein, 3g fat (13 percent calories from fat), 1.5g saturated fat, 38g carbohydrate, 0mg cholesterol, 199mg sodium, 7g fiber.

Note: *For a spicier curry, add more red curry paste.*

EASY ENTERTAINING

Chicken Paprika

Prep time: 10 min • **Cook time:** About 20 min • **Yield:** 4 servings

Ingredients

4 4- to 5-ounce boneless, skinless chicken breasts

2½ teaspoons paprika, divided

½ teaspoon kosher salt

⅛ teaspoon ground black pepper

1 tablespoon olive oil

1 cup chopped onion

1 14½-ounce can no-salt-added diced tomatoes

⅓ cup coffee creamer or light cream

Chopped parsley for garnish if desired

Directions

1 Flatten chicken between two pieces of wax paper until an even thickness (½ inch).

2 Season with ½ teaspoon paprika, salt, and pepper.

3 Heat oil in a large nonstick skillet on medium-high. Add chicken; cook 3 minutes per side or until browned. Remove chicken from skillet; cover to keep warm.

4 Add onion to skillet; cook and stir 4 minutes. Stir in tomatoes and remaining paprika. Bring to boil.

5 Return chicken to skillet. Reduce heat to low; cover and simmer 8 to 10 minutes or until chicken is cooked through.

6 Stir in cream until well-blended. Garnish with parsley as desired.

Per serving: 221 calories, 28g protein, 6g fat (26 percent calories from fat), 0.9g saturated fat, 12g carbohydrate, 66mg cholesterol, 357mg sodium, 3g fiber.

Week 25

 ### Sunday *Family*

Make family day special with **Flank Steak Verde.** Brush 2 1-pound flank steaks (1-inch thick) with canola oil; grill 9 to 11 minutes, turning once, for medium-rare to medium. Remove to cutting board; let stand 5 minutes before slicing. Meanwhile, combine 1 cup salsa verde (green salsa) and 1 cup cilantro leaves in a food processor. Process until smooth, and serve with steak. Serve **roasted red potatoes, tomato wedges,** and **whole-grain bread.** For a special dessert, **cherry cheesecake** is delicious and light. With electric mixer on high, beat 1 8-ounce package softened fat-free cream cheese with ⅓ cup sugar until smooth. Gently stir in 1 8-ounce container fat-free frozen whipped topping (thawed). Spoon into a 6-ounce graham cracker crumb pie crust. Refrigerate 3 hours or until set. Spoon canned light cherry pie filling over top of cheesecake. Slice and serve. *Plan ahead:* Save enough steak, potatoes, and cheesecake for Monday.

 ### Monday *Heat and Eat*

Make **Steak Salad** with Sunday's leftovers. Combine some mixed greens with the leftover potatoes, sliced drained pickled beets, and tomato wedges; toss to coat with a light vinaigrette. Sprinkle with crumbled gorgonzola cheese. Top with thin slices of leftover steak. Serve with **crusty rolls.** For dessert, slice the leftover **cheesecake.**

 ### Tuesday *Express*

For a quick meal, make **Smoked Turkey Pitas**. Fill split warmed pitas with sliced smoked turkey, roasted red peppers (from a jar), sliced onion, watercress, and hummus. Serve with deli **tabbouleh.** Fresh **blueberries** with light **whipped cream** make a great dessert.

 ### Wednesday *Budget*

Ham and Lentil Stew (see recipe) is a low-cost slow-cooker meal. Serve with a **lettuce wedge** and **cornbread** (from a mix). **Peaches** are your dessert.

 ### Thursday *Meatless*

Keep dinner simple with **Mediterranean Quesadillas.** Drain and coarsely chop artichoke hearts. Slice red bell pepper into strips. Place 8 fat-free flour tortillas on a flat surface. Top half of each tortilla with artichokes, peppers, and crumbled feta cheese; fold other half over. Heat a nonstick skillet on medium. Add tortillas, 2 at a time, and cook 3 minutes; flip and cook 1 more minute or until heated. Cut into quarters; serve with **salsa.** (Adapted from *Health* magazine.) Serve with **brown rice.** Enjoy **plums** for dessert.

 ### Friday *Kids*

Celebrate the Fourth like kids! Pile the **burgers** (any kind) on **whole-grain buns** with all the trimmings, such as tomatoes, lettuce, mustard, (low-fat) mayonnaise, ketchup, onion, and pickles. Buy some deli **potato salad** to go with the burgers. For dessert, **Star-Spangled Blueberry Parfaits** (see recipe) are just right for the occasion.

 ### Saturday *Easy Entertaining*

Invite guests for **Island Shrimp with Black Bean Citrus Salsa** (see recipe). Serve with **rice,** a **romaine salad,** and **sourdough bread.** Dessert is **vanilla banana sundaes.** Layer vanilla pudding and banana slices in stemmed glasses. Top with a layer of crushed vanilla wafer cookies and toasted shredded coconut. Garnish with light whipped cream, more banana slices, coconut, and whole cookies.

BUDGET

Ham and Lentil Stew

Prep time: 15 min • **Cook time:** About 7 hr • **Yield:** 8 servings

Ingredients

1 cup diced ham

2 cups lentils, rinsed

2 cups diced carrots

2 cups sliced celery

1 cup chopped onions

1 tablespoon minced garlic

4 cups water

1 teaspoon dried oregano

2¼ cups fat-free chicken broth

¼ teaspoon pepper

1 5- to 6-ounce package baby spinach leaves

2 tablespoons fresh lemon juice

Directions

1 In a 4-quart or larger slow cooker, combine the ham, lentils, carrots, celery, onions, garlic, water, oregano, broth, and pepper.

2 Cover and cook on high 7 hours or until lentils are tender.

3 Stir in spinach; cover and cook 5 minutes or until tender.

4 Stir in lemon juice. Serve.

Per serving: 239 calories, 20g protein, 1g fat (5 percent calories from fat), 0.4g saturated fat, 40g carbohydrate, 9mg cholesterol, 380mg sodium, 9g fiber.

KIDS

Star-Spangled Blueberry Parfaits

Prep time: 20 min • **Yield:** 4 servings

Ingredients

1 10¾-ounce loaf frozen low-fat or regular pound cake

¼ cup red currant jelly or other red fruit jam

2 6-ounce containers low-fat vanilla yogurt

2 cups fresh blueberries

Directions

1 With a serrated knife, cut 14 slices, ¼-inch thick each, from pound cake (return remaining cake to freezer for another time).

2 Spread 7 of the slices with jelly; top with plain slices; trim and discard (or eat!) crusts.

3 With a 1¼-inch star (or a cookie cutter of another shape), cut a star from four sandwiches; set stars aside.

4 Cut sandwich trimmings and remaining whole sandwiches into ¾-inch squares.

5 Into 4 8-ounce stemmed glasses, place half the cake squares, half the blueberries, and 1½ containers yogurt, dividing equally. Top with the remaining cake squares and blueberries.

6 Spoon dollops of the remaining yogurt on top of each parfait; top each with a star and serve.

Per serving: 309 calories, 7g protein, 8g fat (22 percent calories from fat), 4.2g saturated fat, 55g carbohydrate, 59mg cholesterol, 196mg sodium, 2g fiber.

EASY ENTERTAINING

Island Shrimp with Black Bean Citrus Salsa

Prep time: 20 min, plus marinating time • **Cook time:** About 5 min • **Yield:** 4 servings

Ingredients

For the marinade:

2 teaspoons orange zest (orange part only)

¼ cup fresh orange juice

½ teaspoon reduced-sodium seasoned salt

4 cloves minced garlic

1 pound uncooked peeled and deveined medium or large shrimp

1 tablespoon canola oil

For the salsa:

1 19-ounce can black beans, rinsed

1 medium orange

¼ cup thick and chunky salsa

2 tablespoons chopped fresh cilantro

1 teaspoon lime zest (green part only)

2 cloves minced garlic

Directions

1 In a square baking dish, mix orange zest, juice, salt, and garlic.

2 Add shrimp; turn to coat. Cover and refrigerate up to 2 hours.

3 Meanwhile, peel orange, remove membrane, divide orange into segments, and then cut segments in half.

4 In medium bowl, combine beans, orange pieces, salsa, cilantro, lime zest, and garlic. Cover and refrigerate.

5 In a large nonstick skillet, heat oil on medium-high. Drain shrimp; discard marinade. Cook and stir shrimp in oil 2 to 3 minutes or until shrimp are pink.

6 To serve, divide salsa among 4 plates, and arrange shrimp around salsa.

Per serving: 259 calories, 26g protein, 6g fat (20 percent calories from fat), 0.5g saturated fat, 24g carbohydrate, 168mg cholesterol, 633mg sodium, 8g fiber.

Week 26

 Sunday *Family*

Surprise the family with this delicious **Mustard Chicken with Greens** (see recipe). The bright **grape tomatoes** added to the plate, along with **roasted red potatoes,** make a colorful presentation. Add **baguettes.** Buy a **Boston cream pie** for dessert. *Plan ahead:* Save enough pie for Monday.

 Monday *Meatless*

For a no-meat dinner, make **Roasted Red Pepper and Jalapeño Cheese Sandwiches.** Layer roasted red peppers (from a jar), 50-percent-reduced-fat jalapeño cheese, and avocado slices on a hot grilled whole-grain roll. Serve with a **spinach salad.** Leftover **pie** is dessert.

 Tuesday *Budget*

Country singer Trisha Yearwood knows how to make a mean **Meatloaf** (see recipe). Serve Trisha's creation with **mashed potatoes,** tiny **green peas** (frozen), a **mixed green salad,** and **biscuits.** For dessert, make instant **butterscotch pudding** with 1-percent milk. *Plan ahead:* Save enough meatloaf and make extra mashed potatoes for Wednesday.

 Wednesday *Heat and Eat*

Yesterday's meatloaf becomes Trisha's **Meatloaf Sandwiches** today. I asked her how she made her sandwiches, and her reply was, "I just put a little mayo, sometimes cheese, and a little salt and pepper on white or wheat bread." You can add lettuce too. Accompany the sandwiches with **potato patties.** Mix the leftover mashed potatoes with a beaten egg; coat the patties with flour, and brown in a little canola oil until heated through. Add a **romaine salad.** For dessert, fresh **strawberries** are light.

 Thursday *Express*

For a quick meal, try **Tuna-White Bean Salad.** Toss drained canned water-packed tuna, rinsed canned white beans, and chopped red onion with baby spinach leaves and some bottled vinaigrette dressing. Serve with **minestrone soup** and **Italian bread.** Sliced **cantaloupe** makes a refreshing dessert.

 Friday *Kids*

Let the kids help prepare **Piglets in Blankets with Dipping Sauce** (see recipe). Serve this fun food with **green beans.** Frozen **fruit pops** are another kid favorite. Peel a banana and cut in half crosswise. Insert an ice cream stick in the cut end. Dip banana into melted chocolate, roll in chopped nuts, and freeze 1 hour.

 Saturday *Easy Entertaining*

Serve your guests your own **grilled cod** and **grilled vegetables.** Add **orzo salad** to the plate. Cook 8 ounces orzo according to directions; drain and cool. Cut kernels from 1 ear cooked corn on the cob. Combine orzo, corn, juice and zest of ½ lemon, 1 tablespoon extra-virgin olive oil, ¼ cup chopped black olives, 2 tablespoons each chopped fresh cilantro and fresh parsley, ¼ teaspoon each salt and pepper; toss to mix. Serve with a **Boston lettuce salad** and **whole-grain rolls.** Serve **banana crepes** for dessert. Carefully lay 1 package (8 to 10 crepes) on serving plates. Slice 3 ripe bananas into diagonal slices and place down the center of each crepe. Top with banana pudding, covering bananas. Gently fold each crepe like a burrito. Place seam-side down, and add a dollop of light whipped cream. Serve chilled.

FAMILY

Mustard Chicken with Greens

Prep time: 15 min   •   **Cook time:** About 20 minutes   •   **Yield:** 4 servings

Ingredients

4 5- to 6-ounce boneless, skinless chicken breasts

½ cup flour

3 teaspoons olive oil, divided

1 pint grape tomatoes

½ teaspoon minced garlic

¾ cup fat-free chicken broth

3 tablespoons grainy Dijon mustard

3 tablespoons fat-free or low-fat sour cream

Snipped chives for garnish, if desired

1 bunch watercress or 4 cups baby spinach leaves

Directions

1 Flatten chicken to an even thickness (about ½ inch).

2 Put flour in a large plastic bag; add chicken and shake to coat, removing excess flour. Set aside.

3 Heat 1 teaspoon oil in a large nonstick skillet on medium-high. Add tomatoes; cook 3 or 4 minutes or until some of them begin to soften. Add garlic; cook 30 seconds. Remove to bowl.

4 Meanwhile, heat remaining oil in the same skillet on medium. Cook chicken 5 to 6 minutes per side or until no longer pink (160 degrees). Remove to plate; cover.

5 Add broth to skillet, stirring to dissolve browned bits. Whisk in mustard and sour cream. Simmer until slightly thickened; add chives.

6 Place chicken on watercress or spinach leaves; spoon sauce over chicken. Serve with tomatoes.

Per serving: 279 calories, 37g protein, 7g fat (21 percent calories from fat), 1g saturated fat, 17g carbohydrate, 84mg cholesterol, 421mg sodium, 2g fiber.

BUDGET

Meatloaf

Prep time: 10 min • **Cook time:** 1 hr, plus standing time • **Yield:** 8 servings

Ingredients	*Directions*
2 pounds 95-percent-lean ground beef	**1** Heat oven to 350 degrees. In a large bowl, lightly mix beef, crackers, egg, ketchup, mustard, salt, pepper, and onion.
20 crumbled saltine or whole-grain crackers	
1 egg, lightly beaten	**2** Divide evenly, and shape into 2 loaves. Place loaves, side by side crosswise, in a 9-x-13-inch baking dish lined with nonstick foil.
¼ cup ketchup	
1 tablespoon prepared yellow mustard	**3** Bake one hour or until browned or until internal temperature is 160 degrees.
1 teaspoon salt	
½ teaspoon pepper	**4** Remove from oven; transfer to a platter, tent with foil, and let stand 5 minutes before slicing.
1 medium onion, finely chopped	

Per serving: 202 calories, 26g protein, 7g fat (32 percent calories from fat), 2.5g saturated fat, 9g carbohydrate, 89mg cholesterol, 566mg sodium, 1g fiber.

Adapted from Georgia Cooking in an Oklahoma Kitchen *by Trisha Yearwood (Clarkson Potter).*

KIDS

Piglets in Blankets with Dipping Sauce

Prep time: 15 min • **Cook time:** 15 min • **Yield:** 8 servings

Ingredients

1 8-ounce package low-fat or regular crescent roll dough

16 meatless breakfast links (such as Boca)

¾ cup honey

¼ cup Dijon mustard

Directions

1 Heat oven to 375 degrees. Unroll dough; divide along perforations into triangles. Cut each triangle in half to form 2 triangles.

2 Wrap 1 dough triangle around center of each breakfast link, starting at wide end of triangle. Arrange wrapped links on a baking sheet. Bake 15 minutes or until browned.

3 Combine honey and mustard. Serve with piglets.

Per serving: 277 calories, 11g protein, 8g fat (25 percent calories from fat), 1.5g saturated fat, 44g carbohydrate, no cholesterol, 718mg sodium, 2g fiber.

Adapted from Cooking Light *magazine.*

Week 27

Sunday   *Family*

Expect raves from the family with these **Caramelized Lamb Chops** (see recipe). Serve the chops with **grilled carrots, roasted red potatoes, mixed greens,** and **sourdough bread. Strawberry shortcake with chocolate sauce** is a divine ending to a special meal. Spoon fresh strawberries over sliced pound cake; top with chocolate sauce, and add a dollop of light whipped cream. ***Plan ahead:*** Save enough lamb chops and some strawberries for Monday. Save enough chocolate sauce for Saturday.

Monday   *Heat and Eat*

Heat the leftover **lamb chops** and serve them with **couscous,** a **spinach salad,** and **flatbread.** Enjoy the leftover **strawberries** for dessert.

Tuesday   *Meatless*

Grill your favorite **veggie burger** and top with 50-percent-reduced-fat jalapeño cheese. Serve the burgers on whole-grain buns. On the side, add **baked beans** and a **lettuce wedge.** Top fat-free **vanilla ice cream** with **caramel sauce** for dessert. ***Plan ahead:*** Save enough ice cream for Saturday.

Wednesday   *Kids*

Kids of all ages will like **Beef and Bean Chili Verde.** In a large pan, cook 1 pound 93- to 95-percent-lean ground beef, 1 large chopped red bell pepper, and 1 medium chopped onion on medium heat for 6 to 8 minutes, or until beef is no longer pink and vegetables are softened. Add 6 cloves minced garlic, 2 teaspoons chili powder, 2 teaspoons cumin, and ⅛ teaspoon cayenne pepper; cook 15 seconds or until fragrant. Stir in 1 12- to 16-ounce jar salsa verde (green salsa) or taco sauce and ¼ cup water; bring to simmer. Reduce heat to medium-low, cover, and cook, stirring occasionally, 10 minutes. Stir in 1 15-ounce can rinsed pinto beans and cook 1 minute or until heated through. Serve with **carrot sticks** and **cornbread muffins** (from a mix). We're crazy about Brothers-All-Natural **fruit crisps** for dessert.

Thursday   *Express*

Corned Beef Roll-Ups are a quick meal. Spread fat-free flour tortillas with Thousand Island dressing. Top with sliced corned beef and Swiss cheese, along with deli coleslaw. Roll; microwave 1 minute to melt cheese. Serve with deli **German potato salad** and **pickled beets.** Fresh **pineapple** is dessert.

Friday   *Budget*

I really like **Picadillo Stuffed Peppers** (see recipe). Serve them with **mixed greens** and **whole-grain bread.** Try **peaches** for dessert.

Saturday   *Easy Entertaining*

Treat your guests to **Baked Chicken with Yukon Gold Potatoes** (see recipe). Serve the combo with fresh **asparagus,** an **arugula salad,** and **whole-grain rolls.** Top leftover **ice cream** with leftover **chocolate sauce** and **toasted coconut.**

FAMILY

Caramelized Lamb Chops

Prep time: 10 min, plus marinating time • **Cook time:** 7–11 min, plus standing time • **Yield:** 8 servings

Ingredients

1½ tablespoons olive oil

1½ tablespoons red wine vinegar

2½ tablespoons dark brown sugar

2 teaspoons honey mustard

1½ tablespoons fresh lemon juice

8 lamb shoulder chops (about 4 pounds)

Directions

1 Combine marinade ingredients; brush over all sides of the lamb. Cover and refrigerate 30 minutes.

2 Drain any excess marinade. Grill lamb 7 to 11 minutes, turning often, for medium-rare to medium doneness.

3 Transfer to a plate; cover and let stand 5 minutes before serving.

Per serving: 239 calories, 30g protein, 11g fat (43 percent calories from fat), 3.9g saturated fat, 2g carbohydrate, 100mg cholesterol, 91mg sodium, no fiber.

BUDGET

Picadillo Stuffed Peppers

Prep time: 15 min • **Cook time:** 5–6 hr • **Yield:** 4 servings

Ingredients	Directions
1 26-ounce jar no-salt-added or regular marinara sauce	*1* In a large bowl, combine marinara sauce, vinegar, cumin, and cinnamon; mix well.
1 tablespoon red wine vinegar	
½ teaspoon cumin	*2* Spoon 1½ cups mixture into a 4-quart or larger slow cooker.
¼ teaspoon cinnamon	
4 medium green bell peppers	*3* Slice off top ½ inch of peppers; seed peppers and reserve tops.
8 ounces ground chicken	
1 small zucchini, diced	*4* Add chicken, zucchini, barley, onion, and raisins to remaining sauce; mix well. Evenly spoon mixture into peppers (pack filling if necessary); replace tops.
½ cup quick-cooking barley	
⅓ cup finely chopped onion	
¼ cup raisins	
	5 Stand upright in cooker. Cover and cook on low 5 to 6 hours or until tender and internal temperature of filling is 165 degrees. Serve with sauce.

Per serving: 352 calories, 20g protein, 6g fat (16 percent calories from fat), 1.7g saturated fat, 55g carbohydrate, 37mg cholesterol, 102mg sodium, 10g fiber.

EASY ENTERTAINING

Baked Chicken with Yukon Gold Potatoes

Prep time: 10 min • **Cook time:** About 1 hr • **Yield:** 10 servings

Ingredients

2 pounds bone-in skinless chicken breasts

1½ pounds bone-in skinless chicken thighs

3 tablespoons canola oil, divided

1 teaspoon coarse salt

½ teaspoon pepper

2 pounds Yukon gold potatoes, peeled and quartered

1 14½-ounce can no-salt-added or regular diced tomatoes

2 tablespoons chopped fresh Italian parsley

1 tablespoon chopped fresh or 1 teaspoon dried basil

2 cloves minced garlic

¼ cup freshly grated parmesan cheese

Directions

1 Heat oven to 375 degrees. Pat chicken dry. Cover bottom of a large roasting pan with 1 tablespoon oil. Heat on medium-high. Season chicken with salt and pepper.

2 When oil is hot, place chicken in pan. Sear chicken 6 minutes on all sides until golden.

3 Place potatoes around chicken pieces. Add tomatoes, parsley, basil, and garlic. Sprinkle with cheese and drizzle remaining oil over chicken.

4 Cover and bake 1 hour or until chicken thighs are 180 degrees. To serve, spoon vegetables on a serving platter and place chicken on top.

Per serving: 281 calories, 29g protein, 10g fat (32 percent calories from fat), 2g saturated fat, 18g carbohydrate, 78mg cholesterol, 324mg sodium, 3g fiber.

Week 28

 ## Sunday *Family*

Make family day special with **Turkey and Vegetable Skewers with Walnut Lime Curry Sauce** (see recipe). Serve the colorful entree with **brown rice** and **dinner rolls**. Buy a **peach pie** and top each slice with fat-free **vanilla ice cream** for dessert. ***Plan ahead:*** Save enough turkey and vegetables, rice, and pie for Monday; save enough ice cream for Thursday.

 ## Monday *Heat and Eat*

With Sunday's leftover turkey and vegetables, make a quick **stir-fry.** To the leftovers, add thinly sliced carrots and some sliced mushrooms in a large nonstick skillet. Cook 3 minutes. Finish with bottled stir-fry sauce, and serve over leftover **rice.** Add a **mixed green salad** and **baguettes.** Leftover **pie** makes a good dessert.

 ## Tuesday *Meatless*

Confetti Quinoa Salad (see recipe) goes into my favorites file. Serve it with a **spinach salad** and **whole-grain bread.** Fresh **plums** are good for dessert.

 ## Wednesday *Kids*

Baked ziti is all about kids' favorite dishes. Heat oven to 350 degrees. Toss cooked ziti with the kids' preferred pasta sauce and shredded part-skim mozzarella in a baking dish coated with cooking spray. Bake 30 minutes or until the cheese melts and is bubbly. Munch on **celery sticks** on the side and add **soft rolls.** Pop **red and green grapes** in your mouth for dessert.

 ## Thursday *Express*

There will be no cooking tonight with **tuna pitas** for dinner. Stuff whole-grain pitas with deli tuna salad mixed with a little fresh lemon juice and some capers. Add chopped lettuce and cherry tomatoes. Serve with **baked chips** and some **olives.** Scoop the leftover **ice cream** for dessert.

 ## Friday *Budget*

Rosemary Chicken with Cannellini Beans (see recipe) is delicious and low in cost at the same time. Serve the one-dish meal with a **romaine salad** and **crusty rolls.** For dessert, sliced **cantaloupe** is just right.

 ## Saturday *Easy Entertaining*

Invite guests for easy **Garlic Shrimp.** Heat 2 tablespoons butter in a large nonstick skillet on medium; add 1 teaspoon minced garlic. Cook 30 seconds; add 1 pound medium uncooked shelled and deveined shrimp. Cook 2 or 3 minutes or until pink. Serve over **rice;** garnish with fresh chopped parsley. Add **sugar snap peas,** a **Bibb lettuce salad,** and **baguettes** to round out a fine meal. **Chocolate Dipped Strawberries** will wow any guest. Wash and chill 12 large strawberries with caps. Melt 1 cup semi-sweet chocolate chips. Stir in 1 tablespoon shortening until melted. Dip berries into chocolate to come halfway up sides. Place on foil until set. Serve with **almond cookies.**

FAMILY

Turkey and Vegetable Skewers with Walnut Lime Curry Sauce

Prep time: 20 min • **Cook time:** 12–15 min • **Yield:** 8 servings

Ingredients

For the skewers:

2 pounds boneless, skinless turkey breast cut into 1¼-inch pieces

2 red bell peppers cut into 1¼-inch pieces

2 green bell peppers cut into 1¼-inch pieces

2 yellow bell peppers cut into 1¼-inch pieces

16 cherry tomatoes

8 bay leaves

2 tablespoons olive oil

Salt and coarsely ground pepper to taste

For the Walnut Lime Curry Sauce:

1 cup chopped walnuts

2 cups low-fat plain yogurt

Juice and zest of 2 limes

2 tablespoons curry powder

¼ teaspoon salt

Directions

For the skewers:

1 Divide turkey, peppers, tomatoes, and bay leaves among 8 metal skewers, adding them in an alternating pattern.

2 Brush each skewer with olive oil and season with salt and pepper.

3 Grill, turning often, 12 to 15 minutes or until turkey is no longer pink (170 degrees).

For the sauce:

1 In a small bowl, combine walnuts, yogurt, lime juice and zest, and curry powder; mix well. Stir in salt.

2 Serve sauce with skewers.

Per serving: 323 calories, 34g protein, 15g fat (40 percent calories from fat), 1.9g saturated fat, 15g carbohydrate, 78mg cholesterol, 183mg sodium, 4g fiber.

Confetti Quinoa Salad

Prep time: 15 min • **Cook time:** About 30 min • **Yield:** About 6½ cups

MEATLESS

Ingredients	Directions
1 cup quinoa	*1* Rinse quinoa under cold water for 2 minutes or according to directions. Combine quinoa and water in a 2-quart pan and bring to boil. Cover; reduce heat to low, and simmer 20 minutes. Remove from heat; let stand 5 minutes. Fluff with fork.
2 cups water	
3 tablespoons walnut oil	
3 tablespoons fresh lemon juice	
1 teaspoon dried oregano	*2* Meanwhile, in a large bowl, whisk together oil, lemon juice, oregano, cumin, salt, and pepper.
½ teaspoon cumin	
¼ teaspoon salt	*3* Add corn, cucumber, tomatoes, walnuts, feta, olives, parsley, and cooked quinoa; stir gently.
½ teaspoon freshly ground black pepper	
1 cup frozen corn kernels, cooked	*4* Refrigerate until serving time.
1 medium cucumber, peeled, seeded, and thinly sliced	
1 pint grape tomatoes, halved	
½ cup chopped toasted walnuts	
½ cup low-fat crumbled feta cheese	
⅓ cup coarsely chopped kalamata olives	
¼ cup chopped fresh parsley	

Per cup: 303 calories, 9g protein, 18g fat (50 percent calories from fat), 2.5g saturated fat, 30g carbohydrate, 4mg cholesterol, 396mg sodium, 4g fiber.

BUDGET

Rosemary Chicken with Cannellini Beans

Prep time: 15 min • **Cook time:** About 20 min • **Yield:** 4 servings

Ingredients

½ cup Italian dressing

4 boneless, skinless chicken breasts (about 1¼ pounds)

⅓ cup water

1 cup sliced carrots (2 medium)

1 cup sliced celery (2 medium ribs)

¼ cup coarsely chopped sun-dried tomatoes in oil, drained

1 tablespoon finely chopped fresh rosemary or 1 teaspoon dried crushed rosemary

1 19-ounce can cannellini beans, rinsed

Directions

1 In a large nonstick skillet, heat dressing on medium-high.

2 Flatten chicken to an even thickness. Cook chicken in dressing 2 to 3 minutes per side or until lightly browned. Reduce heat to medium-low.

3 Add water, carrots, celery, tomatoes, and rosemary to skillet. Cover; simmer about 10 minutes or until carrots are tender and internal temperature of chicken is 170 degrees.

4 Stir in beans; cook 3 minutes or until beans are heated through.

Per serving: 377 calories, 39g protein, 12g fat (29 percent calories from fat), 2g saturated fat, 27g carbohydrate, 82mg cholesterol, 895mg sodium, 7g fiber.

Week 29

 ## Sunday *Family*

Serve a **spiral-sliced ham** for an easy summer family meal. Add **baked sweet potatoes** on the side, along with **Balsamic and Parmesan Roasted Cauliflower** (see recipe). Add **sourdough bread.** For dessert, top **angel food cake** with fresh **blueberries** and **light whipped cream.** *Plan ahead:* Save some ham and cake, and bake enough potatoes for Monday.

 ## Monday *Heat and Eat*

Enjoy a cool supper with **Summer Subs.** Spread 3 ounces fat-free cream cheese (softened) on a loaf of unsliced French bread halved lengthwise. Layer with leftover ham, sliced provolone cheese, drained sliced mushrooms (from a jar), sliced tomatoes, sliced red onion, banana peppers, and shredded lettuce. Replace top; slice into 1½-inch pieces before serving. Slice the leftover potatoes into lengthwise wedges. Coat with cooking spray; bake in a 425-degree oven for 15 to 20 minutes or until hot. Serve the leftover **cake** with fat-free **chocolate ice cream** for dessert. *Plan ahead:* Save enough ice cream for Thursday.

 ## Tuesday *Budget*

Serve economical **Ravioli with Sausage and Peppers** tonight. Cook 2 9-ounce packages refrigerated cheese ravioli according to directions. Meanwhile, heat 2 teaspoons canola oil in a large, nonstick skillet on medium. Add 2 sliced green bell peppers and 1 small onion cut into wedges; cook 4 minutes. Add 1 12-ounce cooked Italian chicken or turkey sausage cut into ½-inch-thick pieces; cook 2 minutes. Add 1 teaspoon minced garlic; cook 30 seconds. Add ½ cup fat-free chicken broth; remove skillet from heat. Drain ravioli and add to sausage and peppers. Sprinkle with 2 tablespoons fresh sliced basil. (Adapted from *Woman's Day* magazine.) Serve with a **lettuce wedge** and **garlic bread.** Fresh **peaches** are your dessert.

 ## Wednesday *Express*

Make it quick tonight with **Layered Roast Beef Salad.** In a glass bowl, layer shredded lettuce, sliced tomatoes and cucumbers, drained canned artichokes, strips of deli roast beef, and cheese. Top with low-fat **ranch dressing.** Serve with **bean soup** and **flatbread.** Juicy **watermelon** is the perfect dessert.

 ## Thursday *Kids*

Kids are always ready for a burger, and tonight's **Greek Turkey Burgers** (see recipe) will make the adults happy, too. Serve with **oven fries** (frozen). Leftover **chocolate ice cream** with **marshmallow** topping is just for the kids.

 ## Friday *Meatless*

Start your no-meat dinner with refreshing **gazpacho.** Stir finely chopped red onion, seeded cucumbers, tomatoes, and a yellow bell pepper into pureed chilled canned tomatoes. Season with salt and pepper. Serve the hot-weather soup with **egg salad sandwiches** on **whole-grain toast** with **lettuce.** Munch on **peanut butter cookies** for dessert.

 ## Saturday *Easy Entertaining*

Invite guests to a picnic starring **Almond-Crusted Chicken Tenders** (see recipe). Make or buy **potato salad** and **coleslaw** to serve on the side, along with **sliced tomatoes** and **biscuits.** Present **fruit tarts** for dessert.

FAMILY

Balsamic and Parmesan Roasted Cauliflower

Prep time: 10 min • **Cook time:** 20–30 min • **Yield:** 6 servings

Ingredients

1 large head cauliflower, florets cut into 1-inch-thick slices

1 tablespoon extra-virgin olive oil

1 teaspoon dried marjoram

¼ teaspoon salt

Freshly ground black pepper to taste

2 tablespoons balsamic vinegar

½ cup freshly grated parmesan cheese

Directions

1 Heat oven to 450 degrees. In a medium bowl, toss cauliflower with oil, marjoram, salt, and pepper until coated. Spoon onto a large rimmed baking sheet lined with nonstick foil.

2 Bake 15 to 20 minutes or until cauliflower starts to soften and brown. Remove from oven.

3 Toss cauliflower with vinegar and cheese.

4 Return to oven; roast 5 to 10 more minutes or until cheese melts and any moisture has evaporated.

Per serving: 88 calories, 5g protein, 4g fat (40 percent calories from fat), 1.5g saturated fat, 9g carbohydrate, 6mg cholesterol, 242mg sodium, 4g fiber.

Adapted from Eating Well *magazine.*

KIDS

Greek Turkey Burgers

Prep time: 10 min • **Cook time:** 15 min • **Yield:** 4 servings

Ingredients	*Directions*

Ingredients

⅓ cup chopped fresh parsley

1 pound ground turkey breast

2 teaspoons canola oil

¾ teaspoon freshly ground black pepper

¼ teaspoon salt

1 tablespoon Worcestershire sauce

1 tablespoon Dijon mustard

½ teaspoon garlic powder

½ cup crumbled low-fat feta cheese

4 slices red onion

4 toasted whole-grain hamburger buns

Directions

1 In a medium bowl, mix together parsley, turkey, oil, pepper, salt, Worcestershire, mustard, garlic powder, and feta. Divide into 4 patties.

2 Broil 5 to 6 minutes on each side until internal temperature is 165 degrees.

3 Serve with onions on buns.

Per serving: 312 calories, 35g protein, 8g fat (22 percent calories from fat), 2.2g saturated fat, 26g carbohydrate, 84mg cholesterol, 771mg sodium, 4g fiber.

Adapted from Health *magazine.*

EASY ENTERTAINING

Almond-Crusted Chicken Tenders

Prep time: 15 min • **Cook time:** 18–20 min • **Yield:** 4 servings

Ingredients

6 crushed whole-grain crackers

2 tablespoons ground almonds

1 teaspoon paprika

¼ teaspoon salt

¼ teaspoon pepper

1 egg white

3 tablespoons flour

8 chicken tenders (about 1 to 1¼ pounds)

Directions

1 Heat oven to 425 degrees. Mix together crackers, almonds, paprika, salt, and pepper. Place in pie plate or other flat pan; set aside.

2 In another pie plate, whisk egg white until foamy. Place flour in third flat pan.

3 Place a wire rack coated with cooking spray on a foil-lined, rimmed baking sheet.

4 Coat chicken in flour, then in egg white, and finally in cracker mixture. Lightly coat chicken on each side with cooking spray.

5 Arrange chicken on wire rack; bake 18 to 20 minutes, turning after 12 minutes.

Per serving: 187 calories, 29g protein, 4g fat (17 percent calories from fat), 0.5g saturated fat, 9g carbohydrate, 66mg cholesterol, 278mg sodium, 1g fiber.

Adapted from Southern Living *magazine.*

Week 30

Sunday *Family*

Grilled flat iron steaks are a special family summer meal. The steaks go well with **Orzo Salad with Chickpeas, Dill, and Lemon** (see recipe). Add fresh **asparagus** and **whole-grain rolls**. Make **plum cobbler** for dessert. Heat oven to 425 degrees. Put 3 pounds (about 8 medium) ripe, black plums (each one cut into 8 wedges) in an 8-x-8-inch baking dish. Add ¼ cup sugar and 2 tablespoons water; toss gently to mix and coat. Cover with foil; bake 25 minutes. Meanwhile stir 1 bag (7.75 ounces) cinnamon swirl complete biscuit mix (such as Bisquick) and ½ cup water in a medium bowl until a soft dough forms. Drop by spoonfuls in 8 evenly spaced mounds on the fruit. Sprinkle with 1 tablespoon sugar. Bake 15 to 20 minutes until biscuits are golden. Serve warm. (Adapted from *Woman's Day* magazine.) ***Plan ahead:*** Grill enough steak and save enough orzo salad for Monday.

Monday *Heat and Eat*

For a simple meal, prepare **Steak Roll-ups.** Thinly slice leftover steak and place on fat-free whole-grain tortillas. Top with crumbled blue cheese, shredded lettuce, and chopped cherry tomatoes. Roll up and enjoy the simple entree with leftover **orzo salad.** Serve **blackberries** for dessert.

Tuesday *Meatless*

Any burger is a good burger, and tonight's **Grilled Portobello Burgers** (see recipe) are no exception. Serve the no-meat entree with **oven fries** (frozen). Fat-free **strawberry ice cream** is your dessert. ***Plan ahead:*** Save enough ice cream for Thursday.

Wednesday *Budget*

I'm always happy when dinner is low cost and also delicious, as are these **Turkey Enchiladas** (see recipe). Serve them with a **guacamole and shredded lettuce salad**. Make **flan** from a mix for dessert.

Thursday *Express*

Take the night off and buy deli **shrimp salad** and spoon it over a packaged **green salad** for dinner. Start the meal with a glass of chilled **tomato juice.** Scoop leftover **ice cream** for dessert.

Friday *Kids*

Make the kids happy with **Giant Chicken Toast-Achos**. Heat oven to 350 degrees. Lightly brush 4 fat-free flour tortillas with olive oil. Bake 5 minutes. In a large, nonstick skillet on medium, heat 2 cups shredded cooked chicken and 1 cup mild salsa 5 minutes. Top each tortilla (leave on baking sheet) with ½ cup of the chicken mixture and some shredded part-skim mozzarella cheese. Return tortillas to oven and bake 3 to 4 minutes or until cheese melts. Top the tortillas with chopped lettuce, a few chopped green onions, and some sliced olives, and serve. (Adapted from *Yum-O! The Family Cookbook* by Rachael Ray [Clarkson Potter].) Serve the fun kid-food with **carrot sticks.** How about **oatmeal-raisin cookies** for dessert?

Saturday *Easy Entertaining*

Prepare your own **trout almandine** for guests and serve the familiar dish with **parsley buttered brown rice, green beans,** a **spinach salad,** and **whole-grain rolls. Chocolate layer cake** is always good for dessert.

FAMILY

Orzo Salad with Chickpeas, Dill, and Lemon

Prep time: 15 min • **Cook time:** For the pasta • **Yield:** 8 servings

Ingredients

1 cup orzo pasta

½ cup thinly sliced green onions

½ cup low-fat crumbled feta cheese

⅓ cup chopped fresh dill

1 19-ounce can chickpeas, rinsed

3 tablespoons fresh lemon juice

1½ tablespoons extra-virgin olive oil

1 tablespoon cold water

½ teaspoon salt

½ teaspoon minced garlic

Directions

1 Cook orzo pasta according to directions. Drain, rinse in cold water, and rinse again.

2 In a large bowl, combine orzo, onions, cheese, dill, and chickpeas; toss gently to combine.

3 Whisk together juice, oil, water, salt, and garlic. Drizzle over pasta mixture; toss gently to coat.

Per serving: 173 calories, 8g protein, 5g fat (24 percent calories from fat), 1.1g saturated fat, 25g carbohydrate, 3mg cholesterol, 450mg sodium, 3g fiber.

Adapted from Cooking Light Pasta *by Terri Laschober, Editor (Oxmoor House).*

Grilled Portobello Burgers

Prep time: About 10 min • **Cook time:** 10 min • **Yield:** 4 servings

MEATLESS

Ingredients	*Directions*
4 large portobello mushrooms	**1** Heat oven to 425 degrees. Heat ridged grill pan or skillet on medium high until hot.
3 tablespoons balsamic vinaigrette	
⅓ cup low-fat mayonnaise	**2** Place mushrooms, stem side down, in pan. Brush with half of the vinaigrette and grill 5 minutes. Turn; brush with remaining vinaigrette and grill 5 minutes or until very tender.
¼ cup roasted red peppers, drained (jar)	
4 split whole-grain hamburger buns	
Sliced cherry tomatoes	**3** Meanwhile, blend mayonnaise and red peppers in blender, and toast hamburger buns.
Boston lettuce leaves	**4** Spread red pepper mayonnaise on cut sides of bottom buns. Place mushrooms on top. Add tomatoes, lettuce, and bun tops, and serve.

Per serving: 230 calories, 5g protein, 12g fat (45 percent calories from fat), 2.1g saturated fat, 28g carbohydrate, 7mg cholesterol, 482mg sodium, 4g fiber.

Adapted from Good Housekeeping *magazine.*

BUDGET

Turkey Enchiladas

Prep time: 15 min • **Cook time:** 15–20 min • **Yield:** 10 enchiladas

Ingredients

2 cups cooked chopped turkey or chicken

1 8.75-ounce can no-salt-added corn, drained

1 8-ounce container low-fat sour cream

1½ cups low-fat shredded Mexican blend cheese, divided

2 tablespoons chopped fresh cilantro, divided

10 6-inch corn tortillas

1 10-ounce can enchilada sauce

1 cup salsa

Directions

1 Heat oven to 400 degrees. Coat a 9-x-13-inch baking dish with cooking spray. In a large bowl, combine turkey or chicken, corn, sour cream, half of cheese, and half of cilantro.

2 Wrap 5 tortillas in a damp paper towel; microwave them on high (100-percent power) for 30 seconds to soften. Repeat with remaining tortillas.

3 Place about ⅓ cup mixture on each tortilla and roll tightly. Arrange in baking dish, seam side down.

4 In a bowl, combine enchilada sauce with salsa; pour over tortillas. Top with remaining cheese and bake 15 to 20 minutes or until cheese melts and enchiladas are heated through. Sprinkle with remaining cilantro.

Per enchilada: 224 calories, 16g protein, 8g fat (34 percent calories from fat), 4.2g saturated fat, 22g carbohydrate, 43mg cholesterol, 429mg sodium, 2g fiber.

Week 31

 Sunday *Family*

Gather the family for **Malaysian Chicken on Fresh Greens** (see recipe). Serve with **roasted red potatoes** and your own **gazpacho**, fresh **green beans**, and **baguettes**. For dessert, **peach pie** is right in season and is especially good when topped with fat-free **vanilla ice cream**. *Plan ahead:* Buy extra grilled chicken and save some potatoes and pie for Monday.

 Monday *Heat and Eat*

Dinner couldn't be easier than enjoying the leftover **grilled chicken** along with the leftover **potatoes**. Add a **spinach salad** with red onion rings and **whole-grain bread**. Slice the leftover **pie** for dessert.

 Tuesday *Express*

For a quick meal, make **Sausage and Pepper Subs**. Split any sausage and cook it in a hot nonstick skillet on medium. To skillet, add a little canola oil and cook sliced green bell peppers and sliced onions until softened. Spoon onto a split sub bun and top with heated marinara sauce. Serve with **baked chips. Nectarines** make a good dessert.

 Wednesday *Meatless*

Skip meat for a simple meal of **lentil soup** topped with a dollop of fat-free sour cream. Alongside, make **grilled cheese, avocado, and tomato sandwiches**. Fresh **strawberries** are an easy, vitamin C-packed dessert.

 Thursday *Kids*

I wasn't a kid when I lived in Texas, but I sure loved **Chicken Fried Steak** (see recipe), a Texas staple for adults and kids. You'll like this lightened version of the old standard. Buy or make **gravy** and add **mashed potatoes, green beans,** and **soft rolls** on the side. Slice **kiwifruit** for dessert.

 Friday *Budget*

No doubt about it, there's probably a better name for this than **No-Brainer Chicken** (see recipe), but when Weight Watchers leader Lisa Gittleman gave out the recipe, she said it right: "Anyone can make this dish!" Serve it over **brown rice** and top it with fat-free sour cream. Add a **green salad** and **whole-grain rolls,** and you have dinner. A slice of **cantaloupe** completes the meal.

 Saturday *Easy Entertaining*

Invite guests and prepare your own favorite **Grilled Lamb Chop** recipe. Top the chops with **gremolata:** Mix ¼ cup finely chopped parsley, 2 tablespoons lemon zest (yellow part only) and ½ teaspoon minced garlic. Add **corn on the cob, mixed greens,** and **sourdough bread**. For dessert, surprise your friends with **piña colada pineapple**. Sear pineapple slices on the grill quickly (just long enough to get grill marks). Add 2 tablespoons dark rum to ½ cup caramel topping. Drizzle over a scoop of coconut sorbet placed on top of the pineapple. (Adapted from *Woman's Day* magazine.)

FAMILY

Malaysian Chicken on Fresh Greens

Prep time: 15 min, plus marinating time • **Yield:** 4 servings

Ingredients

½ cup unseasoned rice wine vinegar

2 tablespoons sesame oil

2 tablespoons reduced-sodium soy sauce

1 tablespoon peanut butter

1 teaspoon ground ginger

½ teaspoon garlic powder

½ teaspoon crushed red pepper

1 8- to 10-ounce packages grilled chicken strips

6 cups mixed salad greens

½ cup shredded carrots

½ cup alfalfa or bean sprouts

½ cup thinly sliced radishes

Directions

1 In a medium bowl, combine vinegar, oil, soy sauce, peanut butter, ginger, garlic powder, and red pepper; mix well.

2 Stir in grilled chicken strips; toss to coat. Refrigerate up to 1 hour, stirring occasionally.

3 To a large bowl, add salad greens, carrots, sprouts, and radishes. Toss well.

4 Divide salad mixture among 4 serving plates; top with chicken and add some dressing.

Per serving: 239 calories, 30g protein, 11g fat (40 percent calories from fat), 1.8g saturated fat, 6g carbohydrate, 66mg cholesterol, 433mg sodium, 3g fiber.

KIDS

Chicken Fried Steak

Prep time: 10 min • **Cook time:** 12–16 min • **Yield:** 4 servings

Ingredients	Directions
4 4-ounce cubed steaks	**1** Sprinkle steaks with salt and pepper.
¼ teaspoon salt	
¼ teaspoon pepper	**2** Place flour, egg, and cracker crumbs in 3 separate plates. Coat steaks in flour, shaking off excess; dip in egg substitute, and coat in cracker crumbs.
¼ cup flour	
⅓ cup egg substitute	
1 cup coarse cracker crumbs	**3** Lightly coat steaks on each side with cooking spray.
	4 Cook steaks, in batches, in a hot, nonstick skillet on medium 3 to 4 minutes on each side until golden, turning twice. Serve immediately.

Per serving: 265 calories, 30g protein, 6g fat (20 percent calories from fat), 1.9g saturated fat, 22g carbohydrate, 64mg cholesterol, 545mg sodium, 1g fiber.

Adapted from Southern Living *magazine.*

BUDGET

No-Brainer Chicken

Prep time: 10 min • **Cook time:** 6 hr • **Yield:** 4 servings

Ingredients	*Directions*

Ingredients

1 pound frozen boneless, skinless chicken breasts (do not thaw)

2 15-ounce cans black beans, rinsed

2 10-ounce cans diced tomatoes with green chilies, drained (see Note)

1 cup frozen corn

Fresh chopped cilantro

Fat-free sour cream

Directions

1 In a 3-quart or larger slow cooker, combine chicken, beans, tomatoes, and corn. Cover and cook on low 6 hours.

2 Garnish with the cilantro and sour cream.

Per serving: 366 calories, 40g protein, 4g fat (9 percent calories from fat), no saturated fat, 43g carbohydrate, 66mg cholesterol, 1,298mg sodium, 14g fiber.

Note: *I used 1 can of mild and 1 can of regular tomatoes. Adjust to your taste.*

Week 32

 ## Sunday *Family*

Prepare a **marinated flank steak** for the family using a dry or prepared marinade, or make your own. Grill the steak (1 to 1½ pounds) 17 to 21 minutes for medium-rare to medium doneness, using a medium-hot grill. Remove from grill, cover lightly with foil, and let stand 5 minutes. To serve, thinly slice across the grain. Serve with a **Tomato, Chickpea, and Feta Salad:** In a medium bowl, toss 1 15-ounce can rinsed canned chickpeas, 3 sliced green onions, ½ cup halved grape tomatoes, and ¼ cup crumbled reduced-fat feta cheese with ¼ cup Greek salad dressing. Add **corn on the cob** and **sourdough bread.** Buy a **Boston cream pie** for dessert. *Plan ahead:* Save enough pie for Monday.

 ## Monday *Budget*

Try this updated meatloaf, **Herbed Chicken Loaf** (see recipe), for another take on comfort food. Of course, **mashed potatoes** are a must on the side, along with fresh **broccoli**. Add **whole-grain rolls.** Slice the leftover **pie** for dessert. *Plan ahead:* Save enough meatloaf for Wednesday.

 ## Tuesday *Meatless*

Linguine with Spinach-Almond Pesto (see recipe) is knock-your-socks-off delicious. Accompany it with a **romaine salad** and **Italian bread.** Enjoy **peaches** for dessert.

 ## Wednesday *Heat and Eat*

No one minds leftovers when they're as good as these **meatloaf sandwiches.** Slather whole-grain bread with Dijonnaise and top with lettuce. Serve with **baked chips.** Top fat-free **vanilla ice cream** with fresh **strawberries.** *Plan ahead:* Save enough ice cream for Saturday.

 ## Thursday *Express*

For a quick dinner, **Tuna-Bean Salad** is easy. In a large bowl, mix together 1 teaspoon lemon zest (yellow part only), 2 tablespoons each fresh lemon juice and extra-virgin olive oil, 3 ribs thinly sliced celery, 2 thinly sliced green onions, and 1 15- to 19-ounce can each cannelloni beans, chickpeas, and red beans (rinsed and drained); mix well. Gently stir in 2 6-ounce cans drained, flaked light tuna in water and salt and pepper to taste. Spoon into **lettuce cups** to serve. Start your meal with **spicy tomato juice.** Add **whole-grain rolls.** For a cool dessert, **pineapple sherbet** is perfect. *Plan ahead:* Save enough of the tuna mixture for Friday.

 ## Friday *Kids*

Make **Tuna-Bean Rolls** for the kids. Spread fat-free flour tortillas with hummus and top with the leftover tuna-bean mixture. Roll up and eat. Alongside, munch on **celery sticks. Watermelon** is for dessert.

 ## Saturday *Easy Entertaining*

Serve your guests **Grilled Southwestern Chicken** (see recipe) and **Corn and Cucumber Salad.** In a large bowl, combine 2 15-ounce cans rinsed whole-kernel corn; ½ cup diced red bell pepper; 1 cup peeled, seeded, and chopped cucumber; and ¼ cup chopped red onion. In another bowl, combine ⅓ cup low-fat mayonnaise; 2 tablespoons each chopped fresh cilantro, freshly grated parmesan cheese, and fresh lime juice; 1 teaspoon paprika; ½ teaspoon garlic salt; and ¼ teaspoon cumin. Mix well. Add to corn mixture; toss lightly to coat. Refrigerate until serving time. Add **green beans** and **breadsticks.** Top leftover **ice cream** with toasted **walnuts.**

BUDGET

Herbed Chicken Loaf

Prep time: 15 min • **Cook time:** About 1 hr, 10 min, plus standing time • **Yield:** 8 servings

Ingredients

½ **cup frozen diced onion, red and green bell pepper, and celery mixture**

2 **pounds ground chicken**

½ **cup fine dry bread crumbs**

⅓ **cup low-fat mayonnaise**

1 **lightly beaten egg, plus 1 egg white**

2 **tablespoons chopped fresh parsley**

2 **teaspoons Greek seasoning**

¼ **teaspoon salt**

¼ **teaspoon freshly ground black pepper**

Directions

1 Heat oven to 350 degrees. Microwave vegetable combo for 2 minutes on high (100-percent power); drain.

2 In a large bowl, mix together cooked vegetables, chicken, crumbs, mayonnaise, eggs, parsley, Greek seasoning, salt, and pepper until combined.

3 Place mixture in a 9-x-5-inch loaf pan or dish. Bake 1 hour to 1 hour 10 minutes, or until internal temperature is 165 degrees.

4 Let stand 10 minutes; slice and serve.

Per serving: 198 calories, 23g protein, 8g fat (39 percent calories from fat), 2g saturated fat, 6g carbohydrate, 91mg cholesterol, 298mg sodium, no fiber.

Linguine with Spinach-Almond Pesto

MEATLESS

Prep time: 15 min • **Cook time:** For the pasta • **Yield:** 5 servings

Ingredients	*Directions*

Ingredients

10 ounces linguine

½ 6-ounce package fresh baby spinach

½ cup fresh basil leaves

½ cup toasted slivered almonds, divided

1 large clove garlic

3 tablespoons freshly grated parmesan cheese

¼ cup vegetable broth

2 tablespoons extra-virgin olive oil

1 tablespoon fresh lemon juice

2 teaspoons lemon zest (yellow part only)

¼ teaspoon salt

½ teaspoon pepper

1¼ cups halved grape tomatoes

Directions

1 Cook linguine according to directions; drain, reserving ¼ cup pasta water.

2 In a food processor, pulse spinach and basil until finely chopped. Add 6 tablespoons almonds, the garlic, cheese, broth, oil, lemon juice and zest, salt, and pepper. Blend until smooth.

3 Place pasta in a serving bowl (along with a little reserved water, if necessary); add spinach mixture and toss to coat.

4 Top with tomatoes and reserved almonds, and serve.

Per serving: 352 calories, 12g protein, 13g fat (31 percent calories from fat), 1.9g saturated fat, 50g carbohydrate, 3mg cholesterol, 245mg sodium, 5g fiber.

EASY ENTERTAINING

Grilled Southwestern Chicken

Prep time: 10 min, plus marinating time • **Cook time:** 8–12 min • **Yield:** 4 servings

Ingredients	*Directions*
4 5- or 6-ounce boneless, skinless chicken breasts	*1* Flatten chicken to an even thickness (½ inch); set aside.
⅓ cup canola oil	
3 tablespoons cider vinegar	*2* In a small bowl, combine the oil, vinegar, cilantro, chili powder, garlic powder, Italian seasoning, cumin, salt, and pepper; mix well.
1 tablespoon chopped fresh cilantro	
2 teaspoons chili powder	*3* Place chicken in a resealable plastic bag; add marinade. Refrigerate 1 to 2 hours.
1 teaspoon garlic powder	
1 teaspoon Italian seasoning	*4* Remove chicken; discard marinade. Grill 4 to 6 minutes per side or until no longer pink.
½ teaspoon cumin	
½ teaspoon salt	
¼ teaspoon freshly ground black pepper	

Per serving: 187 calories, 33g protein, 5g fat (27 percent calories from fat), 0.7g saturated fat, no carbohydrate, 82mg cholesterol, 165mg sodium, no fiber.

Week 33

Sunday *Family*

The family will welcome **Pork and Supersweet Corn** (see recipe) for a flavorful meal. Serve the savory combo with a **romaine salad** and **whole-grain rolls**. For dessert, buy a **carrot cake** and skip most of the icing. ***Plan ahead:*** Save some cake for Monday.

Monday *Budget*

For a low-cost meal, make a **BLT Pizza.** Top a ready-to-bake pizza crust with 2 cups cooked shredded chicken or turkey, 2 medium sliced green onions, 4 slices cooked crumbled bacon, 1 cup chopped tomato, and 1 cup shredded Colby-Monterey Jack cheese. Bake according to the directions on the pizza crust package until the cheese melts. Remove from oven; top with shredded lettuce. Slice and serve. Enjoy the leftover **cake** for dessert.

Tuesday *Meatless*

You won't care about meat when you have **Bow-Tie Pasta with Spinach and Mushrooms** (see recipe) for dinner. Add a **mixed greens salad** on the side along with **garlic bread**. For dessert, slices of juicy **honeydew melon** are refreshing. ***Plan ahead:*** Prepare enough pasta for Wednesday.

Wednesday *Heat and Eat*

Heat the leftover **pasta** for a quick meal. Add a **lettuce wedge** on the side and garnish with crumbled reduced-fat blue cheese. Fresh **nectarines** are a perfect summer dessert.

Thursday *Kids*

The kids and the adults will enjoy this **Baked Fried Chicken** (see recipe). Enjoy the chicken with **mashed potatoes** and fresh **broccoli,** along with soft **rolls.** For dessert, **watermelon** couldn't be better.

Friday *Express*

Try the **Boca in a Bun Chick'n & Swiss Sandwich** (or another brand) for a quick meal. (Look for the meat alternative in the freezer section.) Serve the sandwiches with **baked chips** and a **lettuce and tomato salad.** For dessert, **kiwifruit** is always good.

Saturday *Easy Entertaining*

Invite friends for a special meal of **Dijon Orange Salmon.** In a small bowl, mix together ¼ cup each orange marmalade and Dijon mustard, and 1 tablespoon fresh lemon juice. Pour over 4 4- to 5-ounce salmon fillets; marinate 30 minutes at room temperature. Heat oven to 400 degrees. Bake salmon 12 to 15 minutes or until salmon flakes easily with a fork. Garnish with lemon wedges. Serve the flavorful salmon with **jasmine rice, snow peas,** a **Bibb lettuce salad,** and **whole-grain rolls.** For dessert, enjoy **peach sorbet** and **chocolate wafer cookies.**

FAMILY

Pork and Supersweet Corn

Prep time: 15 min • **Cook time:** 30 min • **Yield:** 4 servings

Ingredients	Directions

Ingredients

3 ears corn on the cob, cut into 2-inch pieces

4 small zucchini, cut into 1-inch pieces

2 medium red bell peppers, cut into 1-inch pieces

3 tablespoons olive oil, divided

1 tablespoon cumin, divided

1 teaspoon salt, divided

½ teaspoon black pepper, divided

1 pound pork tenderloin, cut into 1-inch pieces

Directions

1 Heat oven to 450 degrees. In a large bowl, combine corn, zucchini, and peppers; add 2 tablespoons oil, 2 teaspoons cumin, ½ teaspoon salt, and ¼ teaspoon pepper. Mix well.

2 Spread mixture on a large, rimmed, nonstick-foil-lined baking pan. Bake 15 minutes; stir after 10 minutes.

3 Meanwhile, toss pork with remaining oil, cumin, salt, and pepper.

4 Remove vegetables from oven; push to one side of pan. Add pork to pan with vegetables; roast 15 more minutes.

5 Spoon vegetables and pork onto a large serving platter.

Per serving: 306 calories, 25g protein, 15g fat (41 percent calories from fat), 2.5g saturated fat, 21g carbohydrate, 58mg cholesterol, 654mg sodium, 5g fiber.

Bow-Tie Pasta with Spinach and Mushrooms

MEATLESS

Prep time: 15 min • **Cook time:** About 10 min, plus pasta • **Yield:** 5 servings

Ingredients

8 ounces bow-tie (farfalle) pasta

1 tablespoon olive oil

8 ounces sliced mushrooms

½ cup sun-dried tomatoes in oil, drained and coarsely chopped

2 cloves minced garlic

¼ cup dry white wine

1 6-ounce package baby spinach

¼ teaspoon salt

½ teaspoon pepper

¾ cup freshly grated parmesan cheese

¼ cup toasted almonds or chopped walnuts

Directions

1 Prepare pasta according to directions; drain.

2 Heat oil in a large nonstick skillet on medium-high. Add mushrooms; cook 5 minutes or until most of the moisture has evaporated.

3 Reduce heat to medium; add tomatoes and garlic. Cook and stir constantly 1 to 2 minutes.

4 Stir in wine; cook 30 seconds and loosen particles from skillet.

5 Stir in hot cooked pasta and spinach. Cook, stirring occasionally, 3 minutes or until spinach is wilted. Stir in salt and pepper.

6 Sprinkle with cheese and nuts, and serve.

Per serving: 333 calories, 14g protein, 11g fat (30 percent calories from fat), 3g saturated fat, 44g carbohydrate, 11mg cholesterol, 390mg sodium, 5g fiber.

KIDS

Baked Fried Chicken

Prep time: 15 min • **Cook time:** 45–50 min • **Yield:** 4 servings

Ingredients

4 boneless, skinless chicken breasts (about 1¼ pounds)

3 tablespoons flour

½ teaspoon kosher salt

⅛ teaspoon pepper

⅔ cup crushed shredded wheat cereal

⅓ cup buttermilk or 1-percent milk

1½ teaspoons Dijon mustard

1½ teaspoons sesame seeds

½ teaspoon paprika

½ teaspoon cayenne pepper (see Note)

⅛ teaspoon ground mustard

Directions

1 Heat oven to 425 degrees. Coat bottom of an 11-x-7-inch baking dish with cooking spray; set aside.

2 Pat chicken dry with paper towels. In a pie plate, combine flour with salt and pepper. Coat each piece of chicken in flour; shake off extra.

3 In a medium bowl, mix milk, mustard, sesame seeds, paprika, cayenne, and ground mustard. Place crushed cereal in another pie plate. Coat chicken in milk mixture and then in cereal crumbs.

4 Arrange chicken in baking dish. Bake 15 to 20 minutes; reduce oven to 375 degrees. Bake 25 to 30 minutes longer or until internal temperature of chicken is 170 degrees and juices run clear.

Per serving: 225 calories, 35g protein, 3g fat (13 percent calories from fat), 0.7g saturated fat, 13g carbohydrate, 83mg cholesterol, 393mg sodium, 2g fiber.

Note: *Adjust the amount of cayenne pepper to your kids' taste.*

Week 34

 ## Sunday *Family*

Enjoy **Grilled Lime Chicken with Avocado Salsa** (see recipe) along with **corn on the cob**, an **arugula salad**, and **baguettes**. **Strawberries in Citrus Syrup** is a refreshing dessert. In a small pan, melt ⅓ cup sugar in 3 tablespoons water on medium heat. Remove from heat; stir in ¼ cup fresh lime juice. Refrigerate until cold. Refrigerate 6 cups halved strawberries. Pour syrup over berries, add some lime zest, and toss to coat. *Plan ahead:* Grill enough chicken and make extra dessert for Monday.

 ## Monday *Easy Entertaining*

Celebrate Labor Day with friends by skipping the labor part and serving the leftover **grilled lime chicken** along with **Barbeque Potato Salad**. Cook 3 pounds red potatoes cut into bite-sized pieces until tender; drain and cool slightly. In a large bowl, mix ⅓ cup olive oil, ½ cup ketchup, ¼ cup cider vinegar, 1½ teaspoons ground mustard, 1 teaspoon pepper, and ½ teaspoon salt; whisk until blended. Add potatoes, 1 cup thinly sliced celery, 1 cup coarsely chopped red bell pepper, and ½ cup chopped red onion; toss to coat. Serve with a **lettuce and tomato salad** and **whole-grain rolls**. For dessert, top the leftover **strawberries** with fat-free **vanilla ice cream**. *Plan ahead:* Save enough ice cream for Wednesday.

 ## Tuesday *Budget*

Serve **Penne Pasta Salad with Spinach and Tomatoes** (see recipe) with a **lettuce wedge** and **garlic bread**. Slice **watermelon** for dessert. *Plan ahead:* Save enough pasta for Wednesday.

 ## Wednesday *Heat and Eat*

Stuffed tomatoes are perfect for a summer meal. Core medium tomatoes. Combine drained flaked tuna packed in water with the leftover pasta salad. Spoon it into the tomatoes. Add deli **coleslaw** and **breadsticks**. Leftover **ice cream** is for dessert.

 ## Thursday *Meatless*

Use your microwave for this really good (and easy) **Risotto with Crimini Mushrooms** (see recipe). Serve with a **romaine salad** and **Italian bread**. For dessert, **peaches** are a favorite.

 ## Friday *Express*

Make it fast and keep the kitchen cool with **chicken salad** for dinner tonight. Stir halved grapes and toasted slivered almonds into the deli salad and spoon it onto **butter lettuce cups**. Alongside, add **tomato wedges**, **olives**, and **pickles**. **Watermelon** is your dessert.

 ## Saturday *Easy Entertaining*

Guests will enjoy your **Scallops with Cherry Tomatoes**. In a small bowl, combine 2 tablespoons olive oil, 1 tablespoon Dijon mustard, 1 teaspoon lemon juice, and ½ teaspoon lemon zest. Brush it on 1 pound sea scallops (reserve remaining mixture). In a large nonstick skillet, heat 2 teaspoons olive oil until hot. Add scallops; cook 1 to 2 minutes per side or until lightly browned. Remove scallops and keep warm. To skillet, add 16 whole cherry tomatoes, 1 cup dry white wine, and remaining mustard mixture; bring to boil and reduce liquid to half. Add scallops to skillet; cook 1 minute or until heated through. Serve scallops with sauce. Add **oven-roasted potatoes**, **spinach salad**, and **sourdough bread**. Buy **fruit tarts** for dessert.

FAMILY

Grilled Lime Chicken with Avocado Salsa

Prep time: 15 min; marinating time, 1 hr • **Cook time:** 6–8 min • **Yield:** 4 servings

Ingredients

4 4- to 5-ounce boneless, skinless chicken breasts

2 tablespoons fresh lime juice

1 tablespoon olive oil

½ teaspoon salt, divided

2 diced ripe avocados

1 chopped tomato

¼ cup finely chopped red onion

1 tablespoon chopped fresh cilantro

Directions

1 In a large baking dish, arrange chicken in a single layer. Add lime juice, oil, and half the salt; turn several times to coat. Refrigerate, covered, 1 hour.

2 To make salsa, in a medium bowl, combine avocados, tomato, red onion, and remaining salt; mix well and stir in cilantro. Set aside.

3 Grill chicken 3 or 4 minutes per side until no longer pink or 170 degrees internal temperature.

4 Remove from heat, slice into strips, and serve topped with avocado salsa.

Per serving: 303 calories, 29g protein, 17g fat (49 percent calories from fat), 2.6g saturated fat, 11g carbohydrate, 66mg cholesterol, 265mg sodium, 7g fiber.

BUDGET

Penne Pasta Salad with Spinach and Tomatoes

Prep time: 15 min • **Cook time:** For the pasta • **Yield:** 5 servings

Ingredients	*Directions*
8 ounces penne pasta	*1* Cook pasta according to directions; drain.
3 tablespoons olive oil	
3 tablespoons white wine vinegar	*2* Meanwhile, to make dressing, whisk oil, vinegar, rosemary, thyme, garlic powder, oregano, and salt in a small bowl.
1 teaspoon finely chopped fresh or ½ teaspoon dried rosemary	
1 teaspoon dried thyme	*3* Mix pasta and spinach in a large bowl. Add dressing; toss to coat. Add tomatoes and cheeses; toss to mix.
½ teaspoon garlic powder	
½ teaspoon dried oregano	
½ teaspoon kosher salt	*4* Serve warm or at room temperature.
1 5- or 6-ounce package baby spinach leaves	
1 pint grape tomatoes, halved	
1 cup bite-size pieces mozzarella cheese	
2 tablespoons freshly grated parmesan cheese	

Per serving: 342 calories, 14g protein, 13g fat (35 percent calories from fat), 3.9g saturated fat, 43g carbohydrate, 16mg cholesterol, 419mg sodium, 4g fiber.

MEATLESS

Risotto with Crimini Mushrooms

Prep time: 15 min • **Cook time:** About 30 min • **Yield:** 4 servings

Ingredients

½ cup finely chopped Vidalia or other sweet onion

2 tablespoons butter

1 tablespoon plus 1 teaspoon olive oil, divided

1 clove minced garlic

1 cup arborio rice

3 to 3½ cups vegetable broth, divided

¼ cup dry white wine

1 8-ounce package sliced crimini mushrooms

3 cups firmly packed fresh spinach

¼ cup freshly grated parmesan cheese

Directions

1 Cover, vent, and microwave the onion, butter, 1 tablespoon oil, and garlic 3 minutes on high (100-percent power) in a large bowl. Stir in rice and microwave for 2 minutes.

2 Stir in 2¾ cups of the broth and the wine. Cover tightly with plastic wrap (do not vent). Microwave on high 9 minutes.

3 Meanwhile, heat 1 teaspoon oil in a large non-stick skillet on medium until hot. Add mushrooms, and cook 5 minutes or until mushrooms release their moisture and are browned.

4 Stir in spinach and cook 1 minute or until wilted.

5 Back at the rice, carefully swirl rice container to combine ingredients. (Do not uncover.) Microwave 8 minutes. Carefully remove and discard wrap.

6 Stir in cheese and ¼ cup of the broth, stirring 30 seconds to 1 minute or until creamy. Add ¼ to ½ cup additional broth, 1 tablespoon at a time, if necessary for desired consistency.

7 Stir mushroom mixture into prepared risotto. Serve immediately.

Per serving: 240 calories, 6g protein, 12g fat (44 percent calories from fat), 5.1g saturated fat, 26g carbohydrate, 20mg cholesterol, 845mg sodium, 1g fiber.

Adapted from Southern Living *magazine.*

Week 35

 ## Sunday *Family*

Enjoy family day with **Caesar Beef Kebabs** (see recipe). Serve the juicy kebabs with **green beans**, a **mixed greens salad**, and **whole-grain rolls**. Buy a **blueberry pie** for dessert. Serve it warm and jazz it up with fat-free **vanilla ice-cream. Plan ahead:** Prepare 2 extra kebabs and save enough pie for Monday.

 ## Monday *Heat and Eat*

Use Sunday's leftover beef for **Steak and Blue Cheese Salad.** Dice steak and vegetables from Sunday's kebabs; mix with packaged greens, cherry tomatoes, drained quartered artichokes, and crumbled blue cheese. Toss with low-fat blue cheese dressing. Add **whole-grain bread**. Serve the leftover **pie** for dessert.

 ## Tuesday *Budget*

Pasta is always a money-saver, as is this **Caramelized Onions with Red Peppers and Balsamic Vinegar over Fettuccine** (see recipe). Serve with a **romaine salad** and **garlic bread**. Enjoy fresh **plums** for dessert.

 ## Wednesday *Express*

For a light and pretty meal, prepare **Asian Spinach and Grape Salad.** For the dressing, combine in a blender ½ cup seasoned rice vinegar, 1 clove minced garlic, 1 tablespoon candied ginger, 2 tablespoons each canola oil and chicken broth, and ½ teaspoon dark (toasted) sesame oil. Blend until smooth. In a large bowl, combine 6 cups baby spinach, 2 8- to 10-ounce packages grilled boneless, skinless, diced chicken breasts, 1 cup green seedless grapes (halved), and ½ cup frozen (thawed) edamame. Toss with dressing. Serve with **red potatoes** (refrigerated) and **sesame breadsticks**. Make instant **butterscotch pudding** with 1-percent milk for dessert.

 ## Thursday *Meatless*

For an easy no-meat dinner, try **creamy mushrooms.** Heat 1 tablespoon canola oil in a large nonstick skillet. Add 1 pound sliced fresh mushrooms; cook and stir 5 minutes or until moisture has evaporated. Meanwhile, mix 1 0.75-ounce package mushroom gravy mix and 1 cup water. Add to skillet; bring to boil. Simmer 1 minute. Mix 2 tablespoons gravy mixture with ¼ cup low-fat sour cream. Slowly stir into gravy. Serve the mushroom mixture over **no-yolk noodles**. Serve with a **green salad** and **sourdough bread**. You'll like **nectarines** for dessert.

 ## Friday *Kids*

For a special treat for the kids, try these **Mexican Meatballs.** In a medium bowl, lightly mix together 12 ounces lean ground pork, ½ cup each grated zucchini and crushed tortilla chips, ¼ cup each thinly sliced green onions and fresh cilantro, 1 egg, and 1 teaspoon each minced garlic, cumin, and dried oregano. Roll into 24 meatballs. Brown in 1 teaspoon canola oil in a large nonstick skillet. Add 1 8-ounce can tomato sauce and 1 10-ounce can enchilada sauce. Cover and simmer for 5 minutes or until meatballs are cooked through (160 degrees). Serve them with **rice, green beans,** and **soft rolls**. For an extra-slurpy dessert, **Choco-Nana Milk Blast** is kid-perfect. For 2 servings: Cut 1 banana into chunks and place in blender; add 1 cup low-fat chocolate milk, 1 cup low-fat chocolate yogurt ,and 1 tablespoon chocolate syrup. Cover and blend until smooth.

 ## Saturday *Easy Entertaining*

Shrimp and Pesto Pasta (see recipe) is an excellent dish for guests and a recipe you'll prepare often. Serve it with an **arugula salad** and **baguettes**. Buy a **coconut meringue pie** for dessert.

FAMILY

Caesar Beef Kebabs

Prep time: 15 min • **Cook time:** About 15 min • **Yield:** 4 servings

Ingredients	Directions
4 small to medium potatoes cut into quarters	**1** Microwave potatoes on high (100-percent power) 3 to 4 minutes or just until tender. Cool slightly.
1 pound boneless beef top sirloin, 1 inch thick	**2** Cut beef into 1½-inch pieces. In a large bowl, combine beef, potatoes, bell pepper, and onion.
1 medium red bell pepper cut into 1-inch pieces	
1 small onion cut into 1-inch pieces	**3** Reserve 2 tablespoons dressing; set aside. Pour remaining dressing over kebab mixture and toss to coat. Alternately thread beef and vegetables onto metal skewers.
½ cup store-bought non-creamy Caesar dressing (such as Ken's), divided	
Salt and pepper to taste	**4** Grill, uncovered, 10 to 12 minutes for medium-rare to medium; turning occasionally.
	5 Season with salt and pepper. Drizzle kebabs with reserved dressing just before serving.

Per serving: 232 calories, 27g protein, 7g fat (30 percent calories from fat), 2.3g saturated fat, 12g carbohydrate, 49mg cholesterol, 275mg sodium, 2g fiber.

Vary it! *To broil instead of grilling, place kebabs on rack in broiler pan and broil 3 to 4 inches from heat for 8 to 10 minutes.*

Caramelized Onions with Red Peppers and Balsamic Vinegar over Fettuccine

Prep time: 15 min • **Cooking time:** 15–20 min, plus pasta • **Yield:** 4 servings

Ingredients	*Directions*
12 ounces spinach or regular fettuccine	**1** Cook pasta according to directions; drain.
1 tablespoon olive oil	**2** Meanwhile, heat oil in a large nonstick skillet on medium. Add onions and sugar, and cook 10 to 15 minutes, stirring occasionally until onions are golden and caramelized.
1 medium onion, halved and sliced	
2 tablespoons sugar	
1 cup sliced roasted red peppers, drained (jar)	**3** Stir in red peppers and vinegar and cook 2 minutes.
2 tablespoons balsamic vinegar	**4** Add broth and pasta; simmer 2 minutes or until heated through.
1 cup fat-free chicken broth	
Salt and pepper to taste	**5** Season with salt and pepper, and serve.

Per serving: 396 calories, 12g protein, 5g fat (11 percent calories from fat), 0.7g saturated fat, 76g carbohydrate, no cholesterol, 136mg sodium, 3g fiber.

Adapted from Robin to the Rescue, *by Robin Miller (The Taunton Press).*

EASY ENTERTAINING

Shrimp and Pesto Pasta

Prep time: 15 min • **Cook time:** About 20 min, plus pasta • **Yield:** 6 servings

Ingredients	*Directions*
8 ounces whole-wheat fettuccine	*1* Cook fettuccine according to directions. Three minutes before end of cooking time, add asparagus and continue cooking 3 minutes or until the pasta and asparagus are just tender. Drain the fettuccine and asparagus and return to the pot.
1 pound fresh asparagus, trimmed and cut into 1-inch pieces (about 4 cups)	
½ cup sliced roasted red peppers (jar)	*2* Stir in peppers and pesto. Cover to keep warm.
¼ cup prepared pesto	*3* Heat oil in a large skillet over medium heat. Add shrimp and cook 2 minutes, stirring occasionally, or until lightly browned.
2 teaspoons extra-virgin olive oil	
1 pound uncooked shrimp (21 to 25 per pound), peeled and deveined	*4* Add wine; increase heat to high and continue cooking 3 to 4 minutes or until the shrimp are opaque and the wine is reduced by about one third.
1 cup dry white wine	
Freshly ground pepper to taste	*5* Add the shrimp to the pasta; toss to coat. Season with pepper and serve immediately.

Per serving: 299 calories, 20g protein, 8g fat (23 percent calories from fat), 1.3g saturated fat, 33g carbohydrate, 115mg cholesterol, 232mg sodium, 7g fiber.

Adapted from Eating Well *magazine.*

Week 36

Sunday *Family*

The family will look forward to your own **grilled chicken breasts with roasted red potatoes** today. Dress up the table with **Fresh and Fruity Salad** (see recipe). Add **crusty bread**. For dessert, slice **Boston cream pie**. *Plan ahead:* Grill 2 extra chicken breasts and save enough pie for Monday.

Monday *Heat and Eat*

Make delicious use of leftover chicken in **Hawaiian Soft Tacos.** Cut chicken into ½-inch strips. Heat 2 16-ounce cans slightly drained chili beans until hot. Spoon about ⅓ cup beans into middle of 8 7- to 8-inch, fat-free flour tortillas. Top with the sliced chicken. Divide and spoon 1 cup diced fresh pineapple and ½ cup chopped green onions onto chicken. Fold tortillas and serve them with **rice**. Leftover **pie** is dessert. *Plan ahead:* Prepare enough rice for Wednesday. Save enough pineapple for Saturday.

Tuesday *Kids*

This **Cheesy Pasta and Bean Bake** is kid-friendly. Heat oven to 375 degrees. Prepare 1 pound penne pasta according to directions; drain and return to pot. Stir in 1 14½-ounce can diced tomatoes, 2 16-ounce cans rinsed and drained kidney beans, and 1 26-ounce jar of red spaghetti sauce. Transfer to a 3-quart baking dish coated with cooking spray, and top with 1 cup shredded part-skim mozzarella cheese. Bake 20 minutes or until cheese is melted and golden. Serve with **red bell pepper sticks** and **ranch dressing** for dipping. Add soft **rolls**. A fun way to eat **kiwifruit** is to halve it and eat it with a spoon for dessert.

Wednesday *Express*

You'll impress everyone with your fast and delicious **Greek-Style Meatball Kebabs.** Heat oven to 350 degrees. Alternately thread meatballs from 1 16- to 18-ounce package turkey or beef meatballs (thawed, if frozen) with 1 red or green bell pepper (cut into ¾-inch pieces) on 4 to 6 skewers. Bake 20 minutes. Meanwhile, make a **yogurt sauce.** Mix together 1 cup plain fat-free yogurt, ¼ cup diced, seeded cucumber, 1 large clove minced garlic, and salt and pepper to taste. Serve the sauce with the meatball kebabs and leftover **rice.** Add a packaged **green salad** and **whole-grain rolls**. Fresh **nectarines** are a refreshing dessert.

Thursday *Budget*

Save money and calories with **Broiled Turkey-Onion Burgers** on hamburger buns. Mix ground turkey with dry onion-mushroom soup mix before broiling. Serve with **Red Cabbage Slaw.** Toss shredded red cabbage with low-fat coleslaw dressing and caraway seeds. Add **corn on the cob.** For dessert, **red and green grapes** are good.

Friday *Meatless*

Start your no-meat dinner with an **Antipasto Platter.** Arrange marinated artichokes, drained roasted red peppers, mushrooms, and olives from the deli (or jars) on a lettuce-lined platter. That was easy, and so will frozen **vegetable lasagna** be for the follow-up. Serve with **garlic bread.** For a simple dessert, **pears** pass the test.

Saturday *Easy Entertaining*

Invite guests for **Pork Stir-Fry** (see recipe). Serve the sweet-hot combo over **cellophane noodles** (or rice). Add a **mixed greens salad** and **crusty bread.** For dessert, **Pineapple Brûlée** (see recipe) will impress any guest. *Tip:* Look for cellophane noodles in the ethnic section of your supermarket.

FAMILY

Fresh and Fruity Salad

Prep time: 10 min • **Yield:** 8 servings

Ingredients

For the dressing:

1 16-ounce jar sliced pickled beets (undrained)

¼ cup orange juice

1 tablespoon finely chopped fresh or 1 teaspoon dried basil

½ teaspoon pepper

¼ cup olive oil

For the salad:

1 5- or 6-ounce package baby spinach leaves or other greens (about 6 cups)

2½ cups bite-size pieces of honeydew melon or cantaloupe

2 fresh peeled peaches, cut into wedges

1 cup fresh blueberries or sliced strawberries

¼ cup toasted sliced almonds

Directions

1 For dressing, drain beets, reserving ¼ cup liquid. Set beets aside.

2 In small bowl, combine reserved beet liquid, orange juice, basil, and pepper. Whisk in oil; set aside.

3 For the salad, arrange spinach, reserved beets, melon, peaches, and berries on a large platter.

4 To serve, drizzle with dressing; toss lightly. Sprinkle with almonds.

Per serving: 161 calories, 2g protein, 9g fat (45 percent calories from fat), 1.1g saturated fat, 22g carbohydrate, no cholesterol, 170mg sodium, 4g fiber.

Note: To toast almonds, spread on a flat baking sheet and bake at 350 degrees for 5 to 10 minutes or until golden; stir once or twice.

Pork Stir-Fry

Prep time: About 15 min • **Cook time:** About 10 min • **Yield:** 4 servings

EASY ENTERTAINING

Ingredients

12 ounces boneless pork loin, sliced into ⅛-x-2-inch strips

1 teaspoon chili powder

½ teaspoon crushed red pepper flakes

¼ teaspoon cumin

1 tablespoon cornstarch

⅓ cup water

2 teaspoons low-sodium soy sauce

1 tablespoon vegetable oil

1 cup thinly sliced fresh carrots

3 cups bok choy

1 small red bell pepper, cut into ½-inch strips

¼ cup walnut pieces

Directions

1 In a resealable plastic bag, combine pork, chili powder, red pepper flakes, and cumin; shake to distribute spices.

2 Mix together cornstarch, water, and soy sauce; set aside.

3 Heat oil in a large nonstick skillet over medium-high heat. Add pork strips and carrots, and stir-fry 4 minutes.

4 Add bok choy and red bell pepper to skillet; stir-fry 4 more minutes or until vegetables are softened.

5 Add soy sauce mixture and walnuts; stir-fry 1 minute or until sauce is thickened and bubbly. Serve immediately.

Per serving: 241 calories, 20g protein, 15g fat (53 percent calories from fat), 2.8g saturated fat, 9g carbohydrate, 48mg cholesterol, 177mg sodium, 3g fiber.

EASY ENTERTAINING

Pineapple Brûlée

Prep time: 10 min • **Cook time:** About 5 min • **Yield:** 4 servings

Ingredients

4 slices peeled fresh pineapple (1-inch thick)

4 tablespoons packed light brown sugar

4 scoops fruit sorbet

Fresh mint sprigs for garnish

Directions

1 Heat broiler. Coat broiler rack with cooking spray. Place pineapple on rack, and place rack on foil-lined broiler pan; sprinkle each slice with 1 tablespoon sugar.

2 Broil 4 inches from heat for 2 to 3 minutes until sugar melts and bubbles.

3 Place on serving plates; top with sorbet. Spoon juices from pan around pineapple. Garnish with mint if desired.

Per serving: 176 calories, 1g protein, no fat, no saturated fat, 45g carbohydrate, no cholesterol, 13mg sodium, 1g fiber.

Adapted from Woman's Day *magazine.*

Week 37

 ## Sunday *Family*

Gather the family for a really good **Grilled Flank Steak with Corn and Avocado Salad** (see recipe). The combo goes well with **roasted red potatoes** and **baguettes.** For dessert, **chocolate layer cake** and fat-free **strawberry ice cream** will be a family favorite. ***Plan ahead:*** Save enough cake for Monday and enough ice cream for Wednesday.

 ## Monday *Express*

For a quick meal, **Cubano Quesadillas** are easy. Spread 8 6-inch fat-free flour tortillas with ¼ cup yellow mustard. Divide 4 ounces sliced ham, 8 dill pickle slices, 4 ounces thinly sliced roast pork (deli or your own) and 4 ounces thinly sliced Swiss cheese on 4 tortillas. Top with remaining tortillas, pressing firmly. Grill in a large nonstick skillet until light brown and cheese melts; turn once. Transfer to cutting board and let stand 1 minute before cutting into wedges; then serve. Add packaged **yellow rice** and **tomato wedges** on the side. Slice the leftover **cake** for dessert.

 ## Tuesday *Kids*

The kids will stand in line for **Tex-Mex Mac and Cheese**. Stir a 14.5-ounce can diced tomatoes with mild green chilies into a prepared mac-and-cheese mix. Heat through. Serve with **celery sticks** and **soft rolls.** Offer the kids **popsicles** for dessert.

 ## Wednesday *Meatless*

Try **Artichokes with Plum Tomatoes over Linguine.** Cook 8 ounces linguine according to directions; drain. Meanwhile, in a medium saucepan, heat 2 tablespoons extra-virgin olive oil on medium until hot. Add 1 large finely chopped sweet onion; cook 8 minutes. Add 1 clove minced garlic; cook 30 seconds. Stir in ¼ cup vegetable broth, ¼ teaspoon salt, and 1 28-ounce can plum tomatoes. Break up tomatoes with a wooden spoon. Simmer, stirring occasionally, 15 minutes. Stir in 1 14-ounce can drained and quartered artichokes packed in water and ½ cup pitted kalamata olives. Cook 1 minute or until heated through. Add a **spinach salad** and **garlic bread,** and enjoy the leftover **ice cream** for dessert.

 ## Thursday *Budget*

No one will be able to resist economical **Moroccan Chicken** (see recipe). Serve it over **couscous.** Add **cucumber spears in cider vinegar** on the side along with **flatbread. Apricots** are good for dessert. ***Plan ahead:*** Save enough Moroccan Chicken for Friday.

 ## Friday *Heat and Eat*

The flavors of the leftover Moroccan Chicken will be even better tonight. For a change, serve it over **brown rice.** Serve with **mixed greens** and **whole-grain rolls.** Fresh **pineapple** is an easy dessert. ***Plan ahead:*** Cook enough brown rice for Saturday.

 ## Saturday *Easy Entertaining*

Invite friends for delicious **Tilapia Gremolata with Vegetable Ribbons** (see recipe). Serve it with leftover **rice,** a **Boston lettuce salad,** and **sourdough bread.** Buy a **cheesecake** for dessert and jazz it up with **cherry topping.**

FAMILY

Grilled Flank Steak with Corn and Avocado Salad

Prep time: 20 min, plus marinating time • **Cook time:** 17–21 min • **Yield:** 4 servings

Ingredients

For the flank steak:

⅓ cup chipotle pepper sauce (such as Tabasco's)

1 tablespoon cumin

1 large garlic clove, crushed

1 pound flank steak

For the corn salad:

2 cups frozen corn or corn cut from 4 ears cooked fresh corn on the cob

2 large tomatoes, chopped

1 small red onion, chopped

1 ripe avocado, diced and peeled

2 tablespoons chopped fresh basil

2 tablespoons fresh lime juice

2 tablespoons extra-virgin olive oil

1 tablespoon chipotle pepper sauce

¼ teaspoon salt

Directions

1 Prepare flank steak: In baking dish large enough to accommodate steak, combine chipotle pepper sauce, cumin, and garlic; mix well. Add steak. Turn to coat; cover and refrigerate at least 30 minutes up to overnight.

2 Meanwhile, for the corn salad: Microwave corn according to package directions; drain. In medium bowl, combine corn, tomatoes, red onion, avocado, basil, lime juice, olive oil, chipotle pepper sauce, and salt; toss to mix well.

3 Preheat grill. Grill flank steak 17 to 21 minutes for medium-rare to medium doneness, turning once.

4 To serve, thinly slice steak across grain. Serve with corn salad.

Per serving: 406 calories, 27g protein, 22g fat (46 percent calories from fat), 4.9g saturated fat, 30g carbohydrate, 45mg cholesterol, 470mg sodium, 7g fiber.

BUDGET

Moroccan Chicken

Prep time: 10 min • **Cook time:** 4 hr on high; 8 hr on low • **Yield:** 8 servings

Ingredients	Directions
2 tablespoons pickling spice (such as McCormick or another brand)	**1** Place pickling spice in the center of a piece of cheesecloth or a coffee filter. Tie tightly with a long piece of string; set aside.
1 large onion, cut into thin wedges	
3 to 3½ pounds bone-in, skinless chicken thighs	**2** Layer onion and chicken in a slow cooker. In a small bowl, mix flour, garlic salt, and turmeric. Sprinkle over chicken.
¼ cup flour	
1 teaspoon garlic salt	**3** Add pickling spice bundle, broth, tomatoes, dates, and almonds.
¼ teaspoon turmeric	
1 14-ounce can fat-free chicken broth	**4** Cover and cook 4 hours on high or 8 hours on low. Remove spice bundle and serve.
1 14.5-ounce can drained no-salt-added or regular diced tomatoes	
1 cup (about 6 ounces) pitted dates	
½ cup sliced almonds	

Per serving: *320 calories, 27g protein, 13g fat (36 percent calories from fat), 3g saturated fat, 25g carbohydrate, 86mg cholesterol, 299mg sodium, 4g fiber.*

EASY ENTERTAINING

Tilapia Gremolata with Vegetable Ribbons

Prep time: 15 min • **Cook time:** About 15 min • **Yield:** 4 servings

Ingredients	Directions
2 tablespoons chopped fresh flat-leaf parsley	*1* For the gremolata: In a small bowl, combine parsley, half of the garlic, and the lemon zest; set aside.
1 clove minced garlic, divided	
1 teaspoon lemon zest	
4 teaspoons extra-virgin olive oil, divided	*2* In a large nonstick skillet, heat 2 teaspoons oil on medium-high; cook zucchini and carrots 8 minutes, stirring occasionally or until tender. Stir in remaining garlic and half the salt; cook 30 seconds.
4 medium zucchini, cut into ribbons (see Note)	
3 medium carrots, cut into ribbons	*3* Arrange vegetables on a serving platter and keep warm.
¼ teaspoon salt, divided	
4 5- or 6-ounce tilapia fillets	*4* Meanwhile, season tilapia with remaining salt. In same skillet, heat remaining oil on medium-high; cook tilapia 5 minutes or until opaque throughout, turning once.
2 tablespoons fresh lemon juice	
	5 To serve, arrange tilapia on vegetables; sprinkle with lemon juice. Evenly top with gremolata mixture.

Per serving: 233 calories, 32g protein, 7g fat (27 percent calories from fat), 1.7g saturated fat, 13g carbohydrate, 71mg cholesterol, 277mg sodium, 4g fiber.

Note: Use a vegetable peeler to make the vegetable ribbons.

Week 38

 ### Sunday   *Family*

Perk up the family day meal with **Turkey Breast and Pineapple-Orange Sauce** (see recipe). On the side, serve **jasmine rice**, fresh **broccoli**, a **spinach salad,** and **dinner rolls.** For dessert, buy a **deep-dish apple cobbler** and sprinkle it with extra cinnamon. ***Plan ahead:*** Save enough turkey and cobbler and prepare enough rice for Monday.

 ### Monday   *Heat and Eat*

Make a quick **stir-fry** using the leftover turkey (cut into strips), frozen stir-fry vegetables, and stir-fry sauce. Serve your creation over leftover **rice.** Add a **lettuce wedge** and **sesame breadsticks.** Heat the leftover **cobbler** for dessert, and top it with fat-free **vanilla ice cream.** ***Plan ahead:*** Save enough ice cream for Tuesday and Thursday.

 ### Tuesday   *Budget*

This **Mediterranean Tuna Salad** has lots of flavor and is easy on the pocketbook. Place 2 6- to 8-ounce packages of Mediterranean or other salad greens in a serving bowl. To bowl, add 8 ounces cooked green beans, 2 peeled, seeded, diced cucumbers, 1 pint halved grape tomatoes, 1 12-ounce can drained flaked tuna in water, 12 pitted kalamata olives, ½ cup reduced-fat crumbled basil and tomato feta cheese, and ½ cup Greek salad dressing; toss to combine the ingredients and coat with dressing. (Adapted from *Woman's Day* magazine.) Serve with leftover **ice cream** for dessert.

 ### Wednesday   *Express*

A **sandwich platter** of fixin's is quick and easy, making it a popular meal. On the platter, include small bowls of **hummus, low-fat mayonnaise,** and various **mustards** for spreads. Add deli **roast beef, Swiss cheese,** and **coleslaw.** Complete the platter with **sliced fennel, tomatoes, lettuce,** and **whole-grain bread.** Add **chips, pickles,** and **olives.** Of course, **cookies** are the right dessert for this simple meal.

 ### Thursday   *Kids*

Here come the kids, ready to eat **Sloppy Joes.** Use a mix and your favorite ground meat. Spoon the kid-food on **whole-grain buns.** Serve with **oven fries** (frozen) and **carrot sticks.** Expect excitement when the kids see **Root Beer Floats** for dessert. Bring 1 cup water to boil. Add ¾ cup sugar; stir until dissolved. Add 1½ teaspoons root beer concentrate; stir until well mixed. Refrigerate until ready to serve. Slowly pour 1 liter cold club soda into root beer mixture. Place 2 scoops ice cream into each of 4 tall glasses. Slowly pour root beer mixture between ice cream and side of glass. Serve immediately. ***Tip:*** Look for root beer concentrate in the spice aisle.

 ### Friday   *Meatless*

Bow-Tie Pasta with Sun-Dried Tomatoes and Arugula (see recipe) is another no-meat meal with great flavor. Serve with steamed **zucchini squash** and **Italian bread.** **Peaches** are your dessert.

 ### Saturday   *Easy Entertaining*

Serve your guests flavor-packed **Greek Chicken with Vegetable Ragout** (see recipe). Add a **romaine salad** and **flatbread.** For dessert, **raspberry sorbet** and **butter cookies** are light and easy.

FAMILY

Turkey Breast and Pineapple-Orange Sauce

Prep time: 15 min • **Cook time:** About 1½ hr, plus standing time • **Yield:** 12 to 18 servings

Ingredients

1 4- to 6-pound frozen bone-in turkey breast, thawed

1⅔ cups pineapple-orange or orange juice

3 tablespoons fresh lemon juice

2 tablespoons cornstarch

1 tablespoon packed light brown sugar

¼ teaspoon ground ginger

1 11-ounce can drained Mandarin orange sections

Directions

1 Heat oven to 450 degrees. Place turkey breast in center of an 18-x-28-inch piece of heavy-duty foil. Close loosely by overlapping ends, turning up short sides to hold in juices. Do not seal airtight.

2 Place turkey in a roasting pan at least 2 inches deep. Insert meat thermometer through foil into thickest part of breast, not touching bone. Roast 45 minutes.

3 Open and turn back foil. Continue roasting 30 to 45 minutes or until thermometer registers 170 degrees and turkey is browned. Let stand loosely covered with foil 10 minutes before slicing.

4 Meanwhile, mix together juices, cornstarch, sugar, and ginger in medium pan. Cook and stir until thickened and bubbly. Cook and stir 2 more minutes. Stir in orange sections; heat through.

5 Serve with turkey.

Per serving: 150 calories, 25g protein, 1g fat (6 percent calories from fat), 0.3g saturated fat, 8g carbohydrate, 71mg cholesterol, 50mg sodium, no fiber.

MEATLESS

Bow-Tie Pasta with Sun-Dried Tomatoes and Arugula

Prep time: 15 min   •   **Cook time:** About 10 min, plus pasta   •   **Yield:** 4 servings

Ingredients	*Directions*
8 ounces bow-tie pasta	*1* Cook pasta according to directions; drain.
4 teaspoons olive oil, divided	
1 medium chopped onion	*2* In a large nonstick skillet, heat half of the oil on medium until hot. Add onion, garlic, salt, and pepper, and cook 5 minutes or until onion is softened, stirring occasionally.
1 clove minced garlic	
¼ teaspoon salt	
¼ teaspoon coarsely ground black pepper	*3* Stir in tomatoes and wine. Bring to boil over medium-high heat and cook, stirring occasionally, for 1 minute.
½ cup chopped, well-drained sun-dried tomatoes packed in oil (see Note)	
¼ cup dry white wine or vegetable broth	*4* Reduce heat to medium and stir in broth. Bring to boil; reduce by half. Add arugula or spinach. Cook 1 minute or until wilted.
1 cup vegetable broth	
1 5- to 7-ounce package coarsely chopped arugula or baby spinach leaves	*5* Remove from heat and stir in pasta, ⅓ cup parmesan cheese, and remaining olive oil.
⅓ cup plus 2 tablespoons freshly grated parmesan cheese	*6* Spoon into serving dishes and sprinkle with remaining cheese.

Per serving: 353 calories, 13g protein, 10g fat (26 percent calories from fat), 2.6g saturated fat, 51g carbohydrate, 8mg cholesterol, 572mg sodium, 4g fiber.

Note: Press tomatoes between layers of paper towels to remove excess oil.

EASY ENTERTAINING

Greek Chicken and Vegetable Ragout

Prep time: 14 min • **Cook time:** About 7 hr • **Yield:** 6 servings

Ingredients

1 pound baby carrots

1 pound (3 or 4 medium) Yukon Gold or other yellow potatoes, peeled and cut lengthwise into 1¼-inch wedges

2 pounds boneless, skinless chicken thighs, trimmed

1 14-ounce can fat-free chicken broth

⅓ cup dry white wine

4 cloves minced garlic

½ teaspoon salt

1 14-ounce can rinsed, quartered artichoke hearts in water

1 egg

2 egg yolks

⅓ cup fresh lemon juice

⅓ cup chopped fresh dill

Freshly ground black pepper

Directions

1 Spread carrots and potatoes over bottom of a 4-quart or larger slow cooker. Arrange chicken on top.

2 Bring broth, wine, garlic, and salt to a simmer in medium pan over medium-high heat. Pour over chicken and vegetables.

3 Cover and cook 6 to 6½ hours on low until chicken is cooked through and vegetables are tender. Add artichokes; cover and cook on high 5 minutes.

4 Meanwhile, whisk egg, egg yolks, and lemon juice in a medium bowl.

5 Transfer chicken and vegetables to serving bowl, using slotted spoon. Cover and keep warm.

6 Ladle about ½ cup cooking liquid into egg mixture. Whisk until smooth. Whisk egg mixture into the remaining cooking liquid in slow cooker.

7 Cover and cook 15 to 20 minutes on high, whisking 2 or 3 times until slightly thickened and sauce reaches 160 degrees. Stir in dill and pepper.

8 Pour sauce over chicken and vegetables, and serve.

Per serving: 369 calories, 33g protein, 14g fat (35 percent calories from fat), 4.1g saturated fat, 25g carbohydrate, 203mg cholesterol, 554mg sodium, 4g fiber.

Week 39

 Sunday *Family*

Impress the family with **Rosemary Lamb Kebabs with Bell Peppers and Mushrooms** (see recipe). Serve the aromatic lamb with **couscous,** an **arugula salad,** and **flatbread.** Buy a **lemon meringue pie** for dessert. **Plan ahead:** Save 2 lamb kebabs and some pie for Monday.

 Monday *Heat and Eat*

Use the leftover lamb for **Lamb Pitas with Cucumber Dressing.** Chop leftover lamb and stuff into whole-grain pitas. Mix 1 cup plain yogurt and diced cucumber with 1 teaspoon cumin, and spoon over lamb in pitas. Add sliced **cucumbers** on the side. Slice the leftover **pie** for dessert.

 Tuesday *Express*

Make it quick tonight with **Taco Veggie Burgers** on whole-grain buns. Brush taco sauce on any brand of veggie burgers during the last 3 minutes of cooking. Serve more sauce on the side, along with sliced **onions** and **avocados.** Add deli **potato salad.** Enjoy **kiwifruit** for dessert.

 Wednesday *Budget*

Careful, or you'll lick your plate of **Pappardelle with Fresh Tomatoes and Basil,** a delicious, low-cost dinner. In a large bowl, add 8 large diced, seeded, and peeled tomatoes (or two drained 14½-ounce cans diced tomatoes with Italian herbs), ¼ to ⅓ cup thinly sliced fresh basil, 1 clove minced garlic, 3 table-spoons extra-virgin olive oil, and ¼ teaspoon each freshly ground black pepper and kosher salt; mix well. Cover and let stand at room temperature 2 hours. Cook 8 ounces pappardelle pasta or no-yolk extra-wide noodles as directed. Top hot pasta with sauce; garnish with freshly grated parmesan cheese. Serve **mixed greens** and **Italian bread.** How about **plums** for dessert? **Tip:** Quickly peel tomatoes by placing whole tomatoes in boiling water for 10 seconds. Remove, run under cold water, and peel.

 Thursday *Kids*

Cheesy Chicken Crunchers (see recipe) are a meal kids of all ages will like. Serve with **barbecue sauce** for dipping. Add **oven fries** (frozen) and **carrot salad. Pears** are your dessert.

 Friday *Meatless*

Take a meat break and enjoy **Vegetable Stew.** In a large nonstick skillet, heat 1 tablespoon olive oil on medium. Add 2 medium zucchini (halved lengthwise and thinly sliced), 1 peeled medium eggplant (cut into ½-inch cubes), 1 medium finely chopped onion, and ¼ teaspoon each salt and pepper. Cook for 15 minutes or until tender; stir occasionally. Stir in 1 26-ounce jar no-salt-added or regular marinara sauce and ¼ cup chopped fresh or 1 tablespoon dried basil. Bring to boil; reduce heat and simmer 10 minutes; stir occasionally. Serve over **couscous;** garnish with crumbled feta cheese. Add **garlic bread.** For dessert, try **red and green grapes.**

 Saturday *Easy Entertaining*

Invite special friends for **Seared Salmon with Spinach and Grapes** (see recipe). Serve with **basmati rice, green beans,** and **crusty rolls.** Spoon **lemon curd** over **angel food cake** for dessert.

FAMILY

Rosemary Lamb Kebabs with Bell Peppers and Mushrooms

Prep time: 25 min • **Cook time:** About 10 min • **Yield:** 6 kebabs

Ingredients

¼ cup balsamic vinegar

3 cloves minced garlic

2 teaspoons chopped fresh rosemary

¾ teaspoon cumin

¾ teaspoon salt

½ teaspoon black pepper

½ teaspoon ground coriander

1¼-pound lamb leg or shoulder, trimmed and cut into 18 cubes

12 medium whole mushrooms

2 bell peppers (any color), each cut into 6 pieces

1 large red onion, cut into 12 pieces

1 large zucchini, cut into 12 pieces

Directions

1 In a small bowl, combine vinegar, garlic, rosemary, cumin, salt, pepper, and coriander.

2 Thread six 12-inch metal skewers alternately with lamb, mushrooms, bell peppers, onion, and zucchini. Baste with sauce.

3 Broil 4 inches from heat source 4 minutes per side or to desired doneness, 145 to 160 degrees for medium-rare to medium.

Per kebab: Per serving: 172 calories, 20g protein, 5g fat (27 percent calories from fat), 1.7g saturated fat, 12g carbohydrate, 54mg cholesterol, 345mg sodium, 3g fiber.

KIDS

Cheesy Chicken Crunchers

Prep time: 10 min • **Cook time:** 25 min • **Yield:** 4 servings

Ingredients	*Directions*
½ cup flour	**1** Heat oven to 375 degrees. Coat a 9-x-13-inch baking dish with foil. Place a rack coated with cooking spray in dish; set aside.
2 egg whites	
⅓ cup 1-percent milk	
½ cup crushed shredded wheat	**2** Place flour in a pie plate. In a second pie plate, mix together the egg whites and milk. In a third pie plate, mix shredded wheat with cheese.
½ cup 50-percent-reduced-fat shredded cheddar cheese	
1 pound chicken tenders	**3** Coat chicken strips in flour (shake to remove excess), then egg-milk mixture.
	4 Roll chicken in cheese-cereal mixture, coating all sides. (Discard any extra coating mixture.)
	5 Place chicken on rack in dish. Bake 15 minutes; increase oven to 450 degrees. Turn chicken; bake 10 more minutes or until no longer pink.

Per serving: 200 calories, 32g protein, 3g fat (15 percent calories from fat), 1.6g saturated fat, 10g carbohydrate, 72mg cholesterol, 160mg sodium, 1g fiber.

EASY ENTERTAINING

Seared Salmon with Spinach and Grapes

Prep time: 15 min • **Cook time:** About 20 min • **Yield:** 4 servings

Ingredients

½ teaspoon salt

1 teaspoon dry mustard

1 teaspoon dried thyme

½ teaspoon pepper

4 5- or 6-ounce salmon fillets

2 teaspoons honey

3 teaspoons olive oil, divided

1 5- or 6-ounce package baby spinach leaves

1 cup seedless red grapes, halved

½ cup dry red wine

Directions

1 Heat oven to 325 degrees. In a small bowl, combine salt, mustard, thyme, and pepper.

2 Drizzle salmon with honey and sprinkle with seasoning mixture. Reserve any remaining seasoning mixture.

3 In a large nonstick skillet, heat 2 teaspoons oil. Brown both sides of salmon on medium-high heat about 2 minutes per side.

4 Meanwhile, toss the spinach with remaining teaspoon oil and arrange in a 9-x-13-inch baking dish. Place salmon on bed of spinach; cover loosely with foil. Bake 8 minutes or until salmon is cooked through.

5 Cook the grapes for 1 minute on medium-high in same skillet. Add wine; bring to boil and cook 4 minutes to reduce by half. Season sauce with remaining spice mixture.

6 Serve the salmon with wilted spinach, topped with grapes and wine sauce.

Per serving: 280 calories, 32g protein, 9g fat (29 percent calories from fat), 1.4g saturated fat, 15g carbohydrate, 81mg cholesterol, 452mg sodium, 2g fiber.

Week 40

Sunday   *Family*

Cooler days call for **Sunday Dinner Pot Roast** (see recipe). Serve the combo meal with **mixed greens** and **whole-grain rolls.** Pair a **yellow layer cake** with fat-free **chocolate ice cream** for an extra-special dessert. *Plan ahead:* Save enough pot roast with vegetables and cake for Monday. Save enough ice cream for Saturday.

Monday   *Heat and Eat*

Use the leftover pot roast and vegetables for **Vegetable Beef Soup.** Dice the meat and vegetables into bite-sized pieces; combine with some low-sodium beef broth, a 14.5-ounce can no-salt-added diced tomatoes, and ½ teaspoon dried thyme. Thin soup with water or broth as desired. Heat soup, ladle into bowls, and top with freshly grated parmesan cheese. Add a **lettuce wedge** and **crackers.** Slice the leftover **cake** for dessert.

Tuesday   *Budget*

Cut food costs and enjoy **Pepper-Potato Cheese Omelet.** Heat some canola oil in a large nonstick skillet. Add 2 cups refrigerated O'Brien potatoes; pat flat into skillet. Cook, uncovered, on low about 7 minutes; turn once. In a small bowl, beat together 4 eggs and ¼ cup milk. Pour over potatoes. Top with 1 cup shredded reduced-fat sharp cheddar cheese and 1 tablespoon crumbled cooked bacon. Cook, covered, 5 to 7 minutes or until mixture is set. Loosen omelet and fold in half onto a serving plate. Cut into wedges to serve. (Adapted from Publix Supermarket recipe.) Serve with a **spinach salad** and **bran muffins** (from a mix). Enjoy **strawberries** for dessert.

Wednesday   *Kids*

Let the kids help prepare **Monster Burgers** (see recipe). Serve the funny creations with frozen **oven fries** and **carrot salad. Tropical fruit** is an easy dessert.

Thursday   *Express*

Make it quick tonight with **Tuna Melts.** Spoon deli tuna salad onto whole-grain English muffins. Top tuna with sliced tomatoes and 50-percent-reduced-fat cheddar cheese. Broil until cheese is melted. Serve with **sweet red pepper soup. Apple slices** sprinkled with cinnamon are a crunchy finish.

Friday   *Meatless*

Forget meat and enjoy **7-Layer Tortilla Pie.** Heat oven to 400 degrees. Mash 2 15-ounce cans rinsed low-sodium pinto beans. Stir in ¾ cup picante sauce and ¼ teaspoon garlic powder. In another bowl, mix another ¼ cup picante, 2 tablespoons chopped fresh cilantro, 1 15-ounce can rinsed black beans, and ½ cup chopped tomatoes. Place 1 8-inch fat-free flour tortilla (7 total) on a baking sheet. Spread ¾ cup pinto bean mixture over tortilla to within ½ inch of the edge. Top with ¼ cup (2 cups total) shredded 50-percent-reduced-fat cheddar cheese. Top with one tortilla and ⅓ of black bean mixture. Repeat layers 2 more times. Top with one more tortilla and the remaining pinto bean mixture. Cover with foil. Bake 40 minutes. Uncover; top with remaining cheese. Cut the pie into wedges and serve with additional picante sauce. Serve with **brown rice** and **sliced avocado.** Make **flan** (from a mix) for dessert.

Saturday   *Easy Entertaining*

Serve your lucky guests **Roasted Shrimp with Spaghetti** (see recipe). Add an **arugula salad** and **garlic bread.** Top leftover **ice cream** with warm fudge sauce and toasted slivered almonds.

FAMILY

Sunday Dinner Pot Roast

Prep time: 15 min • **Cook time:** About 3 hr, plus standing time • **Yield:** 10 servings

Ingredients

1 3-pound boneless beef chuck roast, cut 2 inches thick and trimmed

2 teaspoons 25-percent-less-sodium or regular Montreal Steak Seasoning (such as McCormick)

1¼ cups low-sodium beef broth

¾ teaspoon dried basil

½ teaspoon dried oregano

½ teaspoon dried thyme

4 medium potatoes, peeled and cut into quarters

1 medium onion, cut into ¾-inch wedges

1½ cups baby carrots

Directions

1   Heat oven to 350 degrees. Place beef in a Dutch oven; sprinkle with steak seasoning. Mix broth, basil, oregano and thyme; pour over beef. Cover.

2   Bake 1½ hours. Remove cover. Scatter potatoes, onion, and carrots around roast. Cover.

3   Bake 1½ hours longer or until beef is tender. Remove from oven; remove beef from pan. Let stand 10 minutes before slicing across grain.

4   Arrange on a serving platter with vegetables. Skim fat from broth; serve defatted broth with beef and vegetables.

Per serving: 244 calories, 29g protein, 6g fat (21 percent calories from fat), 2.1g saturated fat, 19g carbohydrate, 52mg cholesterol, 255mg sodium, 2g fiber.

KIDS

Monster Burgers

Prep time: 25 min • **Cook time:** 10–12 min • **Yield:** 8 sandwiches

Ingredients	*Directions*
1½ pounds 93- to 95-percent-lean ground beef	*1* Form beef into 8 thin patties. Place on broiler pan. Broil patties along with bun tops 3 to 4 inches from heat 5 to 6 minutes per side or until burgers are no longer pink and buns are lightly browned.
8 whole-grain burger buns	
8 slices (¾ ounce each) reduced-fat American cheese	
8 thin slices deli ham	*2* Place bottom halves of buns on serving platter. For each monster burger, place 1 cooked patty on bottom half of 8 buns.
16 slices dill hamburger pickles	
Ketchup	*3* Cut cheese slice in half in a zigzag pattern to look like teeth. Place half of cheese slice on burger, with "teeth" hanging off one side of patty.
	4 Loosely fold ham into tongue shape; place on top of "teeth." Place remaining cheese "teeth" on top of "tongue." Top with top half of bun.
	5 Place 2 pickle slices on top of bun for eyes. Dot "eyes" with ketchup for pupils.

Per sandwich: 313 calories, 30g protein, 11g fat (32 percent calories from fat), 4.9g saturated fat, 23g carbohydrate, 90mg cholesterol, 1,032mg sodium, 3g fiber.

EASY ENTERTAINING

Roasted Shrimp with Spaghetti

Prep time: 15 min • **Cook time:** 20 min, plus pasta • **Yield:** 4 servings

Ingredients

8 ounces whole-wheat spaghetti

3 teaspoons olive oil, divided

1 pint grape tomatoes

⅛ teaspoon coarse salt

⅛ teaspoon freshly ground pepper

1 15- to 19-ounce can cannellini beans, rinsed

1 pound uncooked, medium, peeled and deveined shrimp

1 5- to 6-ounce package fresh baby spinach

2 ounces crumbled fat-free or low-fat feta cheese

¼ cup packed fresh dill, chopped, plus more for garnish

Directions

1 Heat oven to 450 degrees. Cook spaghetti according to directions; reserve ¼ cup cooking water. Drain; return pasta to pot.

2 Line a large, rimmed baking pan with nonstick foil. In pan, combine 2 teaspoons oil, tomatoes, salt, and pepper. Roast 15 minutes or until tomatoes begin to collapse.

3 In medium bowl, toss beans, shrimp, and remaining oil. Add to tomato mixture; stir to combine.

4 Spread in a single layer and roast 5 minutes longer or until shrimp are opaque throughout.

5 Add spinach to cooked spaghetti in pot (add reserved water if pasta is stuck together); toss to wilt spinach. Stir in shrimp mixture, feta, and dill.

6 Transfer to serving bowl; garnish with dill sprigs.

Per serving: 437 calories, 36g protein, 7g fat (14 percent calories from fat), 0.8g saturated fat, 61g carbohydrate, 168mg cholesterol, 745mg sodium, 10g fiber.

Adapted from Good Housekeeping *magazine.*

Week 41

 Sunday *Family*

A juicy **turkey breast** for family day is perfect for the cooler temperatures. Keep it simple and follow the directions on the package. Serve it with **mashed sweet potatoes.** Add fresh **zucchini, romaine,** and **crusty bread.** For dessert, treat the family to a slice of warm **apple pie.** *Plan ahead:* Save enough turkey for Monday and enough pie for Tuesday.

 Monday *Heat and Eat*

Use the leftover cooked turkey for **Turkey Enchiladas.** Heat oven to 350 degrees. In a large bowl, mix together 3 cups shredded cooked turkey, ½ cup each low-fat sour cream and chopped fresh cilantro, 1 chopped red bell pepper, 1½ teaspoons garlic, 1 teaspoon cumin, and ¼ cup 50-percent-reduced-fat jalapeño or ched-dar cheese. Puree 2 cups green salsa (salsa verde), ½ cup water, and another ½ cup each sour cream and cilantro in a blender. Spread 1 cup salsa verde mixture over bottom of a 9-x-13-inch baking dish coated with cooking spray. Spoon ⅓ cup turkey mixture down center of each tortilla (from a 10-ounce package of fat-free flour tortillas). Roll and place seam-side-down in dish. Pour remaining salsa verde mixture over top; bake, uncovered, 35 minutes. Sprinkle with ½ cup more of the jalapeño cheese, and bake 15 minutes longer or until bubbly. Serve with **rice** and **mixed greens.** Fat-free **strawberry ice cream** is your dessert. *Plan ahead:* Save enough enchiladas for Wednesday; save enough ice cream for Saturday.

 Tuesday *Meatless*

For a change of pace, try no-meat **Moroccan Vegetable and Pasta Soup** (see recipe). Accompany the flavor-packed soup with a **grilled cheese sandwich** on whole-grain bread. How about leftover **pie** with light **whipped cream** for dessert?

 Wednesday *Express*

Tonight, leftover **enchiladas** are waiting in the fridge for you. Enjoy them with **pinto beans** and **guaca-mole.** Make **flan** from a mix for dessert.

 Thursday *Budget*

Being the frugal type, **Unstuffed Cabbage** (see recipe) caught my eye. Serve it with **mashed potatoes, carrots,** and **whole-grain rolls. Plums** are tonight's dessert.

 Friday *Kids*

Oh, to be a kid again and munch on **Crunchy Nacho Dogs.** Heat oven to 375 degrees. Coat a cookie sheet with cooking spray. Unroll 1 8-ounce can refrigerated low-fat crescent dinner rolls; separate dough into 4 rectangles. Firmly press perforations to seal. Place 4 slices reduced-fat American cheese on rectangles. Place 4 low-fat hot dogs on cheese. Fold short sides of dough over hot dogs; roll up each one. Press edges to seal. Brush rolls with milk; roll in ½ cup crushed baked tortilla chips. Place rolls, seam side down, on cookie sheet. Bake 15 to 22 minutes or until deep golden brown. Serve with ketchup, salsa, and low-fat sour cream. Add **celery sticks. Tropical fruits** are good for dessert.

 Saturday *Easy Entertaining*

Serve your guests easy and delicious **Baked Oregano Chicken and Potatoes** (see recipe). Add **sugar snap peas,** a **Bibb lettuce salad,** and **Italian bread.** For a special dessert, top **coconut cake** with leftover **ice cream.**

MEATLESS

Moroccan Vegetable and Pasta Soup

Prep time: 10 min • **Cook time:** About 30 min • **Yield:** 8 cups

Ingredients

1 tablespoon olive oil

1 medium onion, cut into thin wedges

1 clove minced garlic

3 cups water

1 1-pound package frozen mixed vegetables

2 14.5-ounce cans diced tomatoes

1 15- to 19-ounce can garbanzo beans, rinsed

2 teaspoons dried basil

2 teaspoons turmeric

2 teaspoons paprika

¼ teaspoon pepper

⅛ teaspoon cinnamon

2 tablespoons ketchup

½ cup uncooked whole-wheat rotini pasta or elbow macaroni

Directions

1 In a Dutch oven, heat oil on medium-high. Add onion; cook and stir 4 minutes. Add garlic; cook one more minute.

2 Stir in water, mixed vegetables, tomatoes, beans, basil, turmeric, paprika, pepper, cinnamon, and ketchup. Bring to a boil; reduce heat; cover and simmer 8 to 10 minutes or until vegetables are tender.

3 Add rotini; cook, uncovered, 15 minutes or until rotini is tender. Thin with additional water if desired.

**Per cup:** 148 calories, 6g protein, 3g fat (16 percent calories from fat), 0.3g saturated fat, 27g carbohydrate, no cholesterol, 350mg sodium, 7g fiber.

BUDGET

Unstuffed Cabbage

Prep time: 10 min • **Cook time:** About 25 min • **Yield:** 6 servings

Ingredients

2 teaspoons canola oil

1 pound ground turkey breast or 93- to 95-percent lean ground beef

1 medium onion, thinly sliced

3 cloves minced garlic

1 28-ounce can stewed tomatoes

1 6-ounce can tomato paste

1½ cups water

3 tablespoons chopped fresh parsley

½ teaspoon salt

1 teaspoon dried oregano

1 teaspoon sugar

¼ teaspoon pepper

1 10-ounce package shredded cabbage (for coleslaw)

Directions

1 Heat oil in a Dutch oven on medium. Add turkey or beef; cook 6 minutes or until no longer pink, stirring occasionally. Drain, if necessary.

2 Stir in onion; cook 4 minutes. Add garlic; cook 1 minute. Add tomatoes and tomato paste.

3 Stir in water, parsley, salt, oregano, sugar, and pepper. Simmer 5 minutes.

4 Mix in the cabbage; cook, covered, 6 to 8 minutes or until cabbage is tender, stirring occasionally.

Per serving: 185 calories, 21g protein, 2g fat (11 percent calories from fat), 0.3g saturated fat, 18g carbohydrate, 47mg cholesterol, 608mg sodium, 4g fiber.

Adapted from Family Circle *magazine.*

EASY ENTERTAINING

Baked Oregano Chicken and Potatoes

Prep time: 15 min • **Cook time:** 45–50 min • **Yield:** 4 servings

Ingredients

½ cup freshly grated parmesan cheese

¼ cup unseasoned panko bread crumbs

¾ teaspoon dried oregano

2 cloves minced garlic

¼ teaspoon salt

¼ teaspoon pepper

4 5- to 6-ounce boneless, skinless chicken breasts

4 to 6 medium red potatoes (about 2 pounds), cut into ¼-inch-thick slices

1 14.5-ounce can diced tomatoes, drained

1 tablespoon extra-virgin olive oil

Directions

1 Heat oven to 375 degrees. Line a large, rimmed baking sheet with nonstick foil.

2 In a pie plate, mix the cheese, bread crumbs, oregano, garlic, salt, and pepper.

3 Dip both sides of chicken and potato slices into the mixture. Shake off excess; reserve remaining crumb mixture.

4 Arrange the chicken on one side of pan. Arrange the potatoes on the other side, slightly overlapping. Sprinkle with tomatoes, the remaining crumb mixture, and the oil.

5 Bake 45 to 50 minutes (depending on thickness) or until internal temperature of chicken is 170 degrees and potatoes are tender when pierced with a knife.

Per serving: 439 calories, 42g protein, 8g fat (17 percent calories from fat), 2.7g saturated fat, 47g carbohydrate, 91mg cholesterol, 600mg sodium, 6g fiber.

Week 42

 Sunday *Family*

Pork Tenderloin with Ginger-Peachy Glaze (see recipe) is perfect for family day or even for entertaining. Serve the savory entree with **couscous, green beans, a lettuce wedge salad,** and **sourdough bread.** A piece of **lemon meringue pie** is a delicious dessert. ***Plan ahead:*** Save enough pork for Monday; save enough pie for Tuesday.

 Monday *Heat and Eat*

Use the leftover pork for a quick **stir-fry.** Heat a little canola oil on medium-high in a large nonstick skillet or wok until hot. Choose your favorite combination of frozen stir-fry vegetables, and follow package directions for cooking. Mix in a stir-fry sauce and some leftover cooked pork, cut into strips. Cook until hot throughout. Serve over **brown rice** and garnish with toasted sesame seeds. Serve with **mixed greens** and **breadsticks.** How about **pears** for dessert?

 Tuesday *Budget*

Save money with **Chicken Chili.** In a 4-quart or larger slow cooker, combine 2 pounds boneless, skinless chicken breasts (cubed), 2 15- to 19-ounce cans rinsed white beans, 2 14.5-ounce cans drained diced tomatoes with jalapeño peppers (or other spicy tomatoes), and 1 cup frozen (thawed) corn. Mix together 1 1.25-ounce package slow cooker chili seasoning mix and 1 cup low-sodium chicken broth until blended; add to cooker. Cover and cook 6 hours on low. Serve over **cornbread squares** (from a mix). Add a **romaine salad.** For dessert, slice the leftover **pie.** ***Plan ahead:*** Save enough chili for Thursday.

 Wednesday *Kids*

What kid could resist **Bean and Veggie Wraps?** Heat 4 6- to 8-inch fat-free flour tortillas as directed. In a large nonstick skillet on medium, cook 2 cups sliced fresh mushrooms about 5 minutes or until they lose their moisture. Stir in 1 15-ounce can rinsed black beans; heat through. Stir in 4 cups fresh spinach leaves; remove from heat. Divide bean mixture among tortillas. Sprinkle with 1 cup shredded 50-percent-reduced-fat cheddar cheese. Fold one end of each tortilla about 1 inch over filling; fold right and left sides over folded end, overlapping. Fold remaining end down. Open mouth. Eat. Serve with **corn on the cob** and **celery sticks.** Fresh **pineapple spears** are dessert.

 Thursday *Express*

Heat the leftover **chili** and garnish it with shredded 50-percent-reduced-fat jalapeño cheese, chopped green onions, and low-fat sour cream. Serve with a packaged **green salad** and **baked tortilla chips.** **Kiwifruit** is a simple dessert.

 Friday *Meatless*

This **Chickpea and Tomato Curry** (see recipe) will make you forget about meat tonight. Serve it with **basmati rice,** a **spinach salad,** and **flatbread.** For dessert, make instant **vanilla pudding** with 1-percent milk and top it with **caramel sauce.**

 Saturday *Easy Entertaining*

Your guests will enjoy **Beef Kebabs with Cucumber Yogurt Sauce** (see recipe). Serve it with **rosemary roasted red potatoes, green beans,** and **whole-grain rolls.** For dessert, buy **fruit tarts.**

FAMILY

Pork Tenderloin with Ginger-Peachy Glaze

Prep time: 10 min • **Cook time:** 25–30 min, plus standing time • **Yield:** 8 servings

Ingredients

1½ teaspoons 30-percent-less-sodium seasoned salt

1 teaspoon dried thyme

2 1-pound pork tenderloins

½ cup all-fruit or sugar-free peach preserves

2 teaspoons Worcestershire sauce

1 teaspoon ground ginger

Directions

1 Heat oven to 425 degrees.

2 In a small bowl, mix seasoned salt and thyme. Rub evenly over pork. Place pork on a rack coated with cooking spray in a foil-lined roasting pan.

3 Bake 25 to 30 minutes or until internal temperature is 150 degrees.

4 Meanwhile, in a small bowl, mix preserves, Worcestershire sauce, and ginger. Spoon over pork during the last 10 minutes of cooking.

5 Remove from oven; carefully tent with foil and let stand 5 minutes. Slice and serve.

Per serving: 166 calories, 24g protein, 3g fat (14 percent calories from fat), 0.8g saturated fat, 11g carbohydrate, 74mg cholesterol, 254mg sodium, no fiber.

MEATLESS

Chickpea and Tomato Curry

Prep time: 10 min • **Cook time:** About 20 min • **Yield:** 4 servings

Ingredients	*Directions*
1 tablespoon olive oil	*1* Heat oil in a Dutch oven on medium. Add onion, garlic, ginger, and curry powder; cook 5 minutes or until the onions are softened.
1 medium onion, chopped	
3 cloves minced garlic	
1 tablespoon minced fresh ginger	*2* Stir in chickpeas and tomatoes. Heat to boiling. Reduce heat; simmer, uncovered, 15 minutes, stirring occasionally.
1 tablespoon curry powder	
2 15-ounce cans chickpeas (garbanzo beans), rinsed	*3* Stir in cilantro, juice, and salt.
2 cans regular fire-roasted diced tomatoes	*4* Garnish each serving with yogurt, if desired.
½ cup chopped fresh cilantro	
1 tablespoon fresh lemon juice	
½ teaspoon coarse salt	
Plain yogurt for garnish, if desired	

Per serving: 263 calories, 12g protein, 6g fat (21 percent calories from fat), 0.5g saturated fat, 41g carbohydrate, no cholesterol, 1,036mg sodium, 10g fiber.

EASY ENTERTAINING

Beef Kebabs with Cucumber Yogurt Sauce

Prep time: 20 min • **Cook time:** 7–11 min • **Yield:** 4 servings

Ingredients

Kebabs:

2 tablespoons olive oil

1 teaspoon dried oregano

2 cloves minced garlic

½ teaspoon freshly ground black pepper

1 pound beef top sirloin or beef tenderloin steaks, cut 1 inch thick

8 ounces medium whole mushrooms

2 medium red, yellow, or green bell peppers, cut into 1-inch pieces

Cucumber Yogurt Sauce:

½ cup plain yogurt

⅓ cup finely chopped, seeded cucumber

2 tablespoons crumbled fat-free or low-fat feta cheese

1 clove minced garlic

¼ teaspoon freshly ground black pepper

⅛ teaspoon coarse salt

Directions

1 In a large bowl, combine oil, oregano, garlic, and pepper. Cut beef into 1¼-inch pieces.

2 To bowl, add beef, mushrooms, and bell pepper pieces; toss to coat.

3 Alternately thread beef and vegetables evenly onto 8 12-inch metal skewers, leaving small spaces between pieces.

4 Grill kebabs 7 to 11 minutes for medium-rare to medium doneness, turning once.

5 Meanwhile, combine yogurt, cucumber, feta cheese, garlic, pepper, and salt to make sauce.

6 Serve sauce with kebabs.

Per serving: 248 calories, 28g protein, 12g fat (42 percent calories from fat), 2.7g saturated fat, 9g carbohydrate, 42mg cholesterol, 223mg sodium, 2g fiber.

Week 43

Sunday *Family*

Your family will be impressed with **Steak Kebabs with Long Grain and Wild Rice** (see recipe) for a fall feast. Serve the combo with tiny frozen **green peas** and **sourdough bread.** Dessert is as simple as fat-free **strawberry ice cream.** *Plan ahead:* Save enough ice cream for Tuesday.

Monday *Express*

Make your own quick **Grilled Marguerita Pizza** tonight. Evenly spread 1 cup red pasta sauce on 1 12-inch prebaked pizza crust; top with 4 ounces thinly sliced fresh mozzarella cheese. Grill, covered, on medium heat, rotating pizza occasionally, 10 minutes or until sauce is hot and cheese is melted. Drizzle with a little olive oil, sprinkle with dried or fresh basil, and serve immediately. Add a packaged **green salad.** Enjoy **peaches** for dessert.

Tuesday *Meatless*

Skip meat and go for a **baked potato with vegetables.** Bake the potatoes; slash the tops. Top with mixed vegetables (frozen) and 50-percent-reduced-fat cheddar cheese or ranch dressing. Garnish with freshly grated Parmesan cheese. Add a **spinach salad** with wedges of hard-cooked eggs. Top the leftover **ice cream** with fresh **strawberries** for dessert.

Wednesday *Kids*

We call it kids night, but the adults will want some **Salsa Chili** (see recipe) for themselves. Serve the easy chili with **baby carrots** and a **vegetable dip** along with **tortilla chips.** For dessert, the kids always like **kiwifruit.**

Thursday *Budget*

Stretch your food dollar with **Mexican Lasagna** (see recipe). Serve it with **sliced avocado** on **lettuce** with a fat-free **sour cream** garnish. For dessert, **pears** are easy. *Plan ahead:* Save enough lasagna for Friday.

Friday *Heat and Eat*

Keep dinner simple and heat the leftover **lasagna** for an easy meal. Serve with **mixed greens.** Fresh **pineapple spears** are what you'll want for dessert.

Saturday *Easy Entertaining*

For your special guests, prepare **Lamb Chops with Herbs de Provence.** Nick edges of 8 trimmed ¾- to 1¼-inch lamb chops in several places to prevent curling. Brush some olive oil on both sides of chops. Sprinkle with salt and pepper, and set aside. For the herbs de Provence: Combine 2 tablespoons each basil and thyme, 1 tablespoon savory, 2 teaspoons rosemary, and 1 teaspoon each tarragon, lavender, and fennel. Rub 2 tablespoons of seasoning into chops. Grill on high heat 3 to 4 minutes per side for medium-rare (145 degrees). Transfer to a platter, tent with foil, and let stand 5 minutes before serving. Serve the chops with **roasted red potatoes, green beans,** a **Bibb lettuce salad,** and **baguettes. Fruit tarts** are a very French dessert. *Tip:* Rather than making your own herbs de Provence, you can find them on the spice aisle.

FAMILY

Steak Kebabs with Long Grain and Wild Rice

Prep time: 20 min; marinating time, 6 hr to overnight • **Cook time:** 8–10 min, plus rice • **Yield:** 4 servings

Ingredients

1 pound boneless beef round tip steak, cut 1-inch thick

2 tablespoons water

2 tablespoons coarse-grain Dijon mustard

2 tablespoons red wine vinegar

2 cloves minced garlic

2 teaspoons canola oil

2 cups thinly sliced crimini mushrooms

1 6-ounce package long grain and wild rice blend

½ small red onion, cut into ¾-inch wedges

1 small yellow squash, cut lengthwise in half, then crosswise into 1-inch slices

1 small red or green bell pepper, cut into 1-inch pieces

Directions

1 Cut steak into 1¼-inch pieces. Place beef, water, mustard, vinegar, and garlic in a resealable plastic bag. Turn to coat. Marinate in refrigerator 6 hours to overnight.

2 When ready to grill, heat oil in a large nonstick skillet. Add mushrooms; cook and stir 5 minutes or until mushrooms release their moisture and are tender. Remove and keep warm.

3 Meanwhile, cook rice according to directions without butter or salt. When rice is done, stir in mushrooms.

4 Remove beef from bag; discard marinade. Alternately thread beef, onion, squash, and bell pepper evenly onto 4 skewers.

5 Grill, on medium, 8 to 10 minutes for medium-rare to medium doneness, turning occasionally.

6 Serve kebabs over rice.

Per serving: 336 calories, 32g protein, 7g fat (19 percent calories from fat), 1.4g saturated fat, 36g carbohydrate, 64mg cholesterol, 759mg sodium, 2g fiber.

Salsa Chili

Prep time: 15 min • **Cook time:** 7–9 hr • **Yield:** 4 servings

KIDS

Ingredients

1 pound 95-percent-lean ground beef

1 medium onion, finely chopped

2 medium carrots, shredded

2 cups mild chunky salsa

1 15-ounce can tomato sauce

1 4-ounce can mild chopped green chilies

1 teaspoon chili powder

1 15-ounce can pinto beans, rinsed

Shredded 50-percent-reduced-fat cheddar cheese

Directions

1 In a large nonstick skillet, cook beef, onion, and carrots on medium 8 to 10 minutes or until beef is no longer pink; drain.

2 In a 3- or 4-quart slow cooker, mix beef mixture and remaining ingredients, except beans and cheese. Cover; cook on low 7 to 9 hours.

3 Stir in beans. Cover; cook on low 5 minutes longer or until beans are hot.

4 Top with cheese.

Per serving: 337 calories, 32g protein, 7g fat (18 percent calories from fat), 2.3g saturated fat, 35g carbohydrate, 62mg cholesterol, 1,488mg sodium, 9g fiber.

BUDGET

Mexican Lasagna

Prep time: 20 min • **Cook time:** About 45 min • **Yield:** 8 servings

Ingredients

1½ pounds 95-percent-lean ground beef

2 10-ounce cans mild enchilada sauce

2 15-ounce cans black beans, rinsed

1½ cups frozen corn

2 teaspoons cumin

12 corn tortillas

1½ cups shredded low-fat or regular Mexican cheese blend

1 cup chopped tomato

¼ cup chopped fresh cilantro

Directions

1 Heat oven to 350 degrees.

2 In a large nonstick skillet on medium, cook beef 8 minutes or until beef is no longer pink; drain.

3 Stir in 1 can enchilada sauce, the beans, corn, and cumin; bring to boil. Reduce heat; simmer 5 minutes, stirring occasionally.

4 Coat a 9-x-13-inch baking dish with cooking spray. Arrange 4 tortillas in dish, cutting as needed to cover bottom.

5 Spread ¼ cup remaining enchilada sauce over tortillas; cover with ⅓ beef mixture, then ⅓ cheese. Repeat layers twice, omitting final cheese layer.

6 Pour remaining enchilada sauce over top. Cover with foil. Bake 30 minutes.

7 Remove foil; sprinkle with remaining cheese. Bake, uncovered, 5 minutes or until cheese is melted.

8 Top with tomatoes and cilantro.

Per serving: 369 calories, 32g protein, 10g fat (25 percent calories from fat), 4.3g saturated fat, 38g carbohydrate, 60mg cholesterol, 883mg sodium, 9g fiber.

Week 44

Sunday *Family*

This **Chicken with Caramelized Onions** (see recipe) is just right for a fall family meal. Serve it with **rice, green beans,** and a **mixed green salad.** Add **whole-grain rolls.** Slice **chocolate meringue pie** for dessert. *Plan ahead:* Save enough pie for Tuesday.

Monday *Express*

For a quick meal, try **Baked Beef, Bean, and Corn Quesadillas** (see recipe). Serve with **sliced avocado** topped with **sour cream.** Enjoy fresh **pineapple** for dessert.

Tuesday *Meatless*

You won't miss meat with tonight's **Penne Rustica** for dinner. Cook 8 ounces penne pasta according to directions; drain. Meanwhile, in a large nonstick skillet, heat 1 teaspoon olive oil on medium until hot; add ⅓ cup chopped onion and cook until softened, stirring occasionally. Stir in 1 clove minced garlic; cook 30 seconds. Stir in ¼ cup chopped, well-drained sun-dried tomatoes packed in oil and ¼ cup dry white wine. Bring to boil. Stir in 1 10-ounce container refrigerated light Alfredo sauce and ⅛ teaspoon pepper. Reduce heat to low and simmer, stirring occasionally, until heated through. Stir in ½ teaspoon dried or 2 tablespoons chopped fresh basil. Toss sauce with hot penne and garnish with freshly grated parmesan cheese. Serve with a **spinach salad** and **garlic bread.** How about the leftover **pie** for dessert?

Wednesday *Budget*

I really like this economical, moist **Italian Meatloaf** (see recipe). Serve it with **mashed potatoes,** frozen tiny **green peas** and **whole-grain bread.** **Plums** make an easy dessert. *Plan ahead:* Save enough meatloaf for Thursday.

Thursday *Heat and Eat*

You'll have **Basil-Tomato Spaghetti** ready in no time. Crumble the leftover meatloaf and add to a jar of basil-tomato pasta sauce. Heat and serve over **spaghetti.** Serve with a **lettuce wedge** and **Italian bread.** For dessert, **red and green grapes** are easy.

Friday *Kids*

Kids will love making **Crazy Critter Bagel Sandwiches** for a single-serve pizza meal. Heat oven to 425 degrees. Spread 1 tablespoon pizza sauce over 8 split bagels. Sprinkle each half with 1 tablespoon shredded mozzarella cheese. Arrange your choice of sliced pepperoni, Canadian-style bacon, sliced mushrooms, sliced ripe olives, chopped zucchini, and chopped red bell pepper on sandwiches to look like "critters." Sprinkle with more cheese. Place on ungreased cookie sheet. Bake 5 to 10 minutes or until cheese is melted. Serve with **celery sticks.** Keep up the kid-theme with **fudgsicles** for dessert.

Saturday *Easy Entertaining*

Serve guests your own **grilled salmon.** Jazz up the flavor with **Cucumber-Sour Cream Sauce.** In a small bowl, combine 1 cup fat-free sour cream, 1 medium peeled, seeded and chopped cucumber, 3 tablespoons chopped fresh dill, 1 tablespoon fresh lime juice, 1 teaspoon lime zest, and ¼ teaspoon pepper. Serve with **roasted red potatoes** and buttered fresh **sliced zucchini.** Add **baguettes.** For dessert, a **fruit parfait** is as pretty as it is delicious. Layer fat-free vanilla ice cream with stawberries and blueberries; garnish with light whipped cream.

FAMILY

Chicken with Caramelized Onions

Prep time: 15 min • **Cook time:** About 20 min • **Yield:** 4 servings

Ingredients

4 4- to 5-ounce boneless, skinless chicken breasts

¼ teaspoon salt

¼ teaspoon freshly ground black pepper

2 teaspoons olive oil

½ cup sliced onion

⅓ cup seedless raspberry jam

1 tablespoon red wine vinegar

1 tablespoon low-sodium soy sauce

1 teaspoon bottled minced ginger

1 tablespoon chopped fresh or ½ teaspoon dried rosemary

Directions

1 Sprinkle chicken with salt and pepper.

2 Heat oil in a large nonstick skillet on medium until hot. Add onion and cook 4 minutes.

3 Add chicken; cook 8 minutes, turning once or until chicken is no longer pink. Remove onion and chicken from skillet.

4 Add jam, vinegar, soy sauce, ginger, and rosemary; cook 2 minutes, stirring constantly with a whisk. Return chicken mixture to skillet; cook 2 minutes, stirring occasionally.

5 Serve immediately.

Per serving: 221 calories, 27g protein, 4g fat (15 percent calories from fat), 0.7g saturated fat, 19g carbohydrate, 66mg cholesterol, 317mg sodium, no fiber.

EXPRESS

Baked Beef, Bean, and Corn Quesadillas

Prep time: 10 min • **Cook time:** About 25 min • **Yield:** 4 servings

Ingredients	*Directions*
1 pound 95-percent-lean ground beef	*1* Heat oven to 400 degrees.
Salt and pepper to taste	*2* In a large nonstick skillet on medium, cook beef 8 minutes or until no longer pink; drain. Add salt and pepper to taste.
1 cup salsa	
½ cup canned black beans, rinsed	*3* Stir in salsa, beans, and corn; cook and stir 4 or 5 minutes or until thickened and heated through.
½ cup frozen corn, thawed and drained	
8 fat-free 6- to 7-inch flour tortillas	*4* Coat baking sheet with cooking spray. Arrange 4 tortillas on baking sheet, overlapping slightly, if necessary.
¾ cup shredded 50-percent-reduced-fat cheddar cheese	*5* Sprinkle with ½ of cheese. Spoon beef mixture evenly over cheese; top with remaining cheese and 4 tortillas. Coat top tortillas with cooking spray.
	6 Bake 11 to 13 minutes or until quesadillas are lightly browned and edges are crisp. Remove from oven, cut into wedges, and serve.

Per serving: *457 calories, 38g protein, 13g fat (26 percent calories from fat), 5.6g saturated fat, 46g carbohydrate, 74mg cholesterol, 814mg sodium, 4g fiber.*

BUDGET

Italian Meatloaf

Prep time: 10 min • **Cook time:** About 1 hr, 10 min, plus standing time • **Yield:** 8 servings

Ingredients

2 pounds 95-percent-lean ground beef

1 14½-ounce can diced tomatoes with basil, oregano, and garlic, drained

⅓ cup no-salt-added or regular marinara sauce

⅓ cup Italian-seasoned bread crumbs

1 teaspoon dried or 3 tablespoons chopped fresh basil

1 egg, lightly beaten

¼ teaspoon salt

1 teaspoon pepper

½ cup shredded parmesan cheese

Directions

1 Heat oven to 375 degrees.

2 Place beef in a large bowl; add tomatoes, marinara sauce, bread crumbs, basil, egg, salt, and pepper. Mix until just combined; do not overmix.

3 Shape into a 9-x-5-inch loaf; place on a wire rack (coated with cooking spray) in a foil-lined, rimmed baking sheet. Bake 1 hour.

4 Top with cheese and bake 10 more minutes or until 160 degrees internal temperature.

5 Remove from oven; tent with foil and let stand 5 minutes before slicing.

Per serving: 225 calories, 29g protein, 8g fat (33 percent calories from fat), 3.4g saturated fat, 10g carbohydrate, 93mg cholesterol, 639mg sodium, 1g fiber.

Adapted from Southern Living *magazine.*

Week 45

 ## Sunday *Family*

Make family day extra-special and prepare **Chipotle-Dijon Barbecued Short Ribs.** Heat oven to 350 degrees. Place 6 pounds short ribs, meaty side up, in large roasting pan. Sprinkle with salt. Brush with 2 tablespoons chipotle pepper sauce (such as Tabasco's). Bake 30 minutes. Meanwhile, combine ¼ cup more pepper sauce with 1 cup ketchup and ½ cup Dijon mustard. Reserve ½ cup mixture for later. Brush ribs with remaining pepper sauce mixture; bake 1 more hour, basting occasionally and turning several times during baking. Remove from oven. Adjust rack for broiling; heat broiler. Place ribs in broiler pan, meaty side down. Broil 3 minutes; turn. Broil 5 more minutes, brushing with sauce occasionally. Serve ribs with reserved Dijon chipotle sauce mixture. Serve with deli **potato salad, coleslaw,** and **cornbread** (from a mix). **Apple turnovers** (frozen) are an exceptional dessert. ***Plan ahead:*** Save enough ribs and any leftover sauce for Monday.

 ## Monday *Kids*

Make **barbecue sandwiches** for the kids by pulling the lean meat (discard fat) from the leftover ribs and placing on whole-grain buns. Top with any leftover sauce if desired. Serve with canned **vegetarian baked beans.** Add **carrot sticks** with some **ranch dressing** for dipping. **Peaches** work for dessert.

 ## Tuesday *Express*

You can count on **Chicken Fajita Pizza** (see recipe) for an easy meal. Serve with a packaged **green salad. Kiwifruit** is your dessert.

 ## Wednesday *Budget*

Chicken with Potatoes and Olives (see recipe) is low-cost and tasty. Add a **spinach salad, whole-grain pita bread,** and **pears** for dessert. ***Plan ahead:*** Save enough of the chicken dish for Thursday.

 ## Thursday *Heat and Eat*

The leftover **chicken** dish will taste even better today. This time, serve it over **couscous** and add **flatbread.** Make instant **banana pudding** with 1-percent milk for dessert. Mix in fresh banana slices.

 ## Friday *Meatless*

Raise no-meat dinners to a new flavor level with **Tijuana Torta** (see recipe). Serve with **brown rice** and **banana peppers.** Fresh **tropical fruit** is an easy dessert.

 ## Saturday *Easy Entertaining*

Invite friends for a delicious and easy meal of **Pesto Ravioli.** In a large nonstick skillet, heat 2 teaspoons olive oil on medium heat. Cook 1 pound chicken breast tenders 4 minutes or until brown. Remove from skillet. Add ¾ cup fat-free chicken broth and 1 9-ounce package low-fat or regular cheese-filled ravioli. Heat to boiling; reduce heat. Cover and simmer about 4 minutes or until ravioli are tender. Stir into ravioli 1 medium zucchini, cut into ¼-inch slices, 1 large thinly sliced red bell pepper, and the browned chicken. Cover and cook on medium heat about 4 minutes, stirring occasionally until vegetables are softened and chicken is no longer pink. Stir in ¼ cup refrigerated basil pesto and toss to coat. Sprinkle with freshly grated parmesan cheese and serve. Add an **arugula salad** and **garlic bread.** Buy a **coconut cake** for dessert and serve it with **lemon curd.**

EXPRESS

Chicken Fajita Pizza

Prep time: 20 min • **Cook time:** 26–35 min • **Yield:** 6 servings

Ingredients

1 13.8-ounce can refrigerated classic pizza crust

1 tablespoon canola oil

4 boneless, skinless chicken breasts (about 1¼-pounds, cut into thin bite-size strips)

1 to 2 teaspoons chili powder

¼ teaspoon salt

½ teaspoon garlic powder

1 cup thinly sliced onion

1 cup green or red bell pepper strips (2-x-½ inches)

½ cup chunky-style salsa

2 cups shredded low-fat or regular Monterey Jack cheese

Directions

1 Heat oven to 425 degrees.

2 Coat a 12-inch pizza pan with cooking spray. Unroll dough; place on pan. Starting at center, press out dough to edge of pan.

3 Bake 7 to 9 minutes or until very light golden brown.

4 Meanwhile, in a large nonstick skillet, heat oil on medium-high. Add chicken; sprinkle with chili powder, salt, and garlic powder. Cook and stir 3 to 5 minutes or until lightly browned.

5 Add onions and bell pepper strips; cook and stir 2 or 3 minutes longer or until chicken is no longer pink in center and vegetables are softened.

6 Spoon chicken mixture evenly over partially baked crust. Spoon salsa over chicken; sprinkle with cheese.

7 Bake 14 to 18 minutes or until crust is golden. Cut into wedges and serve.

Per serving: 424 calories, 39g protein, 13g fat (28 percent calories from fat), 4.6g saturated fat, 35g carbohydrate, 75mg cholesterol, 913mg sodium, 2g fiber.

Adapted from Pillsbury Pizza Night *(Wiley).*

Chicken with Potatoes and Olives

Prep time: 15 min • **Cook time:** 5 hr on high; 8 hr on low • **Yield:** 10 servings

BUDGET

Ingredients	Directions
3 pounds bone-in, skinless chicken legs and thighs	*1* Place chicken in a 4½-quart or larger slow cooker.
2 pounds baking potatoes, peeled and cut into ¾-inch pieces	*2* In large bowl, combine remaining ingredients; mix well. Spoon over chicken.
1 large green bell pepper cut into thin strips	*3* Cover and cook 5 hours on high or 8 hours on low until chicken is cooked through and tender, and potatoes are tender.
1 medium onion, chopped	
1 15-ounce can tomato sauce	
½ cup dry white wine or fat-free chicken broth	*4* Discard bay leaf halves, and serve.
½ cup green olives with pimento, rinsed	
1½ tablespoons minced garlic	
1½ tablespoons olive oil	
½ teaspoon salt	
½ teaspoon pepper	
1 bay leaf broken in half	

Per serving: 319 calories, 27g protein, 14g fat (38 percent calories from fat), 3.3g saturated fat, 21g carbohydrate, 89mg cholesterol, 567mg sodium, 3g fiber.

Adapted from Woman's Day *magazine.*

MEATLESS

Tijuana Torta

Prep time: 15 min • **Yield:** 4 servings

Ingredients

1 15-ounce can pinto beans, rinsed

3 tablespoons salsa

1 tablespoon chopped pickled jalapeño

½ teaspoon cumin

1 ripe avocado, pitted and peeled

2 tablespoons minced onion

1 tablespoon fresh lime juice

1 16- to 20-inch long baguette

1⅓ cups shredded green cabbage

Directions

1 In a small bowl, mash beans, salsa, jalapeño, and cumin.

2 In another bowl, mash avocado, onion, and lime juice.

3 Cut baguette into 4 equal lengths. Split each piece in half horizontally. Pull out most of the soft bread from the center so you're left with mostly crust.

4 Divide the bean paste, avocado mixture, and cabbage evenly among the sandwiches.

5 Cut each in half and serve.

Per serving: 349 calories, 14g protein, 9g fat (24 percent calories from fat), 1.4g saturated fat, 54g carbohydrate, no cholesterol, 659mg sodium, 11g fiber.

Adapted from Eating Well *magazine.*

Week 46

Sunday *Express*

Rely on a **spiral-sliced ham,** deli **potato salad,** and canned **baked beans** for a fine meal today. Add **pumpernickel bread.** Finish the easy meal with a **chocolate layer cake.** *Plan ahead:* Cook Monday's rice today. Save enough ham and cake for Tuesday.

Monday *Kids*

If you can't be a cowboy, at least you can eat **Cowboy Beans and Rice with Franks.** Heat 1 teaspoon canola oil in a large nonstick skillet over medium heat until hot. Add 1 medium chopped onion and 1 medium chopped green bell pepper; cook and stir 3 to 5 minutes or until softened. Add 4 fat-free hot dogs (cut into 1-inch pieces), 3 cups cooked rice, 2 15- to 16-ounce cans rinsed pinto beans, and ¾ cup barbecue sauce; mix well. Reduce heat to low and simmer 6 or 7 minutes or until hot. For some extra crunch, dip **celery sticks** into **ranch dressing.** Add **cornbread muffins** (from a mix). **Pears** are dessert. *Plan ahead:* Save enough muffins for Tuesday.

Tuesday *Budget*

Buy canned **lentil soup** and add some chopped (leftover) ham for extra flavor. Serve with a **spinach salad** and leftover **muffins.** Slice leftover **cake** for dessert.

Wednesday *Meatless*

Enjoy the meaty texture of **Barbecue Portobello Mushroom Sandwiches on Focaccia.** Slice focaccia into 6 squares, and then slice horizontally and toast. Brush 6 mushrooms with barbecue sauce, and broil 3 minutes (gill side down) or until tender. To assemble, place 1 mushroom on bottom of focaccia, and top with roasted red bell peppers cut into strips, 5 basil leaves, and 1 tablespoon goat cheese. Top with remaining focaccia, cut in half, and serve. Serve with **baked fries** (frozen). **Peaches** make a good dessert. *Plan ahead:* Cook Thursday's brown rice today.

Thursday *Family*

Lots of us like the traditional **turkey, dressing, gravy,** and **cranberries** for Thanksgiving. This year, try **Harvest Rice** (see recipe) for a little change. Go back to tradition and serve **pumpkin pie** with light whipped cream. *Plan ahead:* Save the leftovers for future feasts.

Friday *Heat and Eat*

Use the leftover turkey for **Asian Turkey Wraps** (see recipe). Heat the leftover **rice.** Leftover **pie** is dessert. That was easy.

Saturday *Easy Entertaining*

For a change of pace, invite your guests for **Mediterranean Shrimp** (see recipe). Serve with **Tomato Caper Salad.** Mix together 2 tablespoons each drained capers and balsamic vinegar, 1 tablespoon olive oil, salt to taste, and ½ teaspoon pepper. Drizzle over 2 cups halved grape tomatoes and let stand for 15 minutes to 1 hour. Sprinkle with 6 shredded basil leaves. Serve over lettuce. Add **garlic bread.** For dessert, sprinkle toasted coconut over fresh **fruit cups.**

FAMILY

Harvest Rice

Prep time: 15 min • **Cook time:** 7–12 min, plus rice • **Yield:** 8 servings

Ingredients	Directions
1 tablespoon canola oil	*1* Heat oil over medium-high heat. Add carrots and cook and stir 3 to 5 minutes until softened.
1 cup shredded carrots	
1 cup sliced green onions	*2* Add green onions and apples; cook 3 to 5 minutes.
2 cups cored and chopped unpeeled apples	
3 cups cooked brown rice	*3* Stir in rice, raisins, sesame seeds, and salt. Cook, stirring, 1 to 2 minutes, or until thoroughly heated.
½ cup raisins	
1 tablespoon sesame seeds	
½ teaspoon salt	

Per serving: 160 calories, 3g protein, 3g fat (17 percent calories from fat), 0.4g saturated fat, 32g carbohydrate, no cholesterol, 160mg sodium, 4g fiber.

HEAT AND EAT

Asian Turkey Wraps

Prep time: 15 min • **Yield:** 4 wraps

Ingredients	Directions

Ingredients

¼ **cup rice wine vinegar**

1 **tablespoon sugar**

1 **tablespoon sesame seeds**

1 **tablespoon dark sesame oil**

½ **teaspoon salt**

4 **cups chopped cooked turkey breast**

¾ **cup sliced celery**

6 **radishes, sliced**

3 **green onions, sliced**

3 **tablespoons toasted slivered almonds**

4 **8- to 10-inch fat-free flour tortillas**

1 **bunch basil leaves, sliced**

Directions

1 Combine vinegar, sugar, sesame seeds, sesame oil, and salt; mix well, then chill.

2 Combine turkey, celery, radishes, green onions, and almonds. Drizzle dressing over turkey mixture and toss to coat.

3 Spoon evenly into tortillas, sprinkle with basil, and wrap.

4 Cut in half and serve immediately.

Per wrap: 424 calories, 49g protein, 10g fat (22 percent calories from fat), 1.4g saturated fat, 31g carbohydrate, 120mg cholesterol, 738mg sodium, 4g fiber.

EASY ENTERTAINING

Mediterranean Shrimp

Prep time: 20 min • **Cook time:** About 10 min, plus pasta • **Yield:** 4 servings

Ingredients	*Directions*
8 ounces orzo pasta	**1** Cook pasta according to directions.
1 teaspoon olive oil	
1 medium red onion, thinly sliced	**2** Meanwhile, heat olive oil over medium heat. Add onion and bell pepper. Cook 4 minutes or until softened.
1 medium red bell pepper, thinly sliced	
1 medium zucchini, thinly sliced	**3** Stir in zucchini and cook 2 minutes or until almost tender.
1 pound shelled and deveined shrimp	**4** Stir in shrimp, dill, and pepper. Cover and cook 1 to 2 minutes, depending on size of shrimp, until cooked through.
¼ cup chopped fresh dill	
¼ teaspoon freshly ground black pepper	
3 ounces crumbled low-fat feta cheese	**5** Spoon over pasta, sprinkle with cheese and olives, and serve.
¼ cup sliced black olives	

Per serving: 414 calories, 35g protein, 7g fat (16 percent calories from fat), 2.3g saturated fat, 51g carbohydrate, 180mg cholesterol, 529mg sodium, 3g fiber.

Week 47

Sunday   *Family*

For a special family meal, try **Mediterranean Pork Kebabs** (see recipe). Serve with **couscous** and add some chopped kalamata olives to it. Alongside, **broccolini** and **dinner rolls** are good. Buy a **chocolate meringue pie** for dessert. ***Plan ahead:*** Broil an extra plain pork loin and save enough pie for Monday.

Monday   *Heat and Eat*

Make a quick **pork stir-fry** with the leftover pork. Add some frozen stir-fry vegetables and teriyaki sauce. Serve your masterpiece over **rice**. Add **sesame breadsticks**. You can have leftover **pie** for dessert.

Tuesday   *Kids*

Kids will love **Beef 'n' Cheese Calzones.** Heat oven to 350 degrees. Coat a pizza pan with cooking spray. Unroll 1 13.8-ounce can refrigerated pizza crust dough on pan; gently stretch dough to form a 12-inch circle. Layer ⅓ cup sliced deli roast beef, 1 thinly sliced green onion, 1 4-ounce can drained mushroom pieces and stems, ½ cup shredded part-skim mozzarella cheese, and ¼ cup shredded 50-percent-reduced-fat cheddar cheese to within 1 inch of edge. Fold crust over filling; fold edge up and seal with fork. Cut slits in top. Bake 20 to 25 minutes or until crust is golden brown and filling is hot. Cool 5 minutes before cutting into wedges. Serve with **mustard**. Add **carrot salad** on the side. For dessert, have fat-free **vanilla ice cream**. ***Plan ahead:*** Save enough ice cream for Saturday.

Wednesday   *Express*

Try one of Campbell's Select Harvest Soups (or another brand). The sodium has been reduced. Alongside, buy egg salad from the deli for **egg salad sandwiches** on whole-grain bread. Add a **lettuce and tomato salad**. Enjoy **orange sections** for dessert.

Thursday   *Meatless*

Tonight's **No-Meat "Jambalaya"** (see recipe) has lots of flavor. Serve it with **mixed greens** and **corn muffins** (from a mix). For a special dessert, top fresh **strawberries** with light **whipped cream**.

Friday   *Budget*

Keep food costs down with **Ham and Potato Frittata.** Brown frozen O'Brien potatoes in a nonstick skillet. Stir in 2 cups diced ham and 6 beaten eggs. Cover and cook until set. Top with sliced tomatoes. Serve with a **lettuce wedge** and **whole-grain rolls**. Make **apple crumble** for dessert. Heat oven to 300 degrees. Coat bottom and sides of an 8-x-8-inch glass baking dish with cooking spray. In large bowl, toss 3 large, peeled and coarsely chopped apples, ½ cup sugar, ¼ cup packed brown sugar, 1 teaspoon cinnamon, and 2 tablespoons cold butter, cut into small pieces. Spread in baking dish. In same bowl, stir 1 1-pound, 1.5-ounce pouch oatmeal cookie mix with ¼ cup melted butter until crumbly. Sprinkle over filling. Bake 40 minutes. Remove from oven; sprinkle with ¼ cup chopped walnuts. Bake 15 more minutes or until topping is golden. Serve warm or at room temperature. ***Plan ahead:*** Save enough dessert for Saturday.

Saturday   *Easy Entertaining*

For special guests, serve **Baked Italian Chicken** (see recipe). Serve with **parsley buttered spaghetti**, a **Bibb lettuce salad**, and **Italian bread**. Warm and top the leftover **apple crumble** with leftover **ice cream**.

FAMILY

Mediterranean Pork Kebabs

Prep time: 15 min, plus marinating time • **Cook time:** 10–15 min • **Yield:** 4 servings

Ingredients

- **1 pound boneless pork loin (see Note)**
- **1 12-ounce jar marinated whole artichoke hearts**
- **1 red bell pepper, cut into 1-inch squares**
- **2 teaspoons hot pepper sauce**
- **1 teaspoon dried oregano**
- **2 tablespoons fresh lemon juice**
- **2 teaspoons black pepper**

Directions

1 Cut pork into 1-inch cubes; place in a resealable plastic bag.

2 Drain artichokes; reserve marinade. Set artichokes and bell pepper squares aside.

3 Add reserved marinade, pepper sauce, oregano, lemon juice, and black pepper to bag; turn to coat and seal. Let stand at room temperature for 30 minutes, turning occasionally.

4 Remove pork; discard marinade. Thread pork, artichokes, and bell pepper onto 4 metal skewers.

5 Grill or broil 10 to 15 minutes or until internal temperature is 155 degrees.

Per serving: 235 calories, 23g protein, 14g fat (49 percent calories from fat), 2.6g saturated fat, 8g carbohydrate, 67mg cholesterol, 304mg sodium, 4g fiber.

Note: Grill or broil 1 pound extra plain pork loin for Monday.

MEATLESS

No-Meat "Jambalaya"

Prep time: 15 min • **Cook time:** About 30 min • **Yield:** 8 servings

Ingredients	Directions
1 tablespoon canola oil 1 medium onion, chopped 1 medium green bell pepper, chopped 2 minced cloves garlic 1 cup rice 1 14-ounce can vegetable broth 1 cup frozen corn, thawed 2 tablespoons Worcestershire sauce ½ teaspoon cayenne pepper 1 15- to 16-ounce can black-eyed peas, rinsed 1 14½-ounce can tomatoes with basil, garlic, and oregano	*1* Heat oil in a large nonstick skillet on medium. Cook onion, bell pepper, and garlic 3 to 5 minutes, stirring often, until softened. *2* Stir in rice; cook 2 to 3 minutes, stirring occasionally, until rice is light golden brown. *3* Stir in broth. Heat to boiling; reduce heat. Cover and simmer 15 minutes. *4* Stir in corn, Worcestershire sauce, cayenne pepper, peas, and tomatoes. Cover and simmer 5 to 10 minutes or until vegetables and rice are tender.

Per serving: 189 calories, 5g protein, 2g fat (9 percent calories from fat), 0.2g saturated fat, 39g carbohydrate, no cholesterol, 682mg sodium, 3g fiber.

EASY ENTERTAINING

Baked Italian Chicken

Prep time: 10 min • **Cook time:** 25 min • **Yield:** 4 servings

Ingredients

2 tablespoons balsamic vinegar

1 tablespoon extra-virgin olive oil

1 teaspoon fresh lemon juice

1 teaspoon dried Italian seasoning

½ teaspoon garlic powder

¼ teaspoon lemon pepper seasoning

4 boneless, skinless chicken breast halves (about 1¼ to 1½ pounds)

Directions

1 Heat oven to 375 degrees.

2 Combine vinegar, oil, juice, Italian seasoning, garlic powder, and lemon pepper seasoning in a 9-x-13-inch baking dish. Add chicken and turn to coat.

3 Bake 25 minutes or until internal temperature of chicken is 170 degrees.

Per serving: 194 calories, 33g protein, 5g fat (25 percent calories from fat), 0.9g saturated fat, 2g carbohydrate, 82mg cholesterol, 114mg sodium, no fiber.

Week 48

 ## Sunday *Family*

For family day, make these extra-special **Moroccan-Style Beef Kebabs with Spiced Bulgur** (see recipe). Serve the savory dish with **sugar snap peas** and **flatbread**. Buy a **carrot cake** for dessert. ***Plan ahead:*** Save 2 kebabs and some bulgur for Monday; save enough cake for Wednesday.

 ## Monday *Heat and Eat*

Make **Stuffed Whole-Grain Pitas** for a quick meal. Heat and chop the leftover kebabs; mix with heated leftover bulgur and moisten with some plain yogurt. Spoon into lettuce-lined pitas. Serve with sliced **cucumbers** marinated in cider vinegar. **Apricots** are your dessert.

 ## Tuesday *Kids*

Call the kids for **Corndog Muffins.** Heat oven to 400 degrees. Lightly coat 18 regular muffin tins with cooking spray. Cut 9 low-fat hot dogs in half. In a large bowl, mix together 2 8.5-ounce packages cornbread mix and 2 tablespoons brown sugar. In a small bowl, whisk 2 eggs and 1½ cups 1-percent milk until smooth. Fold the egg mixture and 1 cup shredded reduced-fat cheddar cheese into the dry mixture until moistened. Spoon mixture into muffin tins until ⅔ full. Add 1 hot dog half to each muffin. Bake 14 to 18 minutes or until golden. Serve with **carrot salad.** For dessert, **red and green grapes** are perfect.

 ## Wednesday *Meatless*

Pasta with Tomatoes, Spinach, and Gorgonzola (see recipe) makes a terrific no-meat meal. Serve it with a **romaine salad** and **Italian bread.** Slice the leftover **cake** for dessert.

 ## Thursday *Budget*

You'll have low-cost **Chicken Chili** on the table in no time. Heat 2 teaspoons chili or canola oil on medium. Add 2 chopped onions and 2 cloves minced garlic. Cook and stir 8 minutes or until onion is softened. Stir in 2 cups cooked chicken breast, 1 tablespoon cumin, 4 15-ounce cans undrained white beans, and 2 4-ounce cans drained diced green chilies. Reduce heat to low. Cover and cook 10 minutes, stirring occasionally. Remove from heat; stir in 1 cup low-fat sour cream. Ladle into bowls. Garnish with these optional toppings: chopped fresh cilantro, chopped tomatoes, crumbled tortilla chips, and shredded Mexican cheese blend. Add a **lettuce wedge** and **cornbread** (from a mix). Add **plums** for dessert. ***Plan ahead:*** Save enough chili for Friday. ***Tip:*** Use canned, rotisserie, or any other cooked chicken breast.

 ## Friday *Express*

You'll have dinner ready faster than a speeding bullet with **chili wraps** on the menu. Spoon some leftover chili onto fat-free flour tortillas; heat. Top with shredded cheese and sour cream. Serve quick-cooking **brown rice** on the side, along with **sliced avocados. Orange sections** are your dessert.

 ## Saturday *Easy Entertaining*

It's fun to have friends for dinner when the cooking is as easy as this **Dilled Shrimp with Lime** (see recipe). Serve the delicious recipe over **rice.** Add **green beans, mixed greens,** and **baguettes.** Buy a **lemon meringue pie** for dessert.

FAMILY

Moroccan-Style Beef Kebabs with Spiced Bulgur

Prep time: 20 min, plus marinating time • **Cook time:** About 30 min • **Yield:** 6 servings

Ingredients

1½ pounds boneless beef top sirloin steak, cut 1-inch thick

For the marinade:

⅓ cup molasses

⅓ cup orange juice

3 cloves minced garlic

½ teaspoon cumin

For the spiced bulgur:

1 cup quick-cooking bulgur

1 cup water

⅔ cup golden raisins

½ cup orange juice

1 teaspoon pumpkin pie spice

1 teaspoon cumin

2 cloves garlic

¼ teaspoon salt

¼ cup chopped fresh parsley

Directions

1 Cut steak into 1¼-inch pieces.

2 Whisk marinade ingredients in a large bowl until smooth. Add beef; toss to coat. Cover and marinate in refrigerator 30 minutes to 2 hours.

3 Meanwhile, prepare spiced bulgur. Combine bulgur, water, raisins, orange juice, pumpkin pie spice, cumin, garlic, and salt in a small saucepan; bring to boil.

4 Reduce heat to low; cover and simmer 15 minutes or until bulgur is tender and water is absorbed. Fluff with fork; stir in parsley. Keep warm.

5 Remove beef; discard marinade. Thread beef onto 6 skewers, leaving a small space between pieces. Grill or broil 6 to 9 minutes for medium-rare to medium, turning occasionally.

6 Serve kebabs with bulgur.

Per serving: 305 calories, 28g protein, 5g fat (15 percent calories from fat), 1.9g saturated fat, 38g carbohydrate, 46mg cholesterol, 159mg sodium, 5g fiber.

Pasta with Tomatoes, Spinach, and Gorgonzola

MEATLESS

Prep time: 15 min • **Cook time:** About 5 min, plus pasta • **Yield:** 4 servings

Ingredients	Directions
8 ounces penne pasta	**1** Cook pasta according to directions; drain.
1 teaspoon extra virgin olive oil	**2** In a large nonstick skillet, heat oil on medium. Add tomatoes, salt, crushed red pepper, and garlic to skillet; cook 1 minute, stirring occasionally.
1 pint cherry tomatoes, halved	
¼ teaspoon salt	
¼ teaspoon crushed red pepper	**3** Stir in half-and-half and cheese; cook 2 minutes or until slightly thickened, stirring constantly.
2 cloves minced garlic	
¾ cup half-and-half	**4** Stir in spinach and pasta; cook 1 minute or until spinach wilts, stirring occasionally.
½ cup low-fat or regular gorgonzola cheese	
2 cups fresh spinach leaves	

Per serving: 350 calories, 13g protein, 10g fat (26 percent calories from fat), 5.3g saturated fat, 52g carbohydrate, 24mg cholesterol, 388mg sodium, 4g fiber.

Adapted from Cooking Light *magazine.*

EASY ENTERTAINING

Dilled Shrimp with Lime

Prep time: 10 min • **Cook time:** About 5 min • **Yield:** 4 servings

Ingredients	Directions
2 teaspoons butter	*1* In a large nonstick skillet, heat butter and oil on medium until hot.
2 teaspoons olive oil	
1 pound uncooked, peeled and deveined shrimp	*2* Add shrimp; cook 1 minute.
Juice of 2 limes	*3* Stir in lime juice and Dijonnaise spread; cook 2 minutes.
2 tablespoons Dijonnaise spread	
2 to 3 tablespoons fresh chopped dill	*4* Stir in dill; cook 1 minute or until shrimp is pink and curled. Serve immediately.

Per serving: 135 calories, 18g protein, 5g fat (35 percent calories from fat), 1.8g saturated fat, 3g carbohydrate, 173mg cholesterol, 312mg sodium, no fiber.

Week 49

Sunday

Family

Prepare your own 5- to 7-pound **roast chicken** for the family. Accompany it with **Seasoned Vegetable Couscous.** Heat 1 tablespoon olive oil in a large saucepan on medium. Add 4 cups finely chopped fresh cauliflower florets (about 1 medium head) and ½ teaspoon salt. Cook 3 minutes, stirring, until softened. Add ¾ cup fat-free chicken broth, 1 teaspoon orange zest, ¼ cup fresh orange juice, and ¼ cup currants or raisins. Bring to boil on medium-high. Stir in ⅔ cup whole-wheat couscous and ½ cup sliced green onions. Remove from heat; let stand, covered, 5 minutes or until liquid is absorbed. Fluff with fork. Serve with **green beans**, a **romaine salad**, and **whole-grain bread**. Buy a **Boston cream pie** for dessert. ***Plan ahead:*** Save enough chicken for Monday; save enough pie for Tuesday.

Monday

Heat and Eat

Take Sunday's leftovers and turn them into **Penne with Chicken, Mushrooms, and Asparagus** (see recipe). Serve the pasta with a **spinach salad** and **garlic bread**. Enjoy **peaches** for dessert.

Tuesday

Budget

Be economical and serve **Huevos Burritos** for a simple meal. Cook sliced onions and bell peppers in a little canola oil until tender. Remove from skillet; scramble some eggs in same skillet. Spoon eggs, onions and peppers, and some salsa into warm, fat-free flour tortillas. Tuck in sides and roll. Serve with **pinto beans** and a **lettuce and tomato salad**. Slice the leftover **pie** for dessert.

Wednesday

Express

Make a quick meal tonight with any **lentil soup** and **roast beef sandwiches.** Mix ¼ cup horseradish mayonnaise with 1 tablespoon mustard. Spread on whole-grain bread. Layer bread with deli roast beef, lettuce, and tomatoes. Finish with **chocolate pudding** (from a mix) made with 1-percent milk. Top it with **strawberry sauce.**

Thursday

Kids

These **"Football" Meat Loaves** are just right for the kids. Heat oven to 350 degrees. Beat ¼ cup milk and 1 egg with a fork in a large bowl. Mix in 1 pound 95-percent-lean ground beef, ¼ cup dry bread crumbs, and 1 0.4-ounce packet ranch dressing mix. Shape into 6 football-shaped loaves. Place in an ungreased 9-x-13-inch pan. Brush loaves with 1 tablespoon Worcestershire sauce. Bake 35 to 40 minutes or until center is 160 degrees or no longer pink, and juices are clear. Decorate with strips of cheese for laces. Let stand 5 minutes. Serve with **mashed potatoes, mixed vegetables,** and soft **rolls**. Halve **kiwifruit** for dessert.

Friday

Meatless

Black Beans and Rice (see recipe) makes an easy no-meat meal. Add **mixed greens** and **flatbread. Apricots** are good for dessert.

Saturday

Easy Entertaining

Spicy Linguine with Shrimp (see recipe) will please any guest. Add a **Bibb lettuce salad** and **Italian bread.** For dessert, keep it simple with **citrus sorbet** and **butter cookies.**

HEAT AND EAT

Penne with Chicken, Mushrooms, and Asparagus

Prep time: 15 min • **Cook time:** About 20 min, plus pasta • **Yield:** About 9 cups

Ingredients

8 ounces multigrain penne pasta

1 tablespoon olive oil

1 clove minced garlic

2 tablespoons thinly sliced green onions

8 ounces sliced crimini mushrooms

1 tablespoon chopped fresh parsley

¼ cup white wine or fat-free chicken broth

½ pound fresh asparagus, cut into 1-inch pieces

2 cups leftover cooked diced chicken breast

¼ cup freshly grated parmesan cheese

Directions

1 Cook pasta according to directions; drain.

2 Heat oil in a large nonstick skillet on medium; add garlic, onions, mushrooms, and parsley. Cook 5 minutes or until mushrooms start to lose their moisture, stirring occasionally.

3 Add wine or broth and asparagus, and cook 8 minutes. Add chicken and cook 3 minutes or until heated through.

4 Add chicken mixture to pasta; toss to mix. Add cheese and toss to coat.

Per cup: 183 calories, 16g protein, 4g fat (20 percent calories from fat), 1g saturated fat, 19g carbohydrate, 28mg cholesterol, 72mg sodium, 3g fiber.

Black Beans and Rice

Prep time: 15 min • **Cook time:** About 50 min • **Yield:** 4 servings

MEATLESS

Ingredients	Directions
1¼ cups brown rice	**1** Cook rice according to directions without salt.
1 medium onion, chopped	
1 medium green bell pepper, chopped	**2** Meanwhile, in a 2-quart sauce pan, heat onion, bell pepper, carrots, juice, paprika, coriander, crushed red pepper, garlic, and tomatoes to boiling; reduce heat. Cover; simmer about 45 minutes or until thickened, stirring occasionally.
2 medium carrots, chopped	
1 cup orange juice	
2 teaspoons paprika	**3** Remove from heat. Stir in beans.
1 teaspoon ground coriander	
¼ to ½ teaspoon crushed red pepper	**4** In a blender or food processor, blend 1 cup of mixture until smooth (see Note).
2 cloves minced garlic	
1 14.5-ounce can diced fire-roasted tomatoes	**5** Stir the mixture into the bean mixture in the pan. Cook on medium 3 minutes or until hot.
1 15-ounce can reduced-sodium black beans, rinsed	
Fat-free sour cream	**6** Serve over rice; garnish with sour cream. Sprinkle with additional paprika if desired. Serve with lime wedges.
Lime wedges	

Per serving: 412 calories, 14g protein, 2g fat (5 percent calories from fat), 0.4g saturated fat, 86g carbohydrate, no cholesterol, 143mg sodium, 12g fiber.

Note: If you have an immersion blender, use it instead of a blender or food processor for easier clean-up.

EASY ENTERTAINING

Spicy Linguine with Shrimp

Prep time: 15 min • **Cook time:** 10 min, plus pasta • **Yield:** 8 servings

Ingredients	*Directions*
1 13.25- to 16-ounce package linguine	*1* Cook pasta according to package directions. Drain and return to pan; keep warm.
1 tablespoon olive oil	
1 cup chopped green, red, or yellow bell pepper	*2* Meanwhile, heat oil in a large nonstick skillet on medium. Cook bell pepper, onions, garlic, parsley, and red pepper flakes 5 minutes or until bell pepper is softened, stirring frequently.
½ cup sliced green onions	
1 tablespoon minced garlic	
1 tablespoon chopped fresh parsley (optional)	*3* Add shrimp; cook 3 to 5 minutes or until shrimp turn pink; stir frequently.
½ teaspoon crushed red pepper	*4* Add shrimp mixture to pasta; toss to combine. Sprinkle with cheese.
1 pound uncooked peeled and deveined shrimp, tails on	
⅓ cup freshly grated parmesan cheese	

Per serving: *248 calories, 19g protein, 4g fat (15 percent calories from fat), 0.9g saturated fat, 34g carbohydrate, 87mg cholesterol, 172mg sodium, 4g fiber.*

Week 50

 Sunday *Family*

Follow the directions on the package and serve a **roast turkey breast** for family day. Everyone will like your own **scalloped potatoes** with the turkey. Serve colorful **green beans with sliced almonds** and a **mixed green salad** on the side. Add **whole-grain rolls**. For dessert, buy a **blueberry pie**. *Plan ahead:* Save enough turkey and potatoes for Monday and enough pie for Tuesday.

 Monday *Heat and Eat*

The best part of the leftover turkey can be **Turkey Melts with Cheddar and Chutney.** Combine 2 cups diced cooked leftover turkey, ⅓ cup finely chopped celery, 3 minced green onions, and ¼ cup chutney. Stir in ½ cup low-fat mayonnaise. Heat broiler. Arrange 4 split English muffins on a baking sheet. Top with turkey mixture and 1 cup shredded reduced-fat sharp cheddar cheese. Broil 3 to 4 minutes or until hot and bubbling. Serve with leftover **potatoes**. Add a **lettuce and tomato salad**. **Grapefruit sections** are good for dessert.

 Tuesday *Meatless*

Skip meat and enjoy **No-Crust Tomato Cheese Pie** (see recipe) for dinner. On the side, add **hash brown potatoes** (frozen), a **lettuce wedge** and **whole-grain bread**. Warm the leftover **pie** and top it with fat-free **vanilla ice cream** for dessert. *Plan ahead:* Save enough ice cream for Saturday.

 Wednesday *Kids*

The kids can help you prepare **Chicken and Rice.** Cook 2 cups quick-cooking brown rice according to directions. When the rice is ready, add 1 5- to 8-ounce can drained chicken breast, 1 10.75-ounce can condensed 98-percent-fat-free cream of chicken soup, and 2 cups frozen (thawed) peas and carrots. Cook on low until heated through. Serve with **celery sticks** and **dip**. For some extra fun, make **Salty "Bones."** Heat oven to 350 degrees. Unroll a tube of refrigerated breadstick dough and separate the rectangle pieces. Working with one piece at a time, stretch the dough to lengthen it a bit, and then cut a 1½-inch slit into the center of each end. Roll or shape the resulting 4 flaps of dough into knobs that look like the ends of a bone. Place dough "bones" on an ungreased baking sheet, a few inches apart; sprinkle with a little coarse salt. Bake 12 minutes or until they are light golden brown. (Adapted from *FamilyFun* magazine.) Sliced **peaches** will be your dessert.

 Thursday *Budget*

Italian Lentil Soup (see recipe) is low-cost and has an excellent flavor. Serve it with a **spinach salad** and **Italian bread**. Make or buy **banana pudding** for dessert. *Plan ahead:* Save enough soup for Friday.

 Friday *Express*

For a fast meal, ladle the leftover **soup** over **brown rice**. Add a packaged **green salad** and **garlic bread**. Fresh **tropical fruits** are a simple dessert.

 Saturday *Easy Entertaining*

Invite friends for **Honey-Ginger Chicken** (see recipe). Serve the chicken with **basmati rice** and **broccoli with sliced water chestnuts**. Add a **red-tipped lettuce salad** and **sourdough bread**. For dessert, top leftover **ice cream** with **caramel sauce** and **toasted coconut**.

MEATLESS

No-Crust Tomato Cheese Pie

Prep time: 15 min • **Cook time:** About 40 min, plus standing time • **Yield:** 4 servings

Ingredients	*Directions*
1 15-ounce container part-skim ricotta cheese	*1* Heat oven to 375 degrees.
4 eggs	*2* In a large bowl, whisk ricotta, eggs, Romano cheese, and pepper until blended.
½ cup freshly grated Pecorino Romano cheese	
⅛ teaspoon pepper	*3* In a measuring cup, stir milk and cornstarch until smooth; whisk into cheese mixture. Stir in basil and mint.
¼ cup skim milk	
1 tablespoon cornstarch	
½ cup loosely packed chopped fresh basil leaves	*4* Pour mixture into a nonstick 10-inch skillet with an oven-safe handle. Arrange tomatoes on top, overlapping slices, if necessary.
½ cup loosely packed chopped fresh mint leaves	
1 pound tomatoes, thinly sliced	*5* Bake 35 to 40 minutes or until lightly browned and set around edge, and center is puffed. Remove from oven; let stand 5 minutes before serving.

Per serving: 257 calories, 21g protein, 15g fat (49 percent calories from fat), 7.7g saturated fat, 14g carbohydrate, 260mg cholesterol, 324mg sodium, 2g fiber.

Adapted from Good Housekeeping *magazine.*

BUDGET

Italian Lentil Soup

Prep time: 15 min • **Cook time:** 5 hr, 30 min • **Yield:** About 13 cups

Ingredients	*Directions*
2 pounds bone-in, skinless chicken thighs	*1* Trim visible fat from chicken; set aside.
1 medium onion, chopped	*2* In a 4-quart or larger slow cooker, combine onion, zucchini, carrots, lentils, broth, salt, and pepper; mix well. Add chicken. Cover and cook on low 5 hours.
2 medium zucchini, sliced lengthwise and then sliced ½-inch thick	
2 cups sliced carrots	
1 cup sorted and rinsed lentils	*3* Remove chicken from cooker; discard bones. Shred chicken and return to cooker. Stir in mushrooms, tomatoes, and basil.
4½ cups fat-free chicken broth	
¼ teaspoon salt	
¼ teaspoon pepper	*4* Cover; cook on low 30 minutes or until thoroughly heated.
1 8-ounce package sliced mushrooms	
1 28-ounce can diced tomatoes with basil, garlic, and oregano or with Italian seasonings	
1 tablespoon dried basil	

Per cup: 201 calories, 19g protein, 6g fat (25 percent calories from fat), 1.5g saturated fat, 19g carbohydrate, 46mg cholesterol, 554mg sodium, 6g fiber.

EASY ENTERTAINING

Honey-Ginger Chicken

Prep time: 10 min • **Cook time:** About 15 min • **Yield:** 4 servings

Ingredients

2 tablespoons ginger spice paste (see Tip)

½ teaspoon kosher salt

¼ teaspoon pepper

¼ cup flour

1½ pounds boneless, skinless chicken breasts

1 tablespoon canola oil

¼ cup fat-free chicken broth

Honey for garnish

Directions

1 In a medium bowl, combine ginger paste, salt, and pepper; mix well.

2 Place flour in a pie plate. Coat chicken in flour; shake off excess. Brush chicken with ginger mixture, coating both sides.

3 Heat oil in a large nonstick skillet on medium-high until hot. Add chicken; cook 3 minutes on each side or until golden.

4 Reduce heat to medium, add broth to deglaze pan. Cover chicken and cook 5 to 7 minutes or until no longer pink (170 degrees).

5 Slice chicken and drizzle lightly with honey. Serve immediately.

Per serving: 237 calories, 40g protein, 6g fat (23 percent calories from fat), 0.8g saturated fat, 4g carbohydrate, 99mg cholesterol, 376mg sodium, no fiber.

Tip: *Look for ginger spice paste in the produce section.*

Adapted from Publix Supermarkets recipe.

Week 51

Sunday   *Family*

Treat the family to **Savory Beef Stew** (see recipe) for a casual family gathering. Serve the meal-in-a-bowl with a **romaine salad**. **Carrot cake** is a perfect dessert. *Plan ahead:* Save enough beef stew for Monday and some cake for Tuesday.

Monday   *Heat and Eat*

Dice the leftover beef and vegetables, combine them with marinara sauce, and heat. Spoon the sauce over spaghetti or any pasta and you have **Beefy Spaghetti** for a quick meal. Add a **spinach salad** and **garlic bread** alongside. Finish with **blueberries** for dessert.

Tuesday   *Meatless*

With all the hustle and bustle this week, no-meat **Spicy Bean Medley,** prepared in the slow cooker, will be stress-free. In a 4-quart or larger slow cooker, stir together 1¾ cups vegetable broth, 1 tablespoon chili powder, 1 teaspoon cumin, 1 15- to 19-ounce can each rinsed black beans, chickpeas, and cannellini beans, and ½ cup dry lentils. Cover and cook on low 6 to 7 hours. Stir in 1 14.5-ounce can diced tomatoes and green chilies; cover and cook on low for last hour or until the lentils are tender. Ladle over **brown rice** and garnish with chopped fresh cilantro. Add a **mixed green salad** and **whole-grain rolls** on the side. Slice the leftover **cake** for dessert.

Wednesday   *Budget*

I'm always glad to save some money, especially around the holidays — and so can you. Make this economical **Southwest Meatloaf** (see recipe) for dinner. Serve it with **baked potatoes, zucchini,** a **lettuce wedge,** and **cornbread** (from a mix) for a fine meal. For dessert, **tropical fruit** is just right. *Plan ahead:* Save enough meatloaf for Thursday and enough cornbread for Friday.

Thursday   *Kids*

Get the kids' attention with **Beef Wraps** for dinner. Crumble and heat the leftover meatloaf; spoon it onto warm, fat-free, whole-grain flour tortillas; top with some shredded 50-percent-reduced-fat cheddar cheese, and roll. Garnish with salsa and guacamole. Serve with canned **mexicorn. Pears** are your dessert.

Friday   *Express*

You'll want a quick meal tonight, so buy a **spiral-sliced ham** and serve it with **mashed sweet potatoes** (refrigerated), **baked apples,** deli **coleslaw,** and leftover **cornbread. Christmas cookies** are always a welcome dessert. *Plan ahead:* Save some ham and cookies for Saturday; make Saturday's brunch entree today.

Saturday   *Family*

Enjoy delicious **Ham and Swiss Christmas Brunch Bake** (see recipe) before the big meal later in the day. Serve the savory dish with **tomato wedges** and **celery sticks**. For dessert, **ambrosia** and leftover **Christmas cookies** fit right into the season.

FAMILY

Savory Beef Stew

Prep time: 10 min • **Cook time:** 8 hr • **Yield:** 8 servings

Ingredients

2 pounds well-trimmed beef stew meat, cut into 1-inch cubes

4 carrots, cut into 1-inch chunks

2 14.5-ounce cans diced no-salt-added tomatoes

1 medium onion, cut into wedges

1 1.5-ounce packet slow cooker beef stew seasoning mix

½ cup water

½ cup dry red wine or low-sodium beef broth

1 tablespoon chopped fresh or 1 teaspoon crushed dried rosemary leaves

8 slices toasted Italian bread

Directions

1 In a 4-quart or larger slow cooker, place beef, carrots, tomatoes, and onion.

2 In a small bowl, blend seasoning mix, water, wine or broth, and rosemary. Pour over beef and vegetables; toss to coat.

3 Cover. Cook 8 hours on low.

4 To serve, place 1 slice toasted bread into each bowl. Spoon stew over bread.

Per serving: 310 calories, 27g protein, 9g fat (26 percent calories from fat), 3.2g saturated fat, 27g carbohydrate, 71mg cholesterol, 742mg sodium, 3g fiber.

Southwest Meatloaf

Prep time: 15 min • **Cook time:** 1 hr, 20 min, plus standing time • **Yield:** 8 servings

BUDGET

Ingredients	*Directions*

2 pounds 93- to 95-percent-lean ground beef

1 cup soft whole-grain bread crumbs (crusts removed)

¾ cup finely chopped onion

½ cup finely chopped red bell pepper

½ cup frozen corn, thawed

½ cup skim or 1-percent milk

1 egg

½ teaspoon salt

1½ teaspoons chili powder

1 teaspoon cumin

¼ teaspoon black pepper

½ cup thick and chunky salsa

Sliced avocado for garnish

1 Heat oven to 350 degrees.

2 In a large bowl, combine beef, crumbs, onion, bell pepper, corn, milk, egg, salt, chili powder, cumin, and pepper; mix thoroughly but lightly.

3 Shape mixture into a 10-x-4-inch loaf. Place on rack coated with cooking spray in broiler pan.

4 Bake 1 hour, 15 minutes to 1 hour, 20 minutes or until internal temperature is 160 degrees. Let stand 5 minutes.

5 Top with salsa and cut into slices. Garnish with avocado and serve.

Per serving: 202 calories, 27g protein, 7g fat (30 percent calories from fat), 2.5g saturated fat, 9g carbohydrate, 89mg cholesterol, 349mg sodium, 1g fiber.

FAMILY

Ham and Swiss Christmas Brunch Bake

Prep time: 15 min; refrigerate 1 hr to overnight • **Cook time:** 30–35 min • **Yield:** 10 servings

Ingredients

20 1-ounce slices (1¼ pounds) dense whole-grain bread, crusts removed

2 to 3 tablespoons Dijon mustard

10 slices cooked ham (about 1 ounce each)

10 slices low-fat or regular Swiss cheese (about ¾ ounce each)

4 eggs

2 cups skim or 1-percent milk

¼ cup freshly grated parmesan cheese

¼ cup plain panko bread crumbs

2 tablespoons chopped fresh parsley

4½ teaspoons butter, melted

Directions

1 In a 9-x-13-inch baking dish coated with cooking spray, arrange half the bread slices, overlapping as necessary. Brush bread in dish with mustard.

2 Top each slice of bread with ham and Swiss cheese, overlapping as necessary.

3 Top with remaining bread slices, arranging them over first layer of bread slices as if making sandwiches.

4 In a medium bowl, beat eggs and milk with whisk until well blended. Carefully pour over "sandwiches."

5 Cover; refrigerate at least 1 hour but no longer than 16 hours.

6 Heat oven to 375 degrees. Just before baking, in a small bowl, mix parmesan, bread crumbs, parsley, and butter. Sprinkle crumb topping over casserole.

7 Bake, uncovered, 30 to 35 minutes or until "sandwiches" are puffed and golden brown.

Per serving: 322 calories, 24g protein, 12g fat (31 percent calories from fat), 4.6g saturated fat, 34g carbohydrate, 117mg cholesterol, 851mg sodium, 4g fiber.

Week 52

 ## Sunday *Family*

Treat the family to a juicy, delicious **grilled pork loin** today. Use your favorite rub on a 3-pound bone-less, well-trimmed pork loin to make it extra special. Serve it with your **potato salad** and deli **coleslaw** along with **whole-grain rolls.** For dessert, try **Baked Apples** (see recipe) for a new flavor. *Plan ahead:* Save enough pork loin, potato salad, and coleslaw for Monday.

 ## Monday *Heat and Eat*

Use the leftovers and make **pork loin sandwiches on rye bread;** spread the bread with chutney and line it with lettuce and slices of pork. On the side, add the leftover **potato salad** and **coleslaw.** For dessert, you'll enjoy fat-free **strawberry ice cream.** *Plan ahead:* Save enough ice cream for Wednesday and Saturday.

 ## Tuesday *Express*

The clock is ticking, and you'll want a quick meal tonight. Buy a frozen **garden pizza** and prepare according to directions. Before slicing, top with a packaged green salad and sliced avocado. Enjoy **pineapple** for dessert.

 ## Wednesday *Easy Entertaining*

Celebrate the New Year with friends and serve elegant **Parmesan-Crusted Tenderloin with Savory Mushroom Sauce** (see recipe). Add a **baked potato,** an **arugula salad,** and **baguettes.** Top the leftover **ice cream** with **hot fudge sauce** for dessert and welcome in the New Year!

 ## Thursday *Budget*

Try the Southern tradition of good luck for the New Year with the popular **Hoppin' John with Mustard Greens** (see recipe). Spice it up with liberal splashes of hot sauce. Serve it with a **lettuce wedge** and **cornbread** (from a mix). Lighten up the New Year with **tropical fruits** for dessert.

 ## Friday *Kids*

For a change of pace, fix the kids **Pluto Pizza Dogs.** Cut crosswise diagonal slices (½ inch apart and ¼ inch deep) into 8 low-fat hot dogs. Heat ½ cup pizza sauce until hot. Boil or grill the dogs until hot and slashes begin to open. Serve the hot dogs on buns. Top with sauce, shredded mozzarella, and mustard. Serve them with vegetarian **baked beans** and **baby carrots. Peaches** are your dessert.

 ## Saturday *Meatless*

For an easy meal after a busy week, serve **split pea soup** along with **grilled tomato and cheese sand-wiches** on whole-grain bread. Scoop some leftover **ice cream** for dessert.

FAMILY

Baked Apples

Prep time: 15 min • **Cook time:** About 45 min • **Yield:** 4 apples

Ingredients

1 cup brown sugar

1 cup water

2 tablespoons butter

Pinch of nutmeg

Pinch of cinnamon

4 baking apples, such as Cortland or Granny Smith

2 tablespoons raisins

2 tablespoons chopped walnuts

Directions

1 Heat oven to 350 degrees.

2 In a small saucepan, stir together sugar, water, butter, nutmeg, and cinnamon. Bring to simmer and cook 5 minutes to make a syrup.

3 Core and peel the top third of the apples. Place them in a baking pan.

4 Divide raisins and walnuts and fill centers of apples. Pour syrup over apples.

5 Bake 40 minutes. Serve warm.

Per serving: 289 calories, 1g protein, 8g fat (25 percent calories from fat), 3.9g saturated fat, 57g carbohydrate, 15mg cholesterol, 52mg sodium, 5g fiber.

Adapted from FamilyFun *magazine.*

Parmesan-Crusted Tenderloin with Savory Mushroom Sauce

EASY ENTERTAINING

Prep time: 25 min   •   **Cook time:** 35–50 min, plus standing time   •   **Yield:** 8–12 servings

Ingredients	Directions
¼ **cup freshly grated parmesan cheese**	*1* Heat oven to 425 degrees.
3 tablespoons chopped fresh thyme, divided	*2* Combine cheese, 2 tablespoons thyme, and ½ teaspoon pepper; roll beef in cheese mixture to cover all surfaces.
½ **teaspoon pepper**	
1 2- to 3-pound center-cut beef tenderloin roast	*3* Place roast on rack in shallow roasting pan. Roast 35 to 40 minutes for medium-rare; 45 to 50 minutes for medium doneness.
1 tablespoon olive oil	
8 ounces sliced crimini mushrooms	*4* Meanwhile, heat oil in a large nonstick skillet on medium until hot. Add mushrooms; cook and stir 5 minutes or until they begin to lose their moisture. Add tomatoes, broth, wine, and remaining 1 tablespoon thyme; bring to boil.
2 cups finely diced fresh tomatoes	
1 cup low-sodium beef broth	
½ **cup dry red wine**	*5* Reduce heat; cook an additional 25 to 30 minutes or until sauce is reduced to 2 cups and it's a rich brown color. Stir occasionally.
	6 Remove roast when meat thermometer registers 135 degrees (medium-rare) to 150 degrees (medium). Transfer to carving board; tent loosely with foil. Let stand 15 to 20 minutes.
	7 Carve into slices; serve with sauce.

Per serving: 211 calories, 27g protein, 9g fat (40 percent calories from fat), 3.2g saturated fat, 3g carbohydrate, 69mg cholesterol, 108mg sodium, 1g fiber.

BUDGET

Hoppin' John with Mustard Greens

Prep time: 20 min • **Cook time:** About 40 min • **Yield:** About 9 cups

Ingredients

2½ cups water

2 tablespoons whole-grain Dijon mustard

⅛ teaspoon salt

¼ teaspoon dried thyme

2 tablespoons canola oil

2 medium onions, chopped

1 cup rice

⅔ cup finely chopped ham

4 minced cloves garlic

4 cups cooked black-eyed peas

4 cups trimmed, chopped mustard greens

Hot pepper sauce, as desired

Directions

1 In a small bowl, combine water, mustard, salt, and thyme; set aside.

2 Heat oil in a Dutch oven on medium. Add onions; cook 6 minutes. Add rice, ham, and garlic; cook 2 minutes, stirring constantly.

3 Stir in water mixture; bring to boil. Cover, reduce heat to low, and simmer 18 minutes.

4 Add peas and greens; cover and cook 5 minutes. Stir; recover and cook 5 more minutes or until greens and rice are tender.

5 Add pepper sauce as desired.

Per cup: 222 calories, 11g protein, 4g fat (17 percent calories from fat), 0.5g saturated fat, 37g carbohydrate, 6mg cholesterol, 238mg sodium, 7g fiber.

Adapted from Cooking Light *magazine.*

Part III
The Part of Tens

The 5th Wave   By Rich Tennant

"Do you want your salad shaken, throttled, or just tossed?"

In this part . . .

Everyone looks forward to dessert; if you could eat it first, you would. In *For Dummies* books, everyone secretly reads the Part of Tens chapters first. Why? Because they can! But also because the chapters are so fun and informative. You're in for a real treat *without* any calories.

You find all sorts of irresistible nuggets here: how to save time in the kitchen, how to save money on meals, what to eat for better health, and meals to save your sanity when you just can't stand to be in the kitchen another night. I also include an appendix that converts standard U.S. measurements to metric.

Chapter 6

Ten Timesaving Techniques

*L*ife is full of ironies. You've heard a few of the contradictions:

✔ Spend money to save money.

✔ Cook more now and eat it later.

✔ All the good ones are married or committed. (Okay, so this one has nothing to do with cooking, but it still seems to be true!)

See? Life is full of 'em. In this chapter, I show you how investing a little time up-front — whether you're learning something new, doing some pre-prep work, or working with others — can save you time in the long-run. Many of these strategies fit seamlessly with your new menu-planning lifestyle!

Take Some Cooking Classes

If you're a mediocre cook and aspire to sharpen your cooking skills, look into taking some cooking classes. They can be expensive, but in many local areas, free demonstrations are sometimes available. Free classes may be offered in a department store, at a farmers' market, or even in a store that also has fee-based classes. Often they're offered on the weekends. Retailers want you in their stores, and teaching you how to do some cooking is a good start. Just think of all the cookbooks and cooking accoutrements that are there to tempt you. These demos can help you get your feet wet before you commit to one of the longer classes. Classes usually last from two to three hours. Some are hands-on (more expensive), and some are strictly the watch-the-teacher type.

You must be asking yourself how spending two hours in a cooking class could save you time. Following are a few ways:

✔ You can find out how to hold a knife properly, use it for the right purpose, and keep it sharp. This is a timesaver in the kitchen.

✔ Classes take you on an eating adventure into some new recipes. No more boring menus — a cooking class helps you out of that rut.

✔ Classes raise your cooking self-esteem, so you're more confident in the kitchen. When you feel like you know what you're doing, you work more efficiently. Plus, folks will fawn over you. Being fawned over is quite nice — or so I've heard. I have no experience of being fawned over either.

✔ You have the opportunity to meet others who share your interest. Who can have too many food friends? They might invite you for dinner, and then you won't have to cook (the ultimate timesaver!).

✔ A cooking class is a good place to meet a cute person (I've been told the fresh produce department is another such place). Theoretically, cooking with someone else saves time — unless you distract each other or start goofing around.

I used to teach cooking classes when I owned a microwave store. At the beginning of each class, I'd ask students if they considered themselves good cooks or bad cooks. There was always a mix of both. I told the good cooks they would continue to be good cooks with the microwave, and the bad cooks that they'd be bad cooks faster. Classes help turn the latter into the former. Expect to learn a lot.

If you don't have cooking classes available in your area, Rachel Ray gets my attention with her TV cooking and user-friendly recipes. She's also interested in lighter, healthier recipes and ingredients. Her recipes are simple, and she teaches you techniques and introduces new foods. She presents the information in a friendly you-can-do-it manner that appeals to viewers (and me). *America's Test Kitchen* on PBS is another reliable source for upping your cooking skills.

Chop Ahead

When preparing vegetables for a recipe, wash and chop what you'll need for several days and store the veggies in the refrigerator. Not only will you save time when you're ready to prepare tomorrow's meals, you'll save time in cleanup. You can do this as soon as you come home from the grocery store.

You can buy fresh or frozen chopped onions and peppers to save time, but not money. I buy and keep frozen peppers and frozen onions for emergencies (for example, when I forgot to buy them). They aren't expensive and keep me from making a last-minute trip to the store.

Onions, peppers, carrots, and green peas freeze well, so you can always chop extras of those (not peas). The more water in the vegetables, the mushier and ickier they'll be after they've spent some time in the freezer. I usually don't chop and freeze, but I do chop and refrigerate for a couple of days. My freezer space is too limited, and it doesn't take that long to chop, either. (See the preceding section on cooking classes if you're chop-a-phobic.)

Look for One-Pot Recipes

One-pot or skillet meals can save you time in more ways than one:

- ✔ You only have to plan for and prepare one dish because it contains most or all of the meal's protein, veggies, and starches. Just add a salad and dinner's ready.

- ✔ You don't have to measure ingredients as precisely; just throw in a couple handfuls of noodles, vegetables, and chunks of meat, and you're good to go.

- ✔ You can throw everything in the pot, slow-cooker, or oven and walk away. Instead of stirring and browning, you can take care of chores, surf the Internet, or do nothing at all while dinner cooks itself.

- ✔ You can cook in larger quantities for a crowd or to have leftovers for another night.

- ✔ You cut down on cleanup time. Fewer pots to start with means fewer pots to wash in the end. (Really hate cleaning up? Check out the "Go for Easy Cleanup" section later in this chapter.)

Slow-cooker recipes are "one-potters," and there are plenty of them in these pages. Besides the slow-cooker ideas, beef stew, all kinds of chili, soups, and skillet dishes that include protein, starch, and vegetables can be one-pot meals too.

Cook Extra

Anytime the grill is heated, the Virgo grills more than we're going to eat for that meal. Sometimes it's better to grill plain chicken or steak than to season it before freezing. Say you're marinating four chicken breasts to grill for a particular recipe, and you want to grill four more for later. By not marinating the additional chicken, you leave your options open. Maybe you'll top that chicken with salsa and a Mexican-blend cheese, or maybe you'll want to use it in a stir-fry that calls for Thai seasonings. Grilling plain chicken would be the best in these two cases.

These simple suggestions apply to cooking extra salmon fillets, flank steaks, and other proteins. If you're cooking pork tenderloins, you can freeze an extra one plain, or you can season it during the cooking process prior to freezing. If you choose to freeze the extra cooked meat, you have to remember how the pork was (or wasn't) seasoned when you want to use the second one.

Always cook more rice than you'll use at one meal, and freeze the rest. I do the same thing with pasta if I know I'll be using it soon. I say soon because pasta takes up more room in the freezer.

Pasta can get mushy when it's frozen (all that water in between those scrumptious starch molecules is the culprit). The pasta I freeze is usually some that I will use in a recipe in four or five days to save another pot to clean. In a combo dish, the texture isn't quite as important as it is in a separate menu item. If the pasta supports a topping such as meat sauce, I recommend cooking to order.

Stay Sharp

Keeping your knives sharpened makes for easier slicing and chopping. Sharp knives are safer than dull ones, too. Remember those cooking classes you're going to sign up for? They'll tell you how to keep your knives sharpened (and how to use them). When I've had cutting accidents involving blood (sorry for the icky part), it has been because my knife wasn't as sharp as it should have been.

Buy a knife sharpener or have a professional do the job. I have an electric sharpener that works fine, when I use it.

Teach Someone Else

There's no reason that the main cook should have to do all the cooking and planning. Interest the kids in learning some kitchen skills. Teach younger ones math skills by measuring. Many recipes give great lessons in fractions. It may take a little investment in time, but it will pay off in the long run, as your "assistant" either helps you or takes over the kitchen one night. Ditto for teaching spouses or partners.

Kid's night is a great way to get some help from the children, and one night a week is devoted to them in the 7-Day Menu Planner. When kids participate in the meal preparation, they are much more likely to enjoy their meals. Participation can be as simple as putting out the placemats, flatware, and napkins. If your kids are ready to get their hands dirty in the kitchen, make Monster Burgers together for dinner. Easy step-by-step instructions are in the recipe in Week 41.

Some stores have cooking lessons or even "camps" to teach kids to cook. Sounds like a fun experience for the kids. My mother held "camp" every night as I helped her prepare dinner.

Bag Like with Like

Tell the person who bags your groceries how you want them separated, for example, all cold things together, all produce together, all groceries together. You may have to guide him, but it pays off when you get home and have to put away what you just toted in. It also tells you which bag needs attention first.

I put items on the belt grouped together so the bagger will have an easier job. You would think this would be a clue, but I came to the conclusion that baggers don't really *know* what goes in the refrigerator when I found a pair of stockings in with the ice cream and canned tomatoes. Do I mention a faux pas like this to the bagger? Why, yes, from time to time. Unfortunately, it's usually younger men or boys who are the culprits, but not always. I am a patient woman, so I continue to instruct the baggers.

For the sake of food safety in hot weather, invest in an insulated bag for cold items, especially meats. This forces the bagger to put all the cold items together. These bags are also handy when you're planning to do more errands than just grocery shopping. Better yet, make the grocery store the last stop on your list.

Reorganize Your Shopping List

Not only do you use your shopping list for what you need to buy, you also can use it to list needed items according to the store's layout. For example, put all the produce together on your list, and do the same for canned vegetables, dairy, meat and fish, and so on. (See Chapter 3 for an example.) This keeps you from running to and fro across the store, especially if you shop in one of those big-box stores. Who has time for that?

Go for Easy Cleanup

Nothing is more discouraging than sitting down to dinner and having a sink full of dirty pans and bowls waiting for cleanup after the meal. To minimize this, try these strategies:

 ✓ **When you're planning meals, take into account the amount of pans and other utensils you'll use.** One-pot or skillet meals save you extra cleanup time.

✔ **Adopt a clean-as-you-go philosophy.** When you're finished using a bowl, dish or utensil, either put it in the dishwasher or wash it if you can. Place trimmings from food or removal of fat or skin in a bowl. If you compost, separate "waste" accordingly. Keep your work space as organized as you can; being organized makes meal preparation more enjoyable.

✔ **Spend a little extra money, and be rewarded by saving time.**

- **Use slow-cooker liners.** Even though the liners cost a little more, the time saved in cleanup (and mess) is amazing. The Virgo, who does the cleaning, thinks they're great. Who's going to argue with that recommendation?

- **Use nonstick or doctored foil.** I use nonstick foil when I'm roasting some foods. If you don't want to use the nonstick kind, coat regular foil with a little cooking spray before you add the food. Cleanup will be faster.

✔ **Recruit help.** If your kids are old enough to learn to cook, they're old enough to help clean up. They can carry dirty dishes to the sink, dry clean dishes, or put them away. And if your spouse or significant other enjoyed the meal, he or she can show undying appreciation for you by doing all the cleanup! Amen!

✔ **If you do have a sink full of dirty dishes, be sure you're sitting with your back to the kitchen or wear very dark sunglasses.** That way, you don't have to see the mess and can enjoy the fruits of your labor.

Love Your Microwave

Every week of the 7-Day Menu Planner includes a Heat and Eat night in which your microwave plays a big part! Go ahead; use your microwave for cooking vegetables, poaching fish or chicken, and making gravy, pudding, and a ton of other foods. You save cooking time and cleanup time.

When reheating foods in the microwave, microwave high-protein foods, such as meats, at lower power (I use 30 percent) and for a longer time. Apply this protein rule when there's a lot of cheese in the reheated item. Protein toughens at higher power. For other foods, heat about 1 minute on high for a mixed dish and about 5 or 6 minutes per pound of fresh vegetables. The more of the food item you have, the longer it will take to heat. Cover all food you're reheating, to hold in the moisture.

Chapter 7

Ten (Plus One) Budget-Friendly Tips

· ·

In This Chapter

▶ Doing the math to save dollars

▶ Using foods you already have

▶ Becoming more self-sufficient

· ·

Are you a multimillionaire? Do you have a six-car garage full of cars? Do you wear a pair of shoes once and then toss them (even if they *don't* hurt your feet)? I don't think so, or you wouldn't be reading this chapter. Here, I tell you how to save money at the grocery store, so you can put the extra money in the bank or plan a trip to Rome. (Can you tell I love to travel?)

Monitor Your Portions

Cut portions to coincide with the nutrition needs of each individual in your family. Not many people need three or four pork chops (unless they're digging ditches). Perhaps Dad can handle two chops, but most likely Mom and the kids can do well with one apiece. You might even split one chop for two smaller children.

It's time to put down those huge portions you've been eating and get a grip on your nutrition needs (not wants). Not only do extra calories run up your weight, they run up your food bill. Using the aforementioned pork chops as an example, take a little trip with me down food budget lane.

Say you have a family of six: three adults (one man, one woman, and one grandparent) and three children (two girls, ages 6 and 8, and a 15-year-old boy). How many chops does the family need (not want)? The dad gets two chops (10 ounces raw total), the mom and grandparent each get one (8 ounces raw total), the girls get a small one apiece (6 ounces raw total) and the teenage boy gets the whole pig (if you know anything about teenage boys, you get the analogy) . . . or, like dad, two chops (10 ounces raw total). That adds up to eight chops weighing a total of 34 ounces, or 2.125 pounds. Round up to 2.2 pounds, and assume the cost per pound for boneless, rather thick chops is $3.50 per pound. The cost is thus $7.70 (2.2 pounds x $3.50 = $7.70). If dad eats a third chop, so does his son (monkey see, monkey do), so there go an extra 20 ounces or 1.25 pounds of chops, which increases the food cost for that meal by $4.38. What if you eat pork chops 20 times a year? $4.38 x 20 meals = $87 more per year spent on pork chops.

To take this concept further, think of all the other meals where folks are eating more than they need — you can do the math this time. Whether you're eating at home or in a restaurant, pay attention to portions for your wallet's sake (not to mention your waistline and overall health).

Watch for Sales

Watch for sales, including buy-one-get-one-free (BOGO in my market). BOGO is an easy way to halve the cost of what you're buying. If you're buying something in the $4 to $5 range, it's worth it if you use the product. Some tuna (albacore) is usually $7.25 per 4-pack. That's a good deal with the BOGO special. Another good deal is the low-fat mayonnaise that can run $4 to $5 per jar. Whether to go for these offers or not depends on whether your family will eat the products on sale.

When is a sale not a sale? When you buy an item because it's on sale and never use it. That's no bargain. (This does *not* include shoes.)

Newspaper ads determine where I do my major grocery shopping for the week. Mostly, I'm talking about the cost of protein — meat, poultry, and fish — and fresh produce. You can also check out online ads to find the best deals.

Personally, I don't go from store to store to save a small amount. For $3 or $4, I could be tempted; for $5, I'm there if the store is very close by! You have to make that decision.

Buy in Quantity

Buy larger quantities of nonperishables if you have the space to store the extras; you'll save money and time. When you run out of something in the kitchen, you can shop in your own basement or garage. My mother was a champ at this.

For me, a big jar of something that I use only occasionally isn't worth it, even if I save a little bit. I usually end up throwing it out anyway, so where are the savings? Also, be smart and check the price per ounce or pound of these so-called "bargains." Sometimes the larger sizes of items are more expensive per ounce than a smaller size. It pays to read the fine print on the shelf tags.

Now, my mother never left the grocery store without a four-pack of toilet tissue (which she always used a coupon for and bought on double green stamp day — do you remember those?). She was smart, because you never know when you might run out of this precious commodity. She also had a place to store it, and it wouldn't spoil — both litmus tests for buying in quantity. After she died, the family had enough tissue for two years! She went a little overboard, but she never ran out. Bless you, Mother.

I guess you know where I got my frugal streak!

Pack a Lunch (or Dinner)

Pack your lunch if possible. It's a good way to use those leftovers from last night. You'll do better nutritionally and certainly eat better than you would by having a burger and fries every day, not to mention how much money you'll save. Over a year, if you eat in *half the time* saving $8 to $10 per day, you'll save $1,040 to $1,300 in a year. Just think of what you could do with a thousand dollars!

Also, a lunch can be more than a sandwich and chips, though turning 7-Day Menu Planner recipes into sandwiches can make for wonderful options: meatloaf, pulled pork, and taco fillings for sandwiches or wraps are some of my favorites. Why not portion your carry-to-work microwavable plate with your dinner's leftovers? Put the plate together after dinner. Make your own TV dinners and reheat the next day for lunch. It's less expensive and healthier.

When I was traveling all the time (in a previous work-life), I'd prepare homemade TV dinners for the Virgo and freeze them. He was working full time and going to grad school, so he got home for dinner late, and I was in Kansas City or Omaha or Paris (Texas), eating in a hotel. With the TV dinners already made by his devoted wife, he could have a meal in no time. We call this love (and frugality, convenience, and a healthier option than driving through a fast-food lane).

Clip Coupons

When it comes to coupon clipping, people range from the if-I-remember-them-I'll-use-them shoppers to the I-won't-buy-it-if-I-don't-have-a-coupon shoppers. The amount of money you can save depends on your interest level. Those who devote their time and energy to clipping coupons save a lot of money. I'm an average, but devoted, clipper. If I save $2 each week, that's another $100-plus per year.

Some wise shoppers use online sites to ferret out valuable coupons. You've read about these amazing folks who get $5,000 worth of groceries for 15 cents. That's a gross exaggeration, but there are those people out there who know how to use coupons to their fullest. They know their shopping stuff. I'm a little more limited because I'm buying for certain recipes for recipe testing, but I'm still looking for the best deal.

One of my personal favorite achievements is to buy something on sale and also have a coupon. This makes me absolutely gleeful!

Plant a Garden

Plant a garden if you have the space and energy to make it work. (Let me know where you are, and I'll buy the house next door.) You save money in the long run when you buy seeds and plants, invest a little time and effort, and then harvest the produce instead of paying Mr. Grocer for fruits and veggies you could have grown yourself. Not only that, but the flavor and quality of home-grown fruits and vegetables are generally better than those of canned or frozen ones.

I grew up working in a very large garden where my mother (and I) canned and froze copious amounts of fruits and vegetables. Even though our family of four was small, we enjoyed the fruits of our labor all winter. Four bushels of peaches for four people was not uncommon. I can still see those beautiful jars lined up, ready to store. We were proud of our work.

I have no room for a garden where I live now, but I do have room for pots of herbs. It tears out my heart to spend $2 for a bunch of a fresh herb when I know I'll use only a stem or two. When the herbs are at home, growing in pots, I feel I've beaten the system. I cut a stem or two and the rest live on, waiting for my next visit.

Wise people in cities are creating community gardens for folks like me who don't have space for a garden but enjoy the experience plus delight in the value of the harvest. All-you-can-pick farms offer another way to buy in quantity, and you can freeze or can the fresh produce.

Think Doggie Bags

You gotta love those doggie bags. We Americans rarely eat all the food at a restaurant and are too proud to carry home (and eat) the leftovers. This has to change! When you bring home restaurant leftovers, you save money (and calories you might eat in one sitting if the original meal is enough to feed 16).

When my husband and I were in the extreme poverty stage of our marriage, we'd eat out at a very inexpensive place (that didn't have plastic chairs), bring the leftovers home, and stretch them into another meal or so. Pasta with sauce was one of our favorites. I once stretched a generous restaurant serving of pasta into three more meals by adding a few ingredients in order to make it into another meal. It was express, efficient, cheap, and delicious!

Clean Out the Freezer and Cabinets

Decrease your inventory. No doubt you and I could live out of our freezer, pantry, and refrigerator for quite a while if we just surveyed it more often. It's a good idea to keep a list of what's in the freezer so food doesn't get buried and become an artifact. (I still have some wedding cake in the freezer — I won't tell you how old it is, but some memory-storage has to be good.)

Anything you find in the freezer or pantry is found money because you've already paid for it. You can dig it out of the freezer, defrost it, and turn it into another meal without spending a dollar from your wallet for the meal. Does that make you as happy as it makes me? I hope so.

Buy Generic

Store or generic brands seem to have improved greatly over the last few years, and I rarely hesitate to buy them. You can sometimes save half versus a branded product. If you're devoted to the flavor of one brand over another, then by all means, buying a store brand isn't worth it.

One-pot meals and skillet dishes provide an excellent home court for generic brands. When I make soups or stews, the canned generic vegetables are just as good as the brand names! I often use generic canola oil, jellies and jams, brown and white sugar, flour, and a number of other staples. Read the ingredients, not just the food label, to compare.

Cut Down on Convenience Foods

Cut down on the use of convenience foods. They may save a little time, but at what price? Convenience dinner portions often aren't enough to fill the heartier eater. If a dinner says it has four servings, at our house it's closer to 2½. Is that a bargain? The flip side of eating convenience foods is that they're less expensive than fast foods such as pizza, burgers, and so on. If you add a big serving of vegetables to the dinners, you can justify them occasionally. Just don't let your freezer look like the freezer section of the grocery store!

One convenience food to consider is prepacked deli items. A pint of chicken salad at $4 is enough to feed four. Don't forget to add a side and a green salad. Chicken salad is delicious in a hollowed out tomato, halved avocado, or on bread for a sandwich.

Sometimes you can make your own convenience food that's just as good as or better than what you'd pick up at the store. For example, you can cut some of the fat you get with premade chicken salad by using the meat from a rotisserie chicken for your own recipe. Add some halved grapes, toasted walnuts or slivered almonds, a little low-fat mayonnaise, and sliced celery, and you have your own chicken salad.

Don't Pay for Waste

Lean meats and fish have little waste because their fat and moisture content are low. Ground beef that's 20-percent fat may be cheaper, but 95-percent-lean ground beef has much less waste. You pay for more good-for-you protein and less unhealthy fat.

Poultry that has been "plumped" with water and salt is the opposite and loses a lot of moisture when cooking. You're paying extra for that water only to watch it cook away.

The devil is in the details. Remember to do the math and compare cost per pound (see Chapter 3). You're better off buying lean meats to keep your ounces on the table rather than watching them go to waste.

Chapter 8

Ten (and an Extra) Family-Friendly Foods for Better Health

In This Chapter

▶ Fighting disease and boosting your health

▶ Getting the biggest bang for your buck

▶ Serving superfoods in kid-friendly ways

*N*utrition experts agree that some foods pack a punch of what's good for us. The experts say these foods are nutrient-dense. I say they're more bang for your buck. It's hard to pick just ten favorites that are both good for you and easy on your wallet, so I've added an extra, eleventh item for good measure. Here are my favorite good-for-you foods in alphabetical order. Before you start reading up on these mouth-watering wonders, I'll tell you why I chose the following: Other than the fact that they're nutrition powerhouses, I just plain like their flavors! I think that with an open mind, your family will too.

Almonds

Almonds are one of the healthiest tree nuts around. Eating just a handful of them a day is a great way to ensure you're getting more of the good things your body needs and wants. Almonds are an excellent source of vitamin E, magnesium, and manganese, and a good source of fiber, copper, phosphorous, and riboflavin.

Guess why I like them so much? The answer: They taste great, especially toasted. Take them with you in a resealable plastic bag (for the ultimate convenience food) or make almond butter to spread on toast or apple slices for a snack. If Elvis had only known, he could have eaten almond butter along with peanut butter sandwiches. I do miss Elvis.

Avocados

Avocados have such a great flavor and nutrition punch that they work for everyone in the family. Mix them with a little low-fat mayonnaise or spread them as they are on bread. For the kids, slice them to make a funny face with avocado eyebrows and raisin eyes. How about a bright red cherry for a mouth? Kids love it!

Why should we eat them (other than because I said so)? These green beauties have nearly 20 vitamins and minerals, such as vitamins C, E, and B6 plus potassium and folate, to name a few. This makes avocados a great food for proper immune function (fighting disease), brain function (we could all use more of that), blood glucose levels (they're very important), blood pressure (you know how I feel about hypertension), and healthy skin. (I hear you can smear avocados on your face for a nice facial. Personally, I wouldn't waste them there, but do what you like.)

Avocados also have those really good-quality fats that give them their creamy, luscious texture. These "good fats," or mono- and polyunsaturated fats, have no cholesterol and can even lower bad cholesterol. Their fat also helps absorb fat-soluble vitamins in other foods, like vitamin A in sweet potatoes. Avocados are a satisfying food, too. As a good source of fiber, they're digested slowly, keeping your hunger at bay longer. I eat them almost every day, as does the Virgo.

Bananas

Everyone's crazy about convenience, and what could be more convenient than a banana, just waiting to be opened and eaten? No need to wash, slice, chop, or do anything else but munch along on this beauty.

Bananas are an excellent source of vitamins B6 and C, fiber, potassium, and manganese. At only 110 calories, a banana is an ideal snack to help you get to your next meal, to fuel up before a workout, or to replenish some nutrients afterward. Bananas are easy on the most sensitive stomachs, young or old, and a favorite fruit of all ages.

Just think, you can have an almond butter and banana sandwich and you'd combine two powerhouse foods. Put it on whole grain raisin bread, and you've hit a home run.

When I have one of those doctor appointments that ends with, "Don't eat after midnight" — you know the ones, where they insist on taking gallons and gallons of your precious blood — you can bet I'm packing a banana or two to scarf down as soon as that needle leaves my arm. Having a banana at that point makes me a much more charming patient. It's a favorite way to use bananas besides as daily snacks.

If you're serving sliced bananas (or avocados or apples) as part of a meal and you want them to keep their pretty color after you peel them, splash them with lemon juice to keep them from turning brown.

When I was a kid, my father had a Tastee Freeze store, the ones that sold "frozen custard" that came out of loud machines. When the men in my family were eating dinner elsewhere, Mother and I would march ourselves to the shop, plop ourselves down in a booth, and each order a banana split for dinner. We were getting so many good nutrients in this "one-dish" meal. This is one of my favorite childhood memories.

Beans (Dried)

I'm known in my home as the bean queen, because I eat beans often simply because I like them. If you've discovered anything in this book, you know my number-one criteria for a food is flavor. I just love beans and the flavor they add to a meal.

Dried beans are extremely beneficial in all diets because they're high in complex carbohydrates, protein, and dietary fiber; low in fat, calories and sodium; and completely cholesterol-free. You can further reduce the sodium in canned beans by thoroughly rinsing them. You'll see that I include "rinsed" in most of the recipes in this book. The rinsing applies to regular or low-sodium canned beans.

Beans are an excellent, nonfat source of protein and complex carbohydrates. Complex carbs are better because they keep you from running to the cookie jar. Beans, like avocados, will stay with you longer and keep you from getting hungry so fast.

Beans are one of the best sources of dietary fiber, containing both insoluble and soluble fiber. Insoluble fiber is generally thought of as roughage, which helps promote a healthy digestive tract (it makes us "go"). Fiber can also reduce the risk of some types of cancer. Soluble fiber helps to lower blood cholesterol levels, especially LDL (the bad guy), one of the main risk factors for a healthy heart.

Mash cooked beans and make them a part of burritos, tacos, or any wrap. They make an excellent paste to hold burritos together. The kids will lap them up. I sometimes add a cup or two of cooked beans and reduce the amount of ground beef or chicken in a recipe. It's healthy and oh, so low-cost! (Did I mention that beans are low-cost and a great way to save money at the grocery store? You *know* how I love to save money too.)

Blueberries

A cup of blueberries has only 80 calories and virtually no fat. Blueberries are a good source of dietary fiber, vitamin C, and manganese. They also contain antioxidants. Talk about a convenience food! The blue-babies never need to be peeled, cored, pitted or sliced — just rinse, and they're ready to enjoy. Best of all, blueberries are readily available year round — fresh, frozen, or dried. Most of the ones you see in the winter come from Chile because their summer is our winter and vice versa.

Sprinkle them over fat-free ice cream, whirl them in a blender with yogurt and a banana to make a smoothie, or toss them in a salad. The possibilities are endless. You can also use them for marbles. I don't encourage this practice, however.

Broccoli

My favorite color is green. I especially like the color of broccoli (I once had a cellphone the color of broccoli). Is that why I love broccoli so much? Yes, but I also like it for its nutrition, year-round availability, reasonable price, and easy prep. Do you need more reasons than that? It fills me up so I don't eat too much of starch-laden foods (which I love).

Broccoli is a member of the cruciferous family of vegetables, containing loads of phytochemicals that may act as antioxidants. Broccoli is also brimming with vitamin C, folate, calcium, potassium, and fiber.

I eat so much of the stuff that it's a wonder I'm not green. Usually I just cook it in the microwave a couple minutes and spritz it with lemon juice or faux butter. Virgo eats it "straight." It's good tossed into a stir-fry or added to any skillet meal. Cut it for finger-food and tell the children they're eating tiny trees. Kids love dips, and broccoli begs to be dipped. Shred it for broccoli slaw.

Milk (Fat-Free or 1-Percent Low-Fat)

Milk is nutrient-rich and an incredible beverage bargain. Low-fat (1-percent) and fat-free milk have the same protein, minerals, and vitamins as whole milk — just fewer calories and fat. Milk has calcium and vitamin D for strong teeth and bones; protein for muscle growth; and calcium, potassium, and magnesium for healthy blood pressure. With all this goodness, I wonder why Superman didn't promote it? Of course, we'd rather kids drink the plain kind that comes straight from the cow (pasteurize it, please), but I'm happy if they drink any flavor. Just drink it! Raise a glass to low-fat and fat-free milk.

I drink milk in the morning on cereal and every day for lunch (unless I'm invited to an expensive restaurant, which doesn't happen too often). I've gotten attached to fat-free Smart Balance milk for its higher protein and calcium, but any fat-free milk is good. Forget soft drinks, people, and go for a glass of fat-free milk.

Milk isn't just a terrific beverage. Use 1-percent milk when making sauces, puddings, and custard — the little extra fat in 1-percent milk gives them a creamier texture. What kid can resist banana or chocolate pudding with marshmallow topping? Not this kid.

Salmon

Salmon is a favorite at my house, and the Virgo can cook it expertly on our indoor grill. Besides its nutritional value with high amounts of omega-3 fatty acids that help to protect our hearts, salmon has a great flavor, is reasonable in cost considering what you get (little waste for one thing), and looks great on the plate. You may have to coax the kids a little to enjoy it, but if their favorite action hero, say, Salmon Man, loves it, the kids may just dive right in. Once in a while, reward them for trying it with a little dessert afterwards or their favorite fruit.

Bake, roast, grill, or pan sauté it, and salmon will "perform" for you. If you can fish for it in Alaska, that's even better. I hear bears like it a lot too, so be careful! I understand bears like people as well, especially if those people are after their salmon.

Sweet Potatoes

Sweet potatoes — sometimes called yams — are chock-full of nutrition and low in fat and sodium. They have twice the daily requirement of vitamin A and almost one-third the recommended daily amount of vitamin C. Also, sweet potatoes are a good source of beta-carotene, which some experts say reduces the risk for certain types of cancer. We know it's important to eat more fruits and veggies, and sweet potatoes are delicious from fries to pies.

I came late to the sweet potato party, but once I got there, I jumped right into their goodness and powerful nutrition content. If you're still on the fence about sweet potatoes, just cut them into wedges, coat them with cooking spray and a little cumin or chili powder, and bake until tender. Kids like them because they equate them with fast food, but these fries are healthier for you.

Tomatoes

Not only do I love tomatoes in any form (as I tell you more than once), I love that they're so nutritious. All forms of tomatoes contain lycopene, a powerful antioxidant, but processed tomatoes (tomato paste, spaghetti sauce, chili sauce, and ketchup) have more lycopene than a raw tomato!

A medium tomato has only 35 calories, is a great source of vitamin C, and also contains vitamin A, fiber, and potassium. Kids already love pasta and pizza with tomato sauce, so adding other tomato recipes to their repertoire is as easy as a tomato tart. Can you imagine life without a BLT sandwich or tomato soup? If I lived on a deserted island, I'd want to be there with tomatoes, peaches, and, of course, the Virgo.

Walnuts

Walnuts are unique among nuts (you've probably said the same thing about some of your relatives) because they're the only ones that contain a significant amount of omega-3 fatty acids — 2.5 grams per ounce. Research has shown that eating walnuts provides many benefits for your health, and the best part is that they taste so good.

Walnuts contain antioxidants. Studies show they can decrease inflammation, which has been linked to many chronic illnesses such as heart disease and diabetes. One study found that including walnuts in a healthy diet improves bone health, and another one says eating walnuts may lead to reduced breast cancer tumor growth. In addition to omega-3s, just one ounce of walnuts provides 2 grams of fiber (I won't say another word about fiber here) and 4 grams of protein, all of which aid in satiety, a key to weight management.

The healthy omega-3s in walnuts can go rancid over time. If you plan to use the walnuts right away, place them in your refrigerator or in a cool, dry pantry. If you'll be storing them for a month or longer, store them in your freezer.

Add walnuts to salads, meatloaf, vegetable dishes, use as a topping for baked salmon and other fish, or just put some toasted walnuts in a snack bag, put the bag in your pocket or purse and you have a perfect, on-the-run convenience food.

If all else fails to get the kids interested in walnuts, bake cookies and add a generous dose of them!

Chapter 9

Ten Meals for "One of Those Days" (Plus a Bonus)

. . . .

In This Chapter

▶ Preparing meals on the spot when you'd rather not

▶ Making meals ahead of time to freeze for a rainy day

. . . .

*E*veryone has them, those days when preparing dinner is the last thing you want to think about. It's the wail of "what's for dinner" heard 'round the world. When I wail, I get no sympathy, nor do I get an invitation to eat out. The Virgo throws it right back at me in an "Aren't you the menu planner?" kind of tone. Boy, does that make me mad. So, what do I do besides whine and complain that I have to fix another meal? I rely on the trusted recipes in this chapter. There's a good chance that one of them will work for you in an emergency. And yes, an emergency can, in fact, be vegging out in front of the television for a night!

Although some of the recipes that follow are quick enough for same-night use, the real key here is to freeze pre-prepped, key ingredients or entire entrees ahead of time. You can devote a block of free time to cooking, or double or triple a recipe the first time you make it, and freeze the extras. That way, when you're having "one of those days," all you have to do is thaw and reheat. What could be easier?

If you want to make sure you're freezing and thawing foods properly, flip to Chapter 2 for more details about these processes.

Meatloaf

I love my meatloaf and always make more so that I can freeze an extra. I once left town, leaving my husband to fend for himself at mealtime. The freezer was full of various meatloaves (leftovers from testing recipes) and he was a happy camper until I returned — or until the meatloaves ran out.

This is the meatloaf recipe that carried us through many dinner crises. It also whisked my mother through a few of her own dinner quandaries. This is one of the best meatloaves you'll ever eat.

Mom's Meatloaf

Prep time: 10 min • **Cook time:** 13–16 min • **Yield:** 4 servings

Ingredients	*Directions*
1 medium green bell pepper, diced	*1* Microwave the bell pepper and onion in a small glass or microwave-safe container on high 4 minutes; drain and set aside.
1 small onion, diced	
2 pounds lean ground beef or turkey, or a combination of both	*2* In a large bowl, combine the onion/pepper mixture, ground meat, whole egg, egg whites, cereal, black pepper, and 1½ cups of the tomato sauce. Mix thoroughly but lightly.
1 whole egg	
3 egg whites	
4 cups "flake" cereal (such as bran flakes or cornflakes), crushed	*3* Divide the mixture into two round loaves with an indention in the center (use a glass — or your fist — and press it into loaf). Brush both tops with remaining tomato sauce.
1 teaspoon ground black pepper	
2 8-ounce cans no-salt-added or regular tomato sauce	*4* Wrap one loaf in heavy-duty foil; label and freeze up to six months.
	5 Place the second loaf in a shallow baking dish; cover with wax paper. Microwave on high 9 to 12 minutes or until internal temperature is 160 degrees. Let stand 5 minutes.

Per serving: 310 calories, 28g protein, 14g fat (41 percent calories from fat), 5g saturated fat, 16g carbohydrate, 103mg cholesterol, 163mg sodium, 3g fiber.

Note: *To defrost, remove from freezer and place in refrigerator the day before cooking.*

Lasagna

Lasagna freezes beautifully. Line the baking dish with foil, assemble the lasagna, and freeze. Once frozen, remove the foil-lined lasagna from the dish to free the dish for other uses. Rewrap the frozen lasagna and pop it back into the freezer. You can cook before freezing or after, whichever you'd like. I tend to cook before freezing, because then all you need to do is thaw and reheat.

Check out Week 43 for Mexican Lasagna.

For another take on lasagna, try this no-meat one. It uses no-cook (or pre-cooked) noodles, which I love. I never could master cooking the other kind. They usually ended up on the floor looking like fish out of water. You wouldn't confuse my skills with one of the famous TV chefs who specialize in Italian cooking, like Lidia Bastianich. She's my favorite.

Black Mean-Bean Lasagna

Prep time: 20 min • **Cook time:** 40–45 min, plus standing time • **Yield:** 8 servings

Ingredients

1 15-ounce can black beans, rinsed

1 28-ounce can crushed tomatoes

1 medium onion, chopped

1 small green bell pepper, chopped

½ cup salsa

1 teaspoon chili powder

½ teaspoon cumin

1 cup reduced-fat ricotta cheese

1 egg

10 no-cook style lasagna noodles, divided

8 ounces shredded 50-percent-reduced-fat cheddar or jalapeño cheese, divided

Directions

1 Heat oven to 350 degrees. Coat a 9-x-13-inch baking dish (or two 8-x-8-inch dishes — see Note) with cooking spray.

2 In large bowl, mash beans slightly. Stir in tomatoes, onions, bell pepper, salsa, chili powder, and cumin; mix well.

3 In small bowl, combine ricotta and egg; blend well.

4 Spread 1 cup of tomato mixture over bottom of dish. Top with half of noodles, overlapping slightly. Top with half of remaining tomato mixture.

5 Spoon ricotta mixture over top; spread carefully. Top with half of cheddar cheese, then with remaining noodles, tomato mixture, and cheddar cheese.

6 Cover with nonstick foil and bake 40 to 45 minutes or until noodles are tender.

7 Uncover; let stand 15 minutes before serving.

Per serving: 338 calories, 19g protein, 9g fat (24 percent calories from fat), 5g saturated fat, 44g carbohydrate, 54mg cholesterol, 755mg sodium, 4g fiber.

Note: *Make two of these — or divide this recipe into two 8-x-8-inch baking dishes — and freeze one. Don't forget to label with date. Thaw in the refrigerator a day ahead.*

Pasta with Sauce

Make a generic pasta sauce that you can turn into many meals. My friend Chet has a great tomato sauce recipe that can be used in many ways. She uses it over pasta and as a sauce for pizza or stuffed shells. To use as a pasta sauce, stir in cooked sausage, some Kalamata olives, or some sautéed garlic. Add a little cream for a richer sauce. Chet's a very good cook (and friend).

Chet makes cauldrons of this sauce, so double or triple it to freeze some for later. I don't own a cauldron or a walk-in freezer, so I make modest amounts. Thaw in the refrigerator.

Chet's Pasta Sauce

Prep time: 10 min • **Cook time:** 20–30 min • **Yield:** About 5 or 6 cups

Ingredients	Directions
2 tablespoons olive oil **2 medium onions, chopped** **4 14.5-ounce cans undrained petite diced tomatoes (fire-roasted for part of them if desired)** **1 to 2 tablespoons dried or 1 bunch of fresh basil leaves**	*1* Heat oil in a large skillet or Dutch oven. Add onions; cook 8 minutes or until softened. Add tomatoes and basil; bring to boil and cook 20 to 30 minutes or until thickened. *2* Blend with immersion blender until mostly smooth. *3* Eat now over pasta of your choice or freeze for later.

Per cup: 137 calories, 3g protein, 6g fat (36 percent calories from fat), 1g saturated fat, 18g carbohydrate, no cholesterol, 735mg sodium, 3g fiber.

Pulled Pork or Beef Barbecue

Pulled pork and barbecued beef make great sandwiches on a moment's notice, as long as you've stored some in the freezer in meal portions (thaw in the refrigerator). Be prepared with the following barbecue recipe. Pull out your slow cooker for this one.

Barbecued Pork or Beef

Prep time: 10 min • **Cook time:** 8 hr • **Yield:** About 12 sandwiches

Ingredients	Directions
3 to 4 pounds trimmed boneless pork shoulder or boneless beef chuck, cut into 3 pieces	*1* Place meat in a 4-quart or larger slow cooker. Scatter onions over meat. Top with barbecue sauce.
1 chopped onion	*2* Cover; cook on low 8 hours. Discard fat.
2 cups of your favorite barbecue sauce	*3* Shred meat; mix with sauce, and serve on buns.

Per serving (excluding bun): 205 calories, 19g protein, 11g fat (47 percent calories from fat), 4g saturated fat, 7g carbohydrate, 66mg cholesterol, 395mg sodium, 1g fiber.

Ground Beef, Chicken, or Turkey for Tacos

Cooked, crumbled ground beef (or chicken or turkey) can be turned into tacos by adding a taco seasoning mix. You can then turn the taco mixture into . . . tacos! When you're feeling a little more creative, Taco Salad is another option. Mix a packaged green salad with tomatoes, avocados, celery, or whatever else is begging to be used. Toss with lemon and olive oil or your favorite vinaigrette. Top the salad with heated taco mixture. Voilà! Another meal.

Tacos!

Prep time: 5–10 min • **Cook time:** 5–6 min • **Yield:** 8 servings

Ingredients	Directions
2 pounds lean ground beef, or ground chicken or turkey breast	*1* Brown the ground beef, chicken, or turkey in a large nonstick skillet over medium-high heat for 5 to 6 minutes or until it is no longer pink. Drain off any fat, if necessary.
2 1.25-ounce packets less-sodium taco seasoning mix	
Your choice of taco shells	*2* Add the taco seasoning mix plus 1⅓ cups water to the meat. Stir to mix and bring the mixture to a boil. Reduce the heat and simmer for 3 to 4 minutes, stirring occasionally.
Shredded 50-percent-reduced-fat cheese (your favorite kind), if desired	
Shredded lettuce, if desired	*3* Serve in taco shells; top with cheese, lettuce, tomatoes, and sour cream, as desired.
Chopped tomatoes, if desired	
Low-fat sour cream, if desired	

Per serving (excluding taco shell and toppings): *235 calories, 24g protein, 13g fat (50 percent calories from fat), 5g saturated fat, 5g carbohydrate, 77mg cholesterol, 466mg sodium, no fiber.*

Note: *Freeze the leftovers; thaw in the refrigerator.*

Diced, Cooked Chicken for Almost Anything

When you have a few minutes, poach or grill extra chicken breasts or thighs. Dice them, and package light and dark meat separately in 1 cup amounts; label and freeze. Just think of the chicken tetrazzini, chicken salad, chicken chili, chicken pot pie, and chicken à la king, you can make. The list goes on. Here's a really easy chili recipe; add or subtract spices or change the beans according to what's on hand. To stretch it, serve over rice.

Chicken Chili

Prep time: 10 min • **Cook time:** 20 min • **Yield:** About 9 cups

Ingredients	Directions
1 medium onion, chopped	*1* In a Dutch oven coated with cooking spray, cook onion 5 minutes until softened.
2 to 3 cups diced cooked chicken (light, dark, or a mixture)	*2* Add chicken, broth, cumin, oregano, pepper sauce, and beans. Cover, bring to boil; reduce heat and simmer 15 minutes.
1¾ cup low-sodium chicken broth	
1 teaspoon cumin	*3* Stir in lime juice and cilantro.
1 teaspoon dried oregano	
1 or 2 teaspoons hot pepper sauce	*4* Garnish with additional cilantro, if desired.
2 15- to 19-ounce cans great northern or other white beans, rinsed	
3 tablespoons fresh lime juice (if available)	
2 tablespoons chopped fresh cilantro, plus more for garnish	

Per cup: 125 calories, 13g protein, 3g fat (21 percent calories from fat), 1g saturated fat, 11g carbohydrate, 28mg cholesterol, 176mg sodium, 4g fiber.

Baked Tilapia

One of my favorite entrees for "one of those days" is Baked Tilapia. (We're having this for dinner tonight; writing is such hard work.) Add a starch and a green salad to round out the meal. This recipe is so easy, you don't need to cook and freeze it ahead of time.

Baked Tilapia

Prep time: 5 min • **Cook time:** 10–12 min • **Yield:** 4 servings

Ingredients	Directions
4 5- or 6-ounce tilapia fillets 3 tablespoons Dijonnaise 4 tablespoons panko bread crumbs 4 tablespoons sliced almonds	**1** Heat oven to 425 degrees. Lay fillets on a foil-lined, nonstick, rimmed baking pan.
	2 Spread Dijonnaise over fillets. Sprinkle with bread crumbs. Top evenly with almonds.
	3 Bake 10 to 12 minutes or until the fillets are opaque.

Per serving: 221 calories, 35g protein, 7g fat (26 percent calories from fat), 2g saturated fat, 6g carbohydrate, 6mg cholesterol, 235mg sodium, 1g fiber.

Salmon Fillets

If you don't like tilapia, as I suggest in the preceding recipe, you can serve salmon fillets instead. The procedure is essentially the same; only the toppings and type of foil differ. The recipe is simple enough to make on the spot, but if you want to keep a couple pieces of salmon for emergencies, wrap them individually in heavy-duty foil, label, and freeze up to two or three months. Thaw in the refrigerator. Sometimes I sprinkle panko bread crumbs over the pesto and sometimes I don't. You can do whichever appeals to you and the family.

When baking salmon with the skin on, don't use nonstick foil because the skin will stick to the foil when you remove the cooked fish. Some stores charge extra for removing the skin. Save some money and do it yourself!

Salmon Fillets à la Pesto

Prep time: 5 min • **Cook time:** 14–16 min • **Yield:** 4 servings

Ingredients	Directions
1½ pounds salmon fillets, cut into 4 pieces	*1* Heat oven to 425 degrees. Lay salmon on rimmed baking sheet lined with regular foil.
3 tablespoons pesto	
¼ cup finely chopped walnuts	*2* Spread with pesto. Top with walnuts.
	3 Bake 14 to 16 minutes or medium doneness, according to thickness. If you want well-done salmon, cook it longer.

Per serving: 323 calories, 40g protein, 17g fat (5 percent calories from fat), 3g saturated fat, 2g carbohydrate, 101mg cholesterol, 214mg sodium, 1g fiber.

Pork Tenderloin

Keep a couple of pork tenderloins in the freezer, wrapped separately. After thawing, cut one into eight medallions, and flatten them between two sheets of plastic wrap. Cut the "rounds" into ¼-inch strips. Brown quickly, add a stir-fry sauce, and cook until hot. Serve with brown rice and yellow squash. Or, bake a thawed tenderloin in a 425-degree oven 20 minutes; tent with foil and let stand 5 minutes. Serve with brown rice and broccoli spears. If you want to doozie (fancy) it up, try the following recipe. Serve it with sweet potatoes and green beans.

Bacon-Wrapped Pork Medallions with Mustard Sauce

Prep time: 10 min • **Cook time:** 21 min, plus standing time • **Yield:** 4–6 servings

Ingredients	Directions
1 1- to 1½-pound pork tenderloin	*1* Cut tenderloin into 2-inch medallions (4 to 6 slices — see Note).
4 to 6 slices bacon (one for each medallion)	*2* Wrap each medallion with a bacon slice around the outer edge (like an equator). Allow the bacon to overlap about ¼ inch and secure with a wooden pick, then trim any excess bacon.
Salt and pepper, to taste	
2 teaspoons canola or olive oil	*3* Season top and bottom of pork medallions with salt and pepper, to taste.
2 tablespoons softened butter	
1 teaspoon Dijon mustard	*4* Preheat oven to 425 degrees.
	5 Meanwhile, heat the oil over medium-high heat in a large ovenproof skillet. (Using a straight-sided skillet to brown the medallions will help the bacon cook faster.) Add medallions to skillet.
	6 Brown pork on each side, about 3 minutes per side. If possible, allow the sides of the medallions to touch the sides of the skillet.
	7 Place skillet in the oven and allow to cook about 10 to 15 minutes, until the internal temperature reaches 155 degrees. Remove skillet from oven and let stand 5 minutes. (The internal temp will continue to increase to 160 degrees.)
Per serving: 230 calories, 25g protein, 14g fat (54 percent calories from fat), 6g saturated fat, no carbohydrate, 85mg cholesterol, 178mg sodium, no fiber.	*8* Meanwhile, mix butter and mustard together. To serve, add a dollop of butter to each medallion.

Note: *If you have a 12-inch skillet, you can fit up to 6 medallions; if you use a 10-inch skillet, you may only be able to fit 4 (5 if the medallions are smaller).*

Stuffed Avocado

Stuffed avocados make an easy meal. For starters, halve an avocado and remove the seed. Spritz with lemon juice. Then stir a little curry sauce into tuna or chicken salad from the deli, or make your own Barbecue Chicken Salad with the recipe that follows. Serve on a plate with hard-cooked egg and tomato wedges. Dinner accomplished!

Barbecue Chicken Salad

Prep time: 15 min • **Cook time:** About 5 min • **Yield:** 4 servings

Ingredients	Directions
2 to 3 cups shredded rotisserie chicken	*1* Toss chicken with barbecue sauce; heat.
½ to ¾ cups barbecue sauce	*2* Serve topped with coleslaw and jalapeño pepper slices on a whole-wheat bun or in an avocado.
2 cups deli coleslaw	
Sliced jalapeño peppers, as desired	

Per serving: 310 calories, 17g protein, 18g fat (54 percent calories from fat), 4g saturated fat, 18g carbohydrate, 15mg cholesterol, 848mg sodium, 2g fiber.

Soup

I never met a soup I didn't like. Make batches and freeze. Thaw and add cooked pasta, rice, or vegetables that need to move out of the refrigerator and into your stomach. I named a soup I make all the time Secret Weapon Soup (see the following recipe). It's frequently my work-day lunch. I add a piece of fruit, a glass of fat-free milk, and sometimes a half slice of bread with spread. Why the name? It fills and holds me until dinner, it's inexpensive and easy to make and reheat, and it has good flavor. It's also loaded with fiber and not so many calories.

When making soup in quantity, freeze it in resealable freezer bags, and lay them on a cookie sheet until frozen. The flat packets store well standing in a freezer basket. My friend Sylvia San Martin taught me this.

Secret Weapon Soup

Prep time: 10 min • **Cook time:** About 30–35 min • **Yield:** About 8 cups

Ingredients	*Directions*
1 to 2 cups sliced fresh carrots	*1* Combine carrots and ½ cup broth in a large glass bowl. Microwave on high 6 minutes.
1 cup (or more) low-sodium chicken or vegetable broth	
1 19-ounce can vegetarian lentil soup (such as Progresso)	*2* Add lentil soup, both types of tomatoes, beans, and chili powder; stir. Rinse cans with remaining broth, swirl it around, and add to the soup. (This way, you don't waste any of the ingredients remaining in the cans.)
1 14.5-ounce can fire-roasted, diced tomatoes (no salt added, if available)	
1 14.5-ounce can no-salt-added or regular diced tomatoes	*3* Cover and microwave on high 15 minutes; micro-wave on medium 10 or 15 minutes or until hot.
1 15-ounce can rinsed cannellini beans	*4* Freeze in 1-cup or meal-sized amounts. The soup will be thick (no need to freeze any more liquid than you need to).
1 teaspoon chipotle chili powder	
	5 When thawed, add a sliced zucchini, green beans, broccoli florets, or another vegetable, and enough broth or water to suit your taste. Heat and enjoy.

Per cup: 92 calories, 5g protein, 1g fat (7 percent calories from fat), no saturated fat, 17g carbohydrate, no cholesterol, 311mg sodium, 5g fiber.

Metric Conversion Guide

· ·

*N**ote:* The recipes in this cookbook were not developed or tested using metric measures. There may be some variation in quality when converting to metric units.

Common Abbreviations

Abbreviation(s)	What It Stands For
C, c	cup
g	gram
kg	kilogram
L, l	liter
lb	pound
mL, ml	milliliter
oz	ounce
pt	pint
t, tsp	teaspoon
T, TB, Tbl, Tbsp	tablespoon

Volume

U.S. Units	Canadian Metric	Australian Metric
¼ teaspoon	1 milliliter	1 milliliter
½ teaspoon	2 milliliters	2 milliliters
1 teaspoon	5 milliliters	5 milliliters
1 tablespoon	15 milliliters	20 milliliters
¼ cup	50 milliliters	60 milliliters

(continued)

Volume *(continued)*

U.S. Units	Canadian Metric	Australian Metric
⅓ cup	75 milliliters	80 milliliters
½ cup	125 milliliters	125 milliliters
⅔ cup	150 milliliters	170 milliliters
¾ cup	175 milliliters	190 milliliters
1 cup	250 milliliters	250 milliliters
1 quart	1 liter	1 liter
1½ quarts	1.5 liters	1.5 liters
2 quarts	2 liters	2 liters
2½ quarts	2.5 liters	2.5 liters
3 quarts	3 liters	3 liters
4 quarts	4 liters	4 liters

Weight

U.S. Units	Canadian Metric	Australian Metric
1 ounce	30 grams	30 grams
2 ounces	55 grams	60 grams
3 ounces	85 grams	90 grams
4 ounces (¼ pound)	115 grams	125 grams
8 ounces (½ pound)	225 grams	225 grams
16 ounces (1 pound)	455 grams	500 grams (½ kilogram)

Measurements

Inches	Centimeters
½	1.5
1	2.5
2	5.0
3	7.5
4	10.0

Inches	Centimeters
5	12.5
6	15.0
7	17.5
8	20.5
9	23.0
10	25.5
11	28.0
12	30.5
13	33.0

Temperature (Degrees)

Fahrenheit	Celsius
32	0
212	100
250	120
275	140
300	150
325	160
350	180
375	190
400	200
425	220
450	230
475	240
500	260

Index

• C •

● **G** ●

• N •

• O •

• P •

• Q •